New Literacies
Second Edition

New Literacies
Everyday Practices and Classroom Learning

Second Edition

COLIN LANKSHEAR and
MICHELE KNOBEL

Open University Press

Open University Press
McGraw-Hill Education
McGraw-Hill House
Shoppenhangers Road
Maidenhead
Berkshire
England
SL6 2QL

email: enquiries@openup.co.uk
world wide web: www.openup.co.uk

and Two Penn Plaza, New York, NY 10121–2289, USA

First published 2006

A catalogue record of this book is available from the British Library

ISBN 10: 0335 220 10X
ISBN 13: 978 0335 220 106

Library of Congress Cataloging-in-Publication Data
CIP data applied for

Typeset by YHT Ltd, London
Printed in Poland by OZGraf S.A. www.polskabook.pl

The **McGraw·Hill** Companies

To JPG
colleague, compañero, friend

Contents

Foreword

The second edition of *New Literacies: Everyday Practices and Classroom Learning* loses no time in establishing itself as the rightful successor to the first edition. Although at first glance this claim might seem an odd, even unnecessary, statement given the fairly common practice of publishing subsequent editions of books that do well initially, I stand by it for several reasons. First and foremost, I want to emphasize that Colin Lankshear and Michele Knobel are once again at their best – doing what they do so well as writers – pulling readers effortlessly through complex ideas made understandable by a lively and engaging style of writing. Their deep and abiding interest in developing a viable concept of new literacies is palpable, and it is this interest that keeps their scholarship fresh and their writing credible.

Another reason for stating what might otherwise seem obvious is this: not all second editions measure up when compared to an earlier edition. *New Literacies: Everyday Practices and Classroom Learning* does, however, and it does so in both practical and pedagogically sound ways. In just the few short years since publication of the first edition, new technologies have appeared that widen the gap between users with insider status and those with relatively little experience in communicating digitally. Rather than leave less experienced users behind, Lankshear and Knobel have taken considerable pains to invite them into the conversation. For example, they pose thoughtful questions throughout each chapter that call for reflection, and they suggest websites where it's possible to experience firsthand a bit of what the new technologies offer.

That the second edition of *New Literacies* does its predecessor proud is due in no small measure to Lankshear and Knobel's ever-increasing visibility globally. Through their travels and invited keynotes, they are in frequent contact with some of the world's other foremost thinkers on new literacies, new technologies, and new social practices involving both. Yet it's not simply a matter of being in touch. What these two authors bring to their work is integrity beyond reproach and an ability to glean insights from new literacy practices worldwide that may (or may not) have applications locally. One of the things I value most about the second edition is that it continues to question the wisdom of change for change's sake. At the same time, it makes clear that changes are afoot – some or all of which will influence how we as educators come to think of, and respond to, new literacies. It is this tension that speaks most provocatively and directly to me, the literacy teacher educator.

But I am more than one kind of person, and hence, more than one kind of reader. As I read and made notes to myself in the margins of the manuscript that would become the second edition of *New Literacies: Everyday Practices and Classroom Learning*, it was clear this was no ordinary professional text. There were just too many interesting topics – written in too engaging a manner – to qualify as such. Thus, with curiosity, I acted on the authors' suggestion to 'have a look' at various web sites featuring fan fiction, a new literacy that heretofore had not appealed to me in the least. In fact, I had on more than one occasion pestered a doctoral advisee to 'let me in' on just what it was that attracted her to writing her own brand of fan fiction. Now, here I was, the person responsible for writing this foreword, engrossed in reading online fan fictions written by authors unknown (to me), while all the time imagining how I might one day soon try my own hand at writing for this new literacy forum.

In a nutshell, this second edition of *New Literacies: Everyday Practices and Classroom Learning* establishes a benchmark against which readers can judge for themselves how prepared they are for a world where relationships – participation, collaboration, and collective intelligence, not information per se – are valued as literate markers; where texts are fluid and subject to change without authoritative mandate; and where productive differences between in-school and out-of-school literacies are yet to be worked out. Lankshear and Knobel amplify with fresh content the message of the first edition – that is, the 'new' in new literacies is with us for the long run. This message, while not for the fainthearted, is one that insiders understand and act on daily. Given that, who among us can afford to be left out?

Donna Alvermann
University of Georgia

List of Figures and Tables

Acknowledgments

This book has been encouraged and supported in diverse ways by many people to whom we are indebted. We want to acknowledge their support and generosity here.

First, several key ideas presented in Part 1 of the book were developed in collaboration with Chris Bigum and Leonie Rowan. We have learned a great deal from working with them over the years and want to express our deep appreciation.

We have also drawn heavily on inspiration from other friends and colleagues with whom we work in different ways and in different contexts. We owe much to Rebecca Black, Kevin Leander, Angela Thomas and, as always, James Paul Gee. In their individual ways they exemplify the critical, inquiring, progressive spirit that seeks to maximize human well-being using the material and non-material resources available to us. Long may they run.

Donna Alvermann and Donald Leu have done much to help us understand more clearly who we are trying to write for and why. They have supported our work in the most generous and unobtrusive ways, while at the same time continuing their own tireless and selfless work in the name of better education for all, and especially for those who have received less than their due share of social benefits from the systems within which they are constrained to live. Despite already having more than enough tasks to complete, Donna generously accepted our invitation to write a foreword for this book. We know what this kind of unsolicited added pressure involves, and treasure the collegiality woven into her text. Don invited us to present the opening Plenary Address at the 2004 National Reading Conference annual meeting in San Antonio, which provided an important motivational opportunity for us to develop material that has been further refined for this book. With Julie Coiro, Don has also extended our range of interest in new literacies through our collaboration in an edited *Handbook of New Literacies Research*, to be published by Erlbaum.

Other colleagues have in various ways made valued contributions to producing this book. As with the people we have already named, they are entitled to enjoy anything in the following pages that may be of educational worth, but share no responsibility for the book's shortcomings. We want especially to thank Neil and Chris Anderson, Dana Cammack, Bill Cope, Christina Davidson, Mary Kalantzis, Chuck Kinzer, Joanne Larson, Lawrence Lessig, Jackie Marsh, Guy Merchant, Michael Peters, and Ilana Snyder. We also thank Johnnycakesdepp and Silver Excel Fox for their contributions to our study of fanfic.

As always, we appreciate greatly the support of Shona Mullen and our other colleagues at Open University Press – in particular, Fiona Richman, Laura Dent and James Bishop. They are a wonderful team to work with, and we hope that our efforts in this book are enough to repay their continuing faith in our work.

Some chapters in this book build on work that has been published in journals and conference proceedings. We have benefited from the opportunities we have had to rehearse ideas in other places. Thanks are due here to *The International Journal of Learning, Literacy Learning in the Middle Years*, and *The 54th Yearbook of the National Reading Conference*.

During the period in which this book has been conceived and written we have enjoyed strong support from friends, colleagues, and institutions in México, Australia and Canada. Without this, our work during the past four years simply would not have been possible. We want to thank Angela Guzmán, Hilario Rivera Rodríguez, Roberto Lugo Lugo, Ma. del Pilar Avila Guzmán, Gustavo Cabrera López, Ana María Salmerón, Toni Chao, Annette Patterson, Roger Slee, la Coordinación de las Humanidades of the National Autonomous University of México (UNAM), the Faculties of Education at Montclair State University and McGill University, the School of Education at James Cook University, and the Faculty of Education and

Creative Arts at Central Queensland University. Special recognition and appreciation are extended to colleagues in the School of Education on the Cairns Campus of James Cook University for their extraordinary kindnesses and friendship during January–March 2006, when Colin was recovering from fracturing two vertebrae. Much of this book was written horizontally on a makeshift bed in an office at all hours of day and night. It could not have been written without much friendship and forbearance, for which we are truly grateful. The same thanks and appreciation go also to the security and cleaning staff on campus whose regular visits and camaraderie provided welcome sparks when the fire was going out.

We wish to thank the following for permission to use material for which they hold copyright: Adbusters Media Foundation for permission to reproduce Figure 4.2, 'The True Colours of Benetton'; Micah Wright for permission to reproduce his image 'Sorry We're Late, New Orleans!' as Figure 4.3; and Lawrence Lessig for permission to reproduce a screen grab of his blog front page as Figure 5.1.

Finally, we wish to thank those anonymous reviewers of the original version of this book who responded to invitations by Open University Press to provide feedback to guide this new edition. We also want to thank the authors of published reviews of the original book for their constructive critical feedback and the boost they gave the original edition of the book in the market place.

Introduction to the Second Edition

When Open University Press mooted a second edition of *New Literacies: Changing Knowledge and Classroom Learning* we welcomed the opportunity to revise and update the original text. Our initial plan was that two or three of the substantive chapters would be replaced by new themes and that the rest of the process would involve smoothing out the original text, bringing key examples up to date, briefly noting some significant recent changes bearing on existing chapter themes, and so on. When it came to actually writing this new edition, however, this scenario changed to such an extent that what we have here is to all intents and purposes a new book. Less than 10 per cent of the content from the 2003 text has made it to this new edition.

The orientation of the book has shifted in ways that have called for a different sub-title. The theme of 'Changing Knowledge' has given way here to 'Everyday Practices', reflecting the way we have taken up the concept of Web 2.0 as a key framing device for our work. Rather than addressing implications for how *knowledge* is understood, approached, generated and evaluated as a result of trends and directions associated with the rise of Web

2.0, we have chosen instead to focus on new literacies as *everyday social practices* and on what these practices might mean for education.

So much had happened in the five-year period between when we began writing the original book (in 2001) and when we began writing this one that we thought it appropriate to tackle a new suite of themes. Some practices that were mere 'side bars' in the first edition – like 'memes' and weblogs – have become the focus for entire chapters here. Other phenomena – like mobile computing and communicating – that were barely on the horizon in 2001 have since become widespread and hugely influential and, accordingly, are taken up at length here.

This is not to say that we think the content of the original book is passé, because we don't. 'Ratings', for example, are more pervasive, pertinent, and diverse today than they were when we looked at participation in ratings systems within spaces like eBay and Plastic.com. Similarly, the points we made about 'schooled' appropriations of new technologies in the chapter on the National Grid for Learning hold with equal force today. On one hand, then, we think there is still plenty in the original book that is current and educationally pertinent and, indeed, that would be worth updating. At the same time, there are many other important matters to talk about. We have chosen the latter option here. We think the original book is still sufficiently current to stand alone as a text, and that the two books can most usefully be read in conjunction with each other. For those reasons we have liaised with Open University Press to keep as much of the first edition available in electronic form as copyright arrangements permit. Substantial portions of the original text can be accessed at http://www.newliteracies.com

Besides these substantive differences in the topics addressed, this new book differs from the first edition in two further ways, both of which we hope will prove useful. First, it develops more fully our views of when it is appropriate to refer to a particular literacy as being a *new* literacy and why the category of *new literacies* may be a useful one. In the first edition we used two main devices for conceptualizing 'new' literacies and distinguishing them from 'conventional' or 'established' literacies. One was a distinction between 'the *ontologically* new' and 'the *chronologically* new'. The other was an account of the difference between what we called 'newcomer' (or 'immigrant') and 'insider' (or 'native') *mindsets*. Each of these devices is developed in much greater conceptual, theoretical, and historical depth here than in the original text. This new work takes up much of Chapters 2 and 3, and is accompanied by a detailed discussion of literacy as social practice. Our account of 'literacy as social practice' draws on pioneering work in sociocultural literacy studies by Silvia Scribner and Michael Cole (1981). It also draws on what we think is an especially fruitful account of 'Discourses' provided by Jim Gee (1997). The net result is a much more *robust* account of new literacies than the original one.

Second, this new edition provides reflection and discussion activities at regular intervals. These suggest ways the text might be used in academic courses as well as by 'private' readers for thinking about new literacies in relation to literacy education in classrooms, and also for reflecting critically upon our own concepts and arguments. We have tried to present these activities as unobtrusively as possible by boxing them off from the rest of the text. Those readers who are not interested in the suggested activities can simply bypass the boxes containing the activities and read on.

One reviewer of the original text recommended that a new edition contain a glossary of terms related to aspects of digital technologies and related social practices that may be unfamiliar to readers with limited experience of new technologies and technocultures. We thought this was a good idea and began to compile a glossary. We abandoned the enterprise, however, because in doing the work we found ourselves returning time and time again to two especially useful resources: *Wikipedia* and *How Stuff Works*. Moreover, when we produced glossary items, they always seemed to offer so much 'less' that could be gained from going directly to these sources. We realized that the convenience of having 'to hand' definitions of terms provided at the end of this book would be greatly outweighed by the rewards to be gained from going online and keying the terms in question into the sites' respective search engines (or, alternatively, into a powerful search tool like Google.com). Indeed, making use of such resources is precisely the kind of initiative this book seeks to encourage.

Consequently, in terms of both enhancing reader understandings and of achieving our own aims, providing a glossary would have subtracted rather than added value. Therefore, at points where readers feel they want clarification of techno terminology and specific aspects of techno culture, we recommend going in the first instance to the following URLs:

- http://en.wikipedia.org
- http://www.howstuffworks.com

;-)

Finally, we are genuinely interested in reader responses to the text: to the argument and position advanced in general, as well as to any experiences readers have of using the reflection and discussion activities. We warmly invite anyone who wants to feed back to us directly to forward their ideas, suggestions, and comments to us at: newliteracies@yahoo.co.uk

Colin Lankshear
Michele Knobel

PART 1

What's New?

CHAPTER 1

From 'Reading' to 'New' Literacies

Introduction

Literacy is now centre stage in education policy, curriculum development, and everyday thinking about educational practice. It is hard to credit that just two or three decades ago the term 'literacy' hardly featured in formal educational discourse. Instead, there was a long-established field known as 'Reading'. This was mainly grounded in psycholinguistics and associated with time-honoured methods of instruction for teaching new entrants into school how to decode printed text and, secondarily, how to encode text.

Prior to the 1970s, 'literacy' was used generally in relation to non-formal educational settings, and, in particular, in relation to adults who were deemed to be *illiterate*. 'Literacy' was the name given to programmes of non-formal instruction – not associated with formal educational institutions like schools – that were offered to illiterate adults to help them acquire basic abilities to read and write. At this time within Britain, North America, Australasia and similar countries, official statistics obtained for census measures and the like indicated almost zero levels of adult illiteracy. Such adult literacy initiatives as existed in these countries were small-scale, largely voluntary endeavours involving adult literacy tutors working with individuals or small groups of learners. Indeed, within First World English-speaking societies, 'literacy teaching' was the name of marginal spaces of non-formal education work intended to provide a 'second chance' for those whose illiteracy was often seen as directly associated with other debilitating or dysfunctional conditions and circumstances. These included 'conditions' like unemployment, imprisonment, drug and alcohol abuse, teenage pregnancy, inferior physical and psychic health, and so on.

The situation was different in the Third World of so-called 'developing countries'. In these countries, relatively few people received formal education. Often as many as 80 per cent or more of the adult population was illiterate relative to popular measures of the day – such as lacking reading abilities roughly equivalent to second or third grade levels of primary school. During the 1950s, and again in the 1990s, it became fashionable among development theorists to associate a country's 'readiness' for 'economic take-off' with attainment of a certain level of adult literacy across the nation. For example, during the 1960s it was widely argued by development theorists that having at least a large minority of the male population achieve literacy was a precondition for underdeveloped nations to 'take off' economically (Anderson 1966). A figure of at least 40 per cent of adults (especially males) deemed literate in a population was seen as the threshold for economic development. This became a rationale for promoting adult literacy campaigns throughout many Third World countries in Africa, Asia, and Latin America as a strategic component of economic and social development policies. Illiteracy was seen as a major impediment to economic development, and literacy campaigns were prescribed as cost-effective measures for developing the minimal levels of 'manpower' needed to give a country a chance for economic take-off. These campaigns were usually undertaken as non-formal programmes aimed at adults – although children often participated – conducted outside the education *system* as such.

Prior to the 1970s, then, neither in the First World nor in the Third World was 'literacy' identified as a formal educational *ideal*. Within formal educational settings, reading and writing were seen as essential tools for learning, and as vehicles for accessing and communicating meanings via printed texts. They were a *means* for learning, not an end – let alone *the* end. Functional mastery of reading and writing was effectively taken for granted as bottom line outcomes of classroom learning for all students other than those designated as intellectually impaired or as having severe learning disabilities. And in any event, so far as curriculum and pedagogy within formal education were concerned, what was talked about, researched, debated and so on was not *literacy* but, rather, *reading* and, to a lesser extent, *writing*.

This changed considerably during the 1970s in the US and, to varying degrees, in other Anglophone countries. All of a sudden, 'literacy' was pushed to the forefront of educational focus and effort. A number of reasons have been linked to this change, three of which seem to us especially interesting.

One was the rise to prominence of Paulo Freire's work within the larger context of the radical education movement of the late 1960s and early 1970s (see Freire 1972, 1973; Freire and Macedo 1987). Freire's work with peasant groups in Brazil and Chile provided an example of how literacy work could be central to radical approaches to education aimed at building critical social praxis. His concept of literacy as 'reading the word and the world' involved much more than merely the ideas of decoding and encoding print. Far from being the sole objective of literacy education, learning how to encode and decode alphabetic print was integrated into an expansive pedagogy in which groups of learners collaboratively pursued critical consciousness of their world via a reflexive or 'cyclical' process of reflection and action. Through their efforts to act on the world, and to analyse and understand the results of their action, people can come to know the world better: more 'deeply' and 'critically'.

From this perspective, 'illiteracy' is seen as a consequence of unjust social processes and relations that have been created historically and become 'woven' (or, as we might say today, 'hard wired') into the social structure. Yet, insofar as these unjust social arrangements have been created and are sustained through human activity, they can equally be *changed* through human action. Before such 'transformative cultural action' can occur, however, it is necessary to understand the nature and origins of social oppression.

In Freire's pedagogy, learning to write and read *words* became a focus for adults in pursuing critical awareness of how oppressive practices and relations operated in everyday life. Words that were highly charged with meaning for them – words that expressed their fears, hopes, troubles and their dreams for a better life – provided the vocabulary by which they learned to write and read. These words were discussed intensively in order to explore how the world 'worked'. In the context of this oral discussion the *written* forms of these words, as well as of other words that could be built out of their syllables and phonemes, were introduced. In the context of discussing and thinking about these words, participants learned what they 'looked like' as text, and how to write and read them.

Within Freire's approach to promoting literacy, then, the process of learning literally to read and write words was an integral part of learning to understand how the world operates socially and culturally in ways that produce unequal opportunities and outcomes for different groups of people. Ultimately, this analysis was to provide a starting point for participants to take action on the world in an attempt to change it in ways that would create social processes and relations that were more just. Groups would undertake cultural action for change in the world in the light of their analysis of their circumstances. They would then analyse and evaluate the results of their action in order to take the next step in cultural action. This *praxis* of reflection and action was the means for knowing the world more deeply and accurately, since it involved 'testing' it to see how it works in the light of concepts and theories developed collaboratively in discussion of experiences and beliefs. Freirean literacy education was, then, an integral component of a radical, politicized pedagogy purposefully designed to stimulate action for change. As a matter of fact, it captured the imagination, respect, and support of many academics and political activists in First World countries – particularly, in North America – as well as being adopted as the philosophical basis for national and regional adult literacy programmes in a number of Third World countries.

A second factor in the development of 'literacy' as a widely used concept in education was the dramatic discovery – although many called it an *invention* – of widespread illiteracy among adults in the US during the early 1970s. This alleged literacy *crisis* coincided with early awareness of profound structural change in the economy, as the US moved toward becoming a post-industrial society. Post-industrialism entailed far-reaching restructuring of the labour market and employment as well as deep changes in major organizations and institutions of daily life. Large numbers of people were seen as poorly prepared for these changes. The 'literacy crisis' quickly spread to other emerging postindustrial societies. Whether it was in Britain, the US, Canada, Australia or New Zealand, much the same storyline emerged: schools were failing to ensure that all learners became literate to the extent required to live 'effectively' under contemporary conditions. Research and reports commissioned by governments claimed relentlessly that standards were falling, that far-reaching educational reform was needed, and that curriculum and pedagogy had to be overhauled in order to ensure that all students would acquire at the very least a *functional* level of literacy. 'Literacy' emerged as the key word here.

A third factor was the increasing development and popularity of a *sociocultural* perspective within studies of language and the social sciences (Gee 1996: Ch. 3; Gee *et al.* 1996: Ch. 1). During the 1980s and 1990s this impacted strongly on conceptual and theoretical understandings of practices involving texts. Early influential works drew on theory and research from different but broadly compatible fields. Gee (1996: Ch. 1) documents these very nicely. For example, Harvey Graff's 1979 book, *The Literacy Myth*, drew on revisionist history. Silvia Scribner and Michael Cole's *The Psychology of Literacy* (1981) drew on concepts and instrumentation that reflected pioneering work in social cognition by Vygotsky and Luria and developed a concept of 'practice' that has evolved into a key construct within sociocultural approaches to literacy. Ron and Suzanne Scollon's *Narrative, Literacy and Face in Interethnic Communication* (1981) worked at complex interfaces between linguistics, anthropology and epistemology to explore relationships among social practices, worldviews, orality and literacy. Shirley Brice Heath (1983) explored the ways literacy is embedded in cultural contexts over an extended period using an ethnographic design and research methods in her major study, *Ways with Words*. Brian Street's *Literacy in Theory and in Practice* (1984) was strongly grounded in anthropology. Together with even earlier work done by scholars in history and cultural studies in Britain, like Robert K. Webb's *The British Working Class Reader* (1955) and Richard Hoggart's *The Uses of Literacy: Aspects of Working Class Life* (1957), among many others (see Lankshear 1999), these studies provided a strong base informed by research from which to challenge established approaches to teaching reading and writing in schools and the growing emphasis on 'literacy basics' and 'functional literacy' fuelled by the alleged literacy crisis.

Reflection and discussion

- Why do you think literacy levels are presumed by many people to be directly related to national economic health and growth? Do you think that they are? If so, what kind of relationship is involved? If not, why do you think there is no direct relationship?

- Consider the results of international literacy tests and cross-comparisons of test results for school students like the Program for International Student Assessment (PISA; see nces.ed.gov/sur-veys/pisa). How and in what ways might these results be used to inform policy or to shape sanctions applied to schools?

- Why do you think some politicians, policy-makers and business interests take international literacy rankings so seriously?

Within this broad historical context, 'literacy' emerged quickly and deci-sively as a key focus of formal education, and for many politicians, policy-makers and administrators it came to comprise *the* key focus. Legislation like the *No Child Left Behind Act* passed in 2001 in the US enshrined literacy as the new 'bottom line' and the new 'centre of gravity' for school education. With hindsight, this dramatic emergence of literacy as an educational focus can be viewed from several angles: (1) 'literacy' replaced 'reading' and 'writing' in educational language; (2) literacy became a considerable industry; (3) literacy assumed a loftier status in the eyes of educationists; (4) 'literacy' came to apply to an ever increasing variety of practices; and (5) literacy is now being defined with the word 'new'.

First, the *educational language* associated with the development of competence with text changed, as we have already noted, from the language of 'reading' and 'writing' to the language of 'literacy'. The term began to figure prominently in school timetables and programme descriptions. The names of professional journals changed. For example, the *Australian Journal of Reading* became the *Australian Journal of Language and Literacy*, the *Journal of Reading* became the *Journal of Adolescent and Adult Literacy*, and the *Journal of Reading Behavior* became the *Journal of Literacy Research*. Likewise, areas of focus for professional and resource development were renamed. For example, 'emergent literacy' subsumed the conventional coverall term, 'reading readiness', and the then new label, 'writing readiness'; 'literacy development' was used in place of reading or writing development; 'literacy studies' instead of 'language arts research' and the like.

The name change did not always count for much, since in many cases people continued doing in the name of 'literacy' much the same as they had always done as 'reading' teachers or researchers. The point is, however, that whereas 'reading' has traditionally been conceived in *psychological* terms, 'literacy' has always been much more a *sociological* concept. For example, 'illiteracy' and 'illiterate' usually carried social class or social group connotations. Being illiterate tended to be associated with being poor, being of marginal status, and so on. In addition, the sociocultural approach to literacy overtly rejects the idea that textual practices are even largely, let alone solely, a matter of processes that 'go on in the head', or that essentially involve heads communicating with each other by means of graphic signs. From a sociocultural perspective, literacy is a matter of social practices. Literacies are bound up with social, institutional and cultural relationships, and can only be understood when they are situated within their social, cultural and historical contexts (Gee *et al.* 1996: xii). Moreover, they are always connected to social identities – to being particular kinds of people. Literacies are always embedded in Discourses (Gee 2000). From around 1992 Gee has distinguished between Discourse (with a big D) and discourse. The former is the notion of ways of being in the world that integrate identities, and the latter refers to the language bits, or language uses, of Discourses – see the discussion of 'powerful literacy' on pp. 17–18.) Texts are integral parts of innumerable everyday '*lived, talked, enacted, value-and-belief-laden* practices' that are 'carried out in specific places and at specific times' (Gee *et al.* 1996: 3; emphasis in original). Reading and writing are not the same things in a youth zine (pronounced 'zeen') culture, an online chat space, a school classroom, a feminist reading group, or in different kinds of religious ceremonies. People read and write differently out of different social practices, and these different ways with words are part of different ways of being persons and different ways and facets of doing life.

This has important implications. From a sociocultural perspective, it is impossible to separate out from text-mediated social practices the 'bits' concerned with reading or writing (or any other sense of 'literacy') and to treat them independently of all the 'non-print' bits, like values and gestures, context and meaning, actions and objects, talk and interaction, tools and spaces. They are all non-subtractable parts of integrated wholes. 'Literacy bits' do not exist apart from the social practices in which they are embedded and within which they are acquired. If, in some trivial sense they *can* be said to exist (e.g., as code), they do not *mean* anything. Hence, they cannot meaningfully be taught and learned as separate from the rest of the practice (Gee 1996).

By adopting and developing 'literacy' as their key word, socioculturally oriented theorists, researchers, and educators sought, among other things, to bypass the psychological reductionism inscribed on more than a century of educational activity associated with 'reading'. They wanted to keep *the social* to the forefront, and to keep the 'embeddedness' of literacy within larger social practices in clear view. This was often subverted, however, when reading specialists and experts simply adopted the term 'literacy' without taking up its substance.

Second, the scope and amount of *formal* educational activity in the name of literacy that was funded and sanctioned by official government policy, guidelines and directives reached impressive levels. Literacy quickly became a considerable *industry*, involving public and private providers of diverse goods and services at different rungs on the education ladder. Adult and workplace literacy programmes received formal recognition, funding, and credentialling in a manner previously unknown. Funding to providers was usually pegged to achievement outcomes and accountability procedures. In countries like Australia, national and state level policies actually factored workplace literacy competencies into the awards and remuneration system, providing incentives for workers to participate in work-related and work-based literacy programmes, many of which were conducted during company time. Adults and workers whose language backgrounds were not in the dominant/official language of the country were often specially targeted.

Resource and professional development activities mushroomed. Literacy educators and literacy programme providers sought curriculum resources, pedagogical approaches, and specialized training for their work. Armies of literacy consultants, resource developers, and professional development experts quickly emerged to meet the market for literacy goods and services. In keeping with the tradition of formal education, the belief that such work should be grounded in research was also officially recognized and, to a greater or lesser extent, funded. Literacy soon emerged as a major focus within educational research. Once again, the Australian case ranks among the most complex and carefully staged responses to the belief that high levels of functional and work-related literacy on the part of all members of a nation's population is a precondition of successful transition to becoming a post-industrial economy and a knowledge society. At the end of the 1980s, the Australian Language and Literacy Policy legislated for competitive research funding to support a national level research programme in the area of Child Literacy. During the 1990s, the National Children's Literacy Projects programme allocated on a highly competitive basis millions of research dollars for targeted projects addressing diverse aspects of school-age children's literacy. These funds counted toward the research quantum of individual universities, which in turn determined the level of government funding they received for general research activity. Research Centres and Schools or Departments specializing in (language and) literacy education became key planks in Education Faculty structures, and often emerged among the top research income earners within their faculties.

Third, at the same time as literacy assumed a larger and larger focal presence within the recognized role and scope of formal education, it also began to assume *loftier* status in terms of how it was defined and understood by many educationists. It was as if educationists who believed that education should involve much more and count for much more than was generally associated with the term 'literacy' responded to its new pride of place by building more into their conceptions of literacy in order to defend and preserve more expansive educational purposes and standards.

This trend is apparent in a variety of areas and initiatives. These include, among others, concepts and ideals of 'cultural literacy', 'critical literacy', 'technoliteracy', 'higher order literacies', 'three-dimensional literacy', 'powerful literacy', 'multiliteracies', and the like.

For example, the urgent interest shown, especially in the US, in relation to cultural literacy in the late 1980s and early 1990s was concerned with the kind of knowledge young people were thought to need in order to participate effectively in social life as active and informed citizens. Advocates of cultural literacy addressed the kinds of approaches and programmes schools should provide to this end. The association of cultural knowledge with literacy was, perhaps, made most clearly by E. D. Hirsch, Jr in his highly influential book *Cultural Literacy: What Every American Needs to Know* (1987). Hirsch argued that students need to be familiar with a cultural canon in order to be able to negotiate their social context effectively. This canon comprises relevant cultural information that has high status in the public sphere. It is assumed that all members of society share this knowledge as part of their cultural heritage. Hirsch discerned cultural *illiteracy* among growing numbers of students who could not contextualize information or communicate with their fellows within the context of a larger national culture because they lacked the common cultural stock presumed to make such communication and meaning making possible. Hirsch regards 'literate Americans' as those who possess a particular body of cultural knowledge, which he itemized in his book.

Reflection and discussion

- To what extent do you think it is possible to itemize definitively the most important elements of cultural knowledge to be known within societies like your own?

- If you had to compile a list of the top ten cultural knowledge items you think all people in your country should know, what would they be? Compare your list with those compiled by two other people. Discuss these three lists in terms of what is included and what is excluded and the implications of both.

An interesting account that builds on a sociocultural perspective to develop a robust conception of literacy can be found in a 'three-dimensional' model (Green 1988, 1997). This view argues that literacy should be seen as having three interlocking dimensions of learning and practice: the operational, the cultural and the critical. These dimensions bring together language, meaning and context (Green 1988), and no one dimension has any priority over the others. In an integrated view of literate practice and literacy pedagogy, all dimensions need to be taken into account simultaneously. The *operational* dimension focuses on the language aspect of literacy. It includes but also goes beyond competence with the tools, procedures and techniques involved in being able to handle the written language system proficiently. It includes being able to read and write/key in a range of contexts in an appropriate and adequate manner. The *cultural* dimension involves competence with the meaning system of a social practice; knowing how to make and grasp meanings appropriately within the practice – in short, it focuses on understanding texts in relation to contexts. This means knowing what it is about given contexts of practice that makes for appropriateness or inappropriateness of particular ways of reading and writing. The *critical* dimension involves awareness that all social practices, and thus all literacies, are socially constructed and 'selective': they include some representations and classifications – values, purposes, rules, standards, and perspectives – and exclude others. To participate effectively and productively in any literate practice, people must be socialized into it. But if individuals are socialized into a social practice without realizing that it is socially constructed and selective, and that it can be acted on and transformed, they cannot play an active role in changing it. The critical dimension of literacy is the basis for ensuring that individuals are not merely able to participate in some existing literacy and make meanings within it, but also that, in various ways, they are able to transform and actively produce it (Green 1988; Gee *et al.* 1996). Hence, rather than focusing on the 'how to' knowledge of literacy, the 3D model of literacy complements and supplements operational or technical competence by contextualizing literacy with due regard for matters of culture, history and power.

During the past two decades various accounts have been provided of concepts like 'powerful literacies', 'higher order literacies' and, more recently, 'multiliteracies'. The pedagogy of multiliteracies focuses strongly on how cultural and linguistic diversity and the burgeoning impact of new communications technologies are changing demands on learners in terms of what we have identified here as the operational and cultural dimensions of literacies. Learners need new operational and cultural 'knowledges' in order to acquire new languages that provide access to new forms of work, civic, and private practices in their everyday lives. At the same time, as the proponents of multiliteracies argue, learners need to develop strengths in the critical dimension of literacy as well. Mary Kalantzis and Bill Cope (1997) make this very clear with respect to literacy demands in relation to work. They note that with a new work life comes a new language, with much of it attributable to new technologies like 'iconographic, text and screen-based modes of interacting with automated machinery' and to changes in the social relations of work (Kalantzis and Cope 1997: 5). This new work life can be even more highly exploitative and unjust than its predecessor. Accordingly, Kalantzis and Cope claim that when responding to radical contemporary changes in working life literacy educators need to walk a fine line. On one side, learners must

> have the opportunity to develop skills for access to new forms of work through learning the new language of work. But at the same time, as teachers, our role is not simply to be technocrats. Our job is not to produce docile, compliant workers. Students need to develop the skills to speak up, to negotiate and to be able to engage critically with the conditions of their working lives.
>
> (ibid.: 6)

Second, it is very clear that literacies, conceived from a sociocultural perspective generally and a multiliteracies perspective specifically, entail a vast amount of knowledge. Being literate involves much more than simply knowing *how* to operate the language system. The cultural and critical facets of knowledge integral to being literate are considerable. Indeed, much of what the proponents of multiliteracies have explicated are the new and changing knowledge components of literacies under contemporary social, economic, cultural, political and civic conditions. In other words, being literate in any of the myriad forms literacies take presupposes complex amalgams of propositional, procedural and 'performative' forms of knowledge. Making meaning is knowledge intensive, and much of the knowledge that school-based learning is required to develop and mobilize is knowledge involved in meaning making.

The idea that literacies can be more or less 'powerful' was developed on a number of rather different fronts during the late 1980s and the 1990s. We will briefly mention two examples here. The first is the account provided by James Gee. The second is a view associated with a group of linguists in Australia whose work was very influential there during the 1990s.

For Gee (1990), a powerful literacy is not a specific literacy *per se* but, rather, a way of using a literacy. He defines being literate as having control, or fluent mastery, of language uses within what he calls secondary Discourses. Gee defines Discourses as 'ways of being in the world', which integrate words, acts, gestures, attitudes, beliefs, purposes, clothes, bodily movements and positions, and so on. Discourses also integrate *identities*, in the sense that through their participation in Discourses individuals are identified and identifiable as members of socially meaningful groups or networks and players of socially meaningful roles (ibid.: 142–3). Language is integral to Discourses, but Discourses are always much more than language alone. Language uses – or what Gee calls the 'language bits' of Discourses – are 'connected stretches of language that make sense', that are meaningful within a Discourse (ibid.: 143). Language uses vary from Discourse to Discourse, but well-known examples include 'conversations, stories, reports, arguments, essays', as well as explanations, commands, interviews, ways of eliciting information, and so on (ibid.: 143).

Gee distinguishes between a person's primary Discourse and its distinctive language use (which he mostly refers to as 'discourse' with a small 'd'), and their secondary Discourses and their respective language uses. Our primary Discourse involves 'face to face communication with intimates', and is the Discourse of our immediate group (ibid.: 143). Primary Discourses differ from social group to social group (e.g., by social class, ethnicity, etc.). We each belong to just one primary Discourse, which shapes who and what we initially are as persons. Members of all social groups that extend beyond immediate, face-to-face encounters also encounter secondary Discourses through their participation in secondary institutions, such as schools, churches, sports clubs, community groups, workplaces, and so on. These secondary Discourses have their own more or less distinctive language uses and they shape our identities in particular ways – as we take on their beliefs, purposes, ways of speaking and acting, moving, dressing, and so on. According to Gee, then, since there are multiple secondary Discourses, and since literacy and being literate are defined in terms of controlling secondary language uses, there are multiple – indeed, *many* – literacies and ways of being literate. In all cases, however, being literate means being able to use the 'right' language in the 'right' ways within a Discourse. This corresponds roughly to command of the 'operational' and 'cultural' dimensions of literacy previously mentioned.

On the basis of these ideas, Gee defines *powerful* literacy in terms of employing a secondary language use as a 'metalanguage' for understanding, analysing and critiquing other Discourses and the way they constitute us as persons and situate us within society (ibid.: 153; see also Gee 1991: 8–9). By a metalanguage, he means, 'a set of meta-words, meta-values [and] meta-beliefs' (Gee 1990: 153). Practising a powerful literacy, so defined, can provide the basis for reconstituting our selves/identities and resituating ourselves within society.

To understand and critique a particular Discourse using a powerful literacy derived from some other Discourse requires understanding both Discourses *as Discourses*: what they are, how they operate, what values and ways of being in the world they promote, how their 'language bits' reflect and enable this. This is metalevel knowledge. In powerful literacy we draw on such knowledge to provide us with a reason, a basis, and an alternative in terms of which we can decide to opt out of another Discourse or work to change it.

Reflection and discussion

Identify and discuss the first time you recall thinking that your home language and social practices (or, your primary Discourse) was not like someone else's. Describe the context in which the thought occurred to you. If you cannot recall a first time, describe any occasion in which you have been strongly conscious of such a difference.

Drawing on resources like those below describe some ways in which a student's primary Discourse might differ significantly from the secondary Discourse they experience in school:

- Heath (1983)

- Hicks (2001)

- Hull and Schultz (2001)

- Knobel (1999)

A rather different account of powerful language was developed in Australia by a school of systemic functional linguists who became known among educators as 'genre theorists'. They adapted Michael Halliday's systemic functional linguistic theory and work in ways intended to invest it with socially transforming possibilities. Their underlying premise was that certain social groups and their characteristic genres enjoy more power than other groups and their genres. They associated social power with mastery of genres which, they believed, could be taught and learned under classroom conditions. They argued that powerful genres and their social purposes can – and *should* – be identified and taught explicitly to students and, particularly, to students from marginalized and/or non-English-speaking backgrounds. From this perspective, genre mastery and successful use of powerful genres depend on one's ability to make the 'right' linguistic choices according to immediate contexts and social purposes. The genre theorists argued that meanings – and the social effects of language use – depend directly on language choices, which in turn, depend on one's purposes. They maintained that language and literacy mastery is properly evaluated according to the repertoire of possible linguistic choices the language user is able to draw on appropriately and that a broad linguistic repertoire can be taught and refined explicitly in classrooms (cf. Christie 1987; Martin 1993; Martin and Rothery 1993).

From the standpoint of these and similar perspectives, it was seen as highly important to ensure that literacy agendas be expansive, because of the way literacy was being prioritized within education policy and the potential that existed for economic and political interests to 'steer' literacy along narrow and minimalist lines.

Fourth, since the 1980s and 1990s the term 'literacy' has been applied to an ever increasing variety of practices. It has reached the point today where it seems that almost any knowledge and learning deemed educationally valuable can somehow or other be conceived as a literacy.

Sometimes this involves 'literacy' becoming a metaphor for 'competence', 'proficiency' or 'being functional'. Concepts like 'being computer literate' or being 'technologically literate' are sometimes used simply to mean that someone is more or less proficient with a computer or some other device like a video recorder: they can 'make sense of' and 'use' computers, or can program their video player or mobile phone. In this sense, talk of being computer literate or technologically literate has become everyday terminology. This is actually an index for just how focal literacy has become as a social issue and an educational ideal during the past two or three decades.

Getting closer to more literal associations with language *per se*, we nowadays hear frequent references to 'oral literacy', 'visual literacy', 'information literacy', 'media literacy', 'science literacy' and even 'emotional literacy'. These uses foreground the notion of being able to communicate or make meaning – as a producer or receiver – using signs, signals, codes, graphic images. In cases like 'science literacy', the concept implies being able to read and write meaningfully the language and literature of science. It is close to the idea advanced in the 1970s by philosophers like Paul Hirst (1974) with respect to knowledge and the academic disciplines. Hirst spoke of 'forms and fields of knowledge' – systematic ways of understanding the world, epitomized by academic disciplines – as having their own discrete 'languages and literatures'. To 'be on the inside' of a form or field of knowledge meant being able to 'speak' its language and 'read and write its literature'. The language comprised the procedures, techniques, standards, methods used by expert practitioners. The literature comprised the products generated by faithful and competent practitioners who spoke the language in question.

In the case of ideas like 'media literacy' or 'information literacy', we sometimes find implications that we need to learn to 'read' media or information sources in specialized ways in order to 'get what is really there' and/or to avoid being 'taken in'. This is the idea that there are ways of deciphering media and information more or less *wittingly* or *critically* as an 'insider' or, at least, as an effective receiver or producer within the media spaces in question. To some extent this implies the ability to identify strategies and techniques being used to produce particular kinds of effects on what we think, believe, or desire.

An example here is provided by David Sholle and Stan Denski's (1993) account of television within their treatment of critical media literacy. They observe that television can be seen as 'a *pedagogical machine*' that operates to construct discourses 'that function primarily in the locus of a mode of transmission where "culture becomes defined solely by markets for culture"' (1993: 309; original emphasis; the quotation is from Wexler 1988: 98). Sholle and Denski argue that if teachers are to educate learners to become media literate,

> we must attend to the multiple references and codes that position them [the learners]. This means paying attention to the manner in which popular culture texts are constructed by and construct various discursive codes, but also how such texts express various contradictory ideological interests and how these texts might be taken up in a way that creates possibilities for different constructions of cultural and political life.
>
> (1993: 309)

At present, one of the hottest 'literacies' going around in this sense is 'digital literacy'. It is emerging in many education policy documents as a core educational goal. This trend is often associated with fears about the emergence of a 'digital divide' – between those who are digitally literate and those who are not. It is feared that a digital divide will create a deep social and economic inequality, in which those who are not digitally literate will be seriously disadvantaged. Those who push a digital literacy agenda to pre-empt inequalities resulting from a digital divide believe we need to capture the essence of what it is to be digitally literate and pass the necessary skills and knowledge on to all who are involved in education and the workforce so that they will not be disadvantaged in learning or at work. Furthermore, those who are not in education or working but who may want to participate in cultural activities using new technologies should also have the opportunity to become digitally literate.

Definitions of digital literacy are of two main kinds: conceptual definitions and standardized sets of operations intended to provide national and international *normalizations* of digital literacy. Two of the best-known conceptual definitions of digital literacy are those provided by Richard Lanham (1995) and Paul Gilster (1997; in Pool 1997).

Lanham (1995: 198) claims that 'literacy' has extended its semantic reach from meaning 'the ability to read and write' to now meaning 'the ability to understand information however presented'. He emphasizes the multimediated nature of digital information, and argues that to be digitally literate involves 'being skilled at deciphering complex images and sounds as well as the syntactical subtleties of words' (ibid.: 200). Digitally literate people are 'quick on [their] feet in moving from one kind of medium to another ... know what kinds of expression fit what kinds of knowledge and become skilled at presenting [their] information in the medium that [their] audience will find easiest to understand' (ibid.). Digital literacy enables us to match the medium we use to the kind of information we are presenting and to the audience to whom we are presenting it.

Gilster defines digital literacy as 'the ability to understand and use information in multiple formats from a wide variety of sources when it is presented via computers' and, particularly, through the medium of the internet (Gilster, in Pool 1997: 6). He emphasizes what he sees as inherent differences between *digital* information media and conventional print media. Digital literacy involves 'adapting our skills to an evocative new medium, [and] our experience of the Internet will be determined by how we master its core competencies' (ibid.). These competencies are not merely 'operational' or 'technical' competencies, however. Digital literacy involves 'mastering ideas, not keystrokes' (ibid.). Gilster identifies four key competencies of digital literacy: knowledge assembly, evaluating information content, searching the internet, and navigating hypertext. He describes each at length in his book, *Digital Literacy* (Gilster 1997). Gilster claims we need to teach and learn 'how to use the Web properly and how to be critical' and that 'we all need to learn that skill' (Gilster, in Pool 1997: 8). Citing the familiar image of students using the internet to find information that they simply cut and paste into a 'cobbled-together collection of quotes or multimedia items', Gilster argues that we need to teach students 'how to assimilate the information, evaluate it, and then reintegrate it' (in Pool 1997: 9).

'Standardised operationalisations' refer to attempts to operationalize what is involved in being 'digitally literate' in terms of certain tasks, performances, demonstrations of skills, etc., and to render these as a standard set for general adoption. Some are little more than codifications of sets of specific operations at the level Gilster refers to as 'keystrokes'. Others are closer to Gilster's idea of 'concern with meanings'.

Toward the 'keystroke' end of the spectrum is the approach of the Global Digital Literacy Council (GDLC). One of the Council's core objectives is to 'review and update the Digital Literacy Standards based on input from subject matter experts worldwide' (gdlc.org). Current GDLC standards are reflected in the Internet and Computing Core Certification (IC^3) program provided by Certiport (certiport.com). This covers Computing

Fundamentals, Key Applications, and Living Online. The Computing Fundamentals test items involve tasks like asking learners to click on all the 'output devices' from a list containing items like joystick, monitor, speakers, keyboard, etc.; to choose among four items (one thousand, one million, one billion, one trillion) for the number of bytes in a megabyte; to create a new folder on the C drive within a simulated file manager; and to match 'operating system', 'application' and 'utility program' to three provided definitions. The items testing Key Applications use a range of simulations and ask learners to insert content from the clipboard at the designated insertion point, and exit Word without using the close box. Items assessing knowledge and skills related to Living Online use simulations to have respondents enter a subject in an email message and send the message, go to a specified address on a webpage, and locate the history of sites visited in a web browser.

Toward the 'concern with meaning' end of a spectrum is an operationalization developed by the US Educational Testing Service (ETS) for higher education environments. From the ETS perspective, digital literacy can be seen as 'the ability to use digital technology, communication tools and/or networks appropriately to solve information problems in order to function in an information society' (ets.org). It comprises 'the ability to use technology as a tool to research, organize, evaluate, and communicate information, and the possession of a fundamental understanding of the ethical/legal issues surrounding the access and use of information'.

The ETS operationalization comprises 12–15 real-time tasks that are 'scenario-based' (for examples of tasks, see ets.org/Media/Tests/ICT_Literacy/pdf/ict_literacy_task_matrix.pdf). Tasks include subject matter from the areas of humanities, natural sciences, social studies, and popular culture and practical affairs, and use a generic version of one or more of 12 named ICT tools (e.g., a word processor, presentation software, a web browser, an email client). Test takers perform a range of 'information management tasks', including 'extracting information from a database, developing a spreadsheet, or composing an e-mail based on research findings'. The seven competencies are: Define, Access, Manage, Integrate, Evaluate, Create and Communicate.

Finally, recently, literacy scholars and researchers have begun using the word 'new' in association with 'literacy' and 'literacies'. This has occurred in two main ways, which we call *paradigmatic* and *ontological* respectively.

The *paradigmatic* sense of 'new' occurs in talk of the 'New Literacy Studies' (Gee 1996, 2000; Street 1993). This refers to a particular sociocultural approach to understanding and researching literacy. The 'New Literacy Studies' can be seen as a new theoretical and research *paradigm* for looking at literacy: a new alternative to the previously established paradigm that was based on psycholinguistics. The use of 'new' here parallels that which is involved in names for initiatives or movements such as the New School of Social Research, the New Science, the New Criticism (and New Critics). In all such cases, the proponents think of their project as comprising a new and different paradigm relative to an existing orthodoxy or dominant approach.

This paradigmatic sense of 'new' in relation to literacy is not concerned with new literacies as such but, rather, with a new approach to thinking about literacy as a social phenomenon. As it happens, numerous scholars who are associated with the New Literacy Studies paradigm are researching and writing about the kinds of practices we are calling new literacies. But that is simply a contingency. The 'New' of New Literacy Studies and the 'new' of new literacies in the sense we are discussing here are quite distinct ideas. By the same token, and for reasons we hope become apparent in this book, we think that new literacies in the way we understand and describe them here can really only be researched effectively from a sociocultural perspective, of which the New Literacy Studies is an example.

Our idea of the *ontological* sense of 'new' is intended to relate directly to new literacies of the kinds under discussion here. The terms 'ontological' and 'ontology' are being used in multiple ways in the context of talk about new technologies and new social practices involving new technologies, so it is necessary that we spell out what we mean by our use of 'ontological'. In simple language, we are using 'ontological' here to refer to the 'nature' or 'stuff' of new literacies. To say that 'new' literacies are ontologically new is to say that they consist of a different kind of 'stuff' from conventional literacies we have known in the past. It is the idea that changes have occurred in the character and substance of literacies that are associated with larger changes in technology, institutions, media and the economy, and with the rapid movement toward global scale in manufacture, finance, communications, and so on. As we see things, this idea can be broken down into two parts.

The first part has to do with the rise of digital-electronic technologies and, with this, the emergence of 'post-typographic' forms of texts and text production. It is the idea that 'new' literacies are different kinds of phenomena – are made of different stuff, or are significantly different in their nature – from 'conventional' print-based literacies. The argument is that contemporary changes have impacted on social practices in all the main areas of everyday life within modern societies: in work, at leisure, in the home, in education, in the community, and in the public sphere. Established social practices have been transformed, and new forms of social practice have emerged and continue to emerge at a rapid rate. Many of these new and changing social practices involve new and changing ways of producing, distributing, exchanging and receiving texts by *electronic* means. These include the production and exchange of multimodal forms of texts that can arrive via digital code – what Richard Lanham (1994) calls 'the rich signal' – as sound, text, images, video, animations, and any combination of these.

In the ontological sense of 'new', the category of 'new literacies' refers to practices that are mediated by 'post-typographic' forms of texts. 'Ontologically new' literacies involve things like using and constructing hyperlinks between documents and/or images, sounds, movies, etc.; text messaging on a mobile phone; using digital semiotic languages (such as those used by the characters in the online episodic game *Banja*, or emoticons used in email, online chat space or in instant messaging); manipulating a mouse to move around within a text; reading file extensions and identifying what software will 'read' each file; navigating three-dimensional worlds online; uploading images from a camera or digital phone to a computer or to the Internet; inserting text into a digital image or animation, attaching sound to an image, or inserting sound into an image; building multimedia role play universes online; choosing, building or customizing a weblog template.

The second part of the idea of new literacies as ontologically new is a little more complex, and will be discussed at length in Chapter 2. Let's think of the points made in the previous paragraph as having mainly to do with ontologically new literacies involving a different kind of *'technical stuff'* from conventional literacies: for example, screens and pixels rather than paper and type, digital code rather than material print (whether printed by hand, typewriter or press), seamlessly multimodal rather than distinct process for distinct modes (text, image, sound), etc. What we want to say here is that in addition to being made of different 'technical' stuff from conventional literacies, new literacies are also made of what we might call different *'ethos* stuff' from what we typically associate with conventional literacies. For example, they are often more 'participatory', more 'collaborative', and more 'distributed', as well as less 'published', less 'individuated' and less 'author-centric' than conventional literacies. When we spell this out in the following chapter we will be saying that the 'stuff' of what we think of as new literacies reflects a different *mindset* from the stuff of which conventional literacies are largely composed. They involve different kinds of social and cultural *relations*, they flow out of different kinds of priorities and values, and so on. At least, they do so up to an extent that makes it plausible to distinguish between conventional and new literacies in a broad way. The different 'ethos' of new literacies seems to us to be linked to the different 'technical' character of new literacies in complex ways, but it is useful to separate these aspects out as two dimensions of what we see as *ontologically* new about new literacies.

The following chapters focus overwhelmingly on literacies that are associated with the massive growth of electronic information and communications technologies and their increasing role and place within our everyday lives. To a large extent it is literacies in this post-typographic sense that schools have identified as their main challenge as far as incorporating 'new literacies' into their programmes and as media for learning are concerned.

At the same time, as our earlier reference to the 'multiliteracies' project suggests, the relationship between 'new literacies' and new digital electronic technologies does not seem to us to be a one-to-one relationship. In other words, we want to argue here for the view that it is possible to think of some literacies being 'new' *without them necessarily involving the use of new digital electronic technologies*. The 'multiliteracies' project reminds us that there are any number of recently-emerged literacy practices associated with contemporary changes in our institutions and economy that do not necessarily involve using new technologies, or at the very least where we can say that using new technologies in these literacies is optional or, at any rate, not an especially important aspect of them. This is especially true of some important work-related literacies. It is also true of the massive uptake in many Western countries of print format manga comics, of the popular use of scenario building activities by businesses, political organizations, governments, non-government organizations, and educational institutions, and of the still large-scale involvement of mainly young people in a range of highly sophisticated card games like *Pokémon, DragonBall Z* and *Yu-Gi-Oh!*.

In arguing for this position we do not in any way underestimate the huge significance of post-typographic, electronically-mediated literacies within everyday life, and their leading place within any useful conception of 'new literacies'. By the same token, we think it would unjustifiably marginalize the status of many 'new' literacy practices as social phenomena were the link between 'new' literacies and digital electronic technologies to be made necessary by fiat. Consequently, we want to leave some space for a *chronological* dimension in our account of new literacies, such that it is possible for some literacies to qualify as 'new' even if they are not ontologically new with respect to their 'technical stuff'. Examples of new literacies of this kind include scenario building, paper zines, and print-based fan fiction and manga.

The significance of this third idea of the new was underscored, by utter coincidence, within an hour of the two previous paragraphs being composed, when *Yahoo News* ran an online version of a story from *USA Today* (see Memmott, 29 December 2005: n.p.). The story reports that beginning 8 January 2006 the *Los Angeles Times* and the *Seattle Intelligencer* would be running a manga strip called *Peach Fuzz*. According to the report, other US newspapers were expected to start running manga strips during 2006. Personnel from both newspapers referred to the wish to attract new readers, and 'especially younger ones who might otherwise turn to online news and entertainment' as a key reason for the decision to run the manga strips. The report also cited manga as currently being among 'the fastest growing genres in US publishing' (Memmott, 29 December 2005: n.p.).

There is one final important point to be made here, which we think is interesting and which we will develop further in Chapter 3. When we look at literacies that are chronologically recent, that we want to call 'new' literacies but that are not made of new 'technical stuff', what we find is that they *are* made of new 'ethos stuff'. So, if we take examples like scenario building and paper-based fanfiction and printed zines, we find that they reflect key features of the mindset we associate with new literacies. They emphasize relations of collaboration, participation, dispersion, distributed expertise. In other words, even though such new literacies are not new in the 'technical stuff' aspect of their ontology, they *are* ontologically new in terms of their 'ethos stuff'. This will allow us in Chapter 3 to distinguish between paradigm cases of new literacies – ones that are new in *all* their ontology – and peripheral cases of new literacies.

In Chapter 2 we continue our discussion of what counts as 'new' in terms of literacies by addressing the theme of mindsets that relates to what we have called the 'ethos stuff' of new literacies.

Reflection and discussion

Using the discussion in this chapter as a basis for deciding, which of the following would not be considered 'new' literacies, and why?

- Reading any or all of Shakespeare's plays online.

- Contributing to a wiki, such as Wikipedia.org.

- Accessing a portable document file (pdf) of a student assignment archived online.

- Watching digitized versions of old television shows online (e.g., use video.google.com to search for shows like *The Mary Tyler Moore Show* or *Lost in Space*).

- Playing a massively multi-player online game, like Kingdomof loathing.com.

- Using an educational CD-ROM package like the *Reader Rabbit* series to practise reading and spelling skills.

- Creating fan-based animations that remix clips from a range of animation shows and movies.

- Blogging (see Technorati.com).

- Scanning a handwritten and self-illustrated story and posting it online.

- Using image manipulation software like *Photoshop* to alter, enhance, or spoof an image as part of contributing to a set of images similarly altered around a given theme or message.

Repeat this activity after you have read Chapters 2 and 3 and compare your responses and reasons with those provided here.

CHAPTER 2

New Literacies and the Challenge of Mindsets

Introduction

This chapter argues that 'new' literacies are related to an emerging and evolving mindset and that the idea of 'new' literacies is a useful way to conceptualize what might be seen as one component of an unfolding 'literacy dialectic'. By a *dialectic* we mean a kind of transcendence, in which two forces that exist in tension with one another 'work out their differences', as it were, and evolve into something that bears the stamp of both, yet is qualitatively different from each of them.

Since the eighteenth century and particularly since the Industrial Revolution, Western industrialized countries have developed along a broad trajectory in conjunction with a characteristic way of thinking about the world and responding to it. We can refer to this general way of thinking about the world as a *mindset*. Part of this trajectory and its associated mindset included the development of certain kinds and qualities of literacy practices and ways of thinking about literacy. Recently, however, important changes have occurred on a historical scale. These are associated with the development and mass uptake of digital electronic technologies and the rise of a new mode of development of a broadly 'post-industrial' kind (e.g., Castells 1996, 2000). These changes have been accompanied by the emergence of different (new) ways of thinking about the world and responding to it. A new kind of mindset has begun to emerge and some new kinds of *literacies* have begun to evolve. We call these 'new' literacies. While these 'new' literacies share some features in common with conventional forms of literacy that developed throughout the modern era, they also differ from conventional literacies in some very important ways.

We are presently at a point in the historical-cultural development of literacy where we don't really know how to deal educationally with these new literacies. What seems to be happening is that the day-to-day business of school is still dominated by conventional literacies, and engagement with the 'new' literacies is largely confined to learners' lives in spaces outside of schools and other formal educational settings. Insofar as schools try to get to grips with the changing world of literacy and technology (often seen in terms of using computers in the production of texts and textual representations), they often simply end up reproducing familiar conventional literacies through their uses of new technologies. Learners who have access to *both* realms of literacy – the conventional and the 'new' – experience parallel 'literacyscapes' (Leander 2003). At school they operate in one literacy 'universe', and out of school they operate in another. For some learners this experience is confusing and/or frustrating. Learners who do not have out-of-school access to 'new' literacies may escape this kind of confusion or frustration, but at the expense of not encountering forms of practice that are becoming increasingly prevalent in everyday life.

While at present it is possible to carve our lives up in ways that accommodate the different kinds of literacies and confine them to different spaces – at schools and universities and, in many cases, at work we operate with conventional literacies, but at home and in various public and community spaces we engage in 'new' as well as conventional literacies – it will almost certainly *not* be like this in the future. Rather, social routines and their embedded literacies will draw on elements of both what is currently familiar and what is currently 'new' in ways that perhaps we can scarcely begin to imagine now. Part of making a successful transition to this future state of affairs will involve understanding *both* 'literacy legacies' – the conventional and the 'new' – from the inside, and knowing how to draw on them productively and creatively as a necessary condition for participating effectively in social routines. This will require us to develop conceptions and arrangements of literacy education that enable learners to negotiate the kind of transcendence – the dialectic – that seems most likely to occur.

'Mindsets' and 'the contemporary fracturing of space'

The idea of a mindset usually refers to a point of view, perspective, or frame of reference through which individuals or groups of people experience the world, interpret or make sense of what they encounter, and respond to what they experience. Mindsets can be thought of as sets of assumptions, beliefs, values, and ways of doing things that orient us toward what we experience and incline us to understand and respond in some ways more than others.

In addition, however, the 'set' in 'mindset' usually refers to the sense of someone's mind being *set* or *fixed* – as in 'set in stone' – in the way they approach the world. For example, the definition of 'mindset' provided by Roger Caldwell in a course on futures offered at the University of Arizona states that a mindset is 'a person's frame of reference that is fixed'. Moreover, someone

> can have a particular 'mindset' that is so strong in a specific outlook that they do not see other perspectives, even though they might hear them and believe they have been given consideration. This prevents looking at new options in a realistic sense.
>
> (Caldwell, no date or page)

This coheres with the use of 'mindset' in decision theory and system theory as described by *Wikipedia*, according to which a mindset

> refers to a set of assumptions, methods or notations held by one or more people or groups of people which is so established that it creates a powerful incentive within these people or groups to continue to adopt or accept prior behaviours, choices, or tools.
>
> (wikipedia.org/wiki/Mindset, accessed 30.12.05)

The concept of mindsets is useful for thinking about literacy education specifically, and learning more generally, under current historical conditions. At present, schools and classrooms can be seen as a specific instance of a more general phenomenon that involves a 'fracturing of space' accompanied by a striking divergence in mindsets (Lankshear and Bigum 1999: 457).

The idea of space having been fractured refers to the emergence of *cyberspace* as a distinctively new space that co-exists with physical space (ibid.). Cyberspace has not *displaced* physical space, of course, and will not displace it. Nor, however, can physical space 'dismiss' cyberspace. For the majority of young people in so-called developed countries who are now in adolescence, cyberspace has been integral to their experience of 'spatiality' since their early years. In these same countries an entire generation has grown up in a world saturated by digital electronic technologies that cyberspace links to each other as an enormous network. Co-existence is the destiny of these two spaces. Neither is about to disappear.

The idea of a striking divergence in mindsets accompanying this contemporary fracturing of space refers to the difference between people who continue to approach the world in familiar ways because they see the current world as essentially unchanged, and others who see the world as being significantly different now from how it was until recently, and who approach it differently. The former, in various ways, continue to view the world from a perspective based on the constitution and mastery of the *physical* world throughout the modern era and within the industrial mode of development (Lankshear and Bigum 1999). The latter view the contemporary world as being significantly different from how it was before the 'advent' of digital electronic technologies, the transition toward a new mode of development (Castells 1996, 2000), and the explosion of *cyberspace*.

An indicative example: from atoms to bits

A specific example of the kind of qualitative differences that are involved between the divergent mindsets is apparent in Nicholas Negroponte's example of different perceptions of a computer's value. Negroponte recalls checking in at a place where he was asked if he had a laptop computer with him. He was asked how much it was worth (in case it got lost or stolen). Negroponte valued it at 1 to 2 million dollars. The check-in person disputed the possibility of the machine having such a high value, and asked what kind it was. On being told the brand and model she assigned it a $2000 value. Negroponte says this exchange reflects the distinction between *atoms* and *bits* as different kinds of stuff.

Atoms belong to the physical world we have always known, and to the world which can be captured in 'analogue' forms. Bits (binary units) belong to the non-physical digital world. They are 'states of being' like 'on or off, true or false, up or down, in or out, black or white' which can be represented in binary code of 0s and 1s in a colourless, sizeless, weightless form that can be 'moved' at the speed of light (Negroponte 1995: 14).

We are, of course, well used to dealing with atoms. Over the centuries humans have developed concepts, frameworks, laws, assumptions and procedures for handling the myriad aspects of the physical world. Thinking in atomic terms has become a kind of 'baseline' in our everyday approach to the world. Many things are changing, however, as our everyday environments become increasingly digitized. This invites us – indeed, *challenges* us – to develop new conceptual beliefs and knowledge orientations and approaches to our everyday world.

Not unreasonably, the person in the position of responsibility for property was thinking in terms of atoms, in the form of the physical computer. The laptop was atom stuff, of a particular make and vintage, and its value as such was $2000. Being 'digital' in his orientation to the world, Negroponte approached the value of the machine in terms of its 'bits'. That is, he thought of the machine in terms of its 'contents' in the form of ideas or patents potential and the like that were 'contained' or 'stored' (even the language gets tricky) as binary code some 'where' on the hard disk. Depending on what was on the disk at the time, the value of the 'computer' could have amounted to practically anything at all in dollar terms, not to mention in terms of potential human benefits and the like.

This example gives a sense of the degree of qualitative differences in mindset involved when reading, respectively, out of a physical/material/industrial mindset (including what we will later refer to as a 'newcomer' mindset), and when reading out of a mindset (that we will later refer to as an 'insider' mindset) informed by a sense of cyberspace and the digital. It only takes us part of the way, however, because while it addresses the all important ontological difference between atoms and bits as different kinds of 'stuff', it does *not* yet speak to the fracturing of space at the level of a new co-existent space (i.e., cyberspace). Negroponte's example could refer to a universe in which there were only standalone computers, with no networks: no cyberspace. We would certainly have to deal with different kinds of *stuff* under those conditions, but we would not have to deal with different kinds of *'space'* – or, at least, not to the same extent. Yet as we will see, it is the interconnectedness of phenomena in cyberspace, enabled by technologies of 'bits' and 'bytes', that is what is really at stake in these two diverging mindsets. The information contained on the computer hard disk can take on a completely new kind of life – and engender completely new kinds of lives – when that computer is part of a global internet(work) from what it can have when it is 'confined' to the space of a standalone machine.

The two diverging mindsets

At their most general level the two divergent mindsets can be stated as follows (see Lankshear and Bigum 1999). The first mindset assumes that the contemporary world is essentially the way it has been throughout the modern-industrial period, only now it is more technologized or, alternatively, technologized in a new and very sophisticated way. To all intents and purposes, however, the world on which these new technologies are brought to bear is more or less the same economic, cultural, social world that has evolved throughout the modern era, where things got done by means of routines that were predicated on long-standing assumptions about bodies, materials, property and forms of ownership, industrial techniques and principles, physical texts, face-to-face dealings (and physical proxies for them), and so on.

The second mindset assumes that the contemporary world is different in important ways from the world we have known, and that the difference is growing. This is related to the development of new digital electronic internetworked technologies and new ways of doing things and new ways of being that are enabled by these technologies. More and more the world is being changed as a result of people exploring hunches and 'visions' of what might be possible given the potential of digital technologies and electronic networks. The world is being changed in some fairly fundamental ways as a result of people imagining and exploring how using new technologies can become part of making the world (more) different from how it presently is (second mindset), rather than using new technologies to do familiar things in more 'technologized' ways (first mindset).

At an early point in the development of the internet, Nat Tunbridge (1995) interviewed Electronic Frontier Foundation co-founder John Perry Barlow on the theme of issues arising around the internet at that time, and how Barlow understood and responded to those issues. We will draw on ideas from that interview at several subsequent points in this chapter. In the course of the interview Barlow drew a distinction that suggests convenient labels for the two mindsets. He distinguished between people who have been born into and have grown up within the context of cyberspace, on one hand, and those who come to this new world from the standpoint of a life-long socialization in physical space, on the other. Barlow refers to the former as 'natives' and the latter as 'immigrants'. We prefer to call them 'insiders' and 'newcomers' to cyberspace and, on this basis, to identify the two broad mindsets spelled out above as a *Newcomer* or *Outsider* mindset (Mindset 1) and an *Insider* mindset (Mindset 2), respectively.

This distinction marks off those who 'understand the Internet, virtual concepts and the IT world generally' from those who do not (Barlow, in Tunbridge 1995: 2). That is, it distinguishes mind*sets*, even though Barlow does not refer to mindsets *per se*. Newcomers to cyberspace don't have the experiences, history and resources available to draw on that insiders have. And so, to that extent, they cannot understand and respond to the space as insiders do. Barlow believes this distinction falls very much along age lines. If we update his numbers to allow for the decade that has passed since he was interviewed by Tunbridge, Barlow would be saying that, generally speaking, people over the age of 35 are 'newcomers' and, conversely, that those in societies like our own who are under 35 are closer to being 'insiders' in terms of understanding what the Internet is 'and having a real basic sense of it' (ibid.: 2).

Reflection and discussion

- To what extent do you see yourself as a 'newcomer' or an 'insider' with respect to Barlow's classification with respect to new technology practices?

- To what extent is it possible for a 'newcomer' to ever become an 'insider'?

- To what extent do *all* people born in First World countries after 1985 have an 'insider' mindset by default?

Barlow is suggesting that without the appropriate mindset people will approach the tools and environments of the digital technology revolution in inappropriate ways. Moreover, he believes that in the current context, legions of 'newcomers' ('immigrants') are doing precisely that.

In the same interview Barlow also provided a colourful and enthusiastic statement of what it is like to approach the world from the insider mindset. Barlow said of the internet, 'Technologically. Philosophically. Socially. I ... believe this is the biggest technological event since the capture of fire in terms of what it will do to the basic look and feel of being a human being' (ibid.: 4). Such a general statement tells us very little on its own, but we can begin to get a sense of the ways 'the look and feel of being a human being' might change by reference to such concrete and prosaic examples as what it is like, say, to be a consumer (or, for that matter, to be a retailer) under conditions where thinking from the second mindset is applied to internet space. Let's, for example, consider Jeff Bezos's description of the kind of thinking that went into creating Amazon.com. Robert Spector's (2000) account of the creation and rise of Amazon.com provides some interesting insights into how Bezos, the CEO of Amazon.com, thinks about information space and how to 'live' there. Spector describes how Bezos wanted to establish the kind of enterprise that Amazon.com has since become, and had made it known to corporate headhunters that he wished 'to hook up with a technology company, where he could chase his real passion [of] "second-phase" automation' (2000: 16).

Bezos identifies second-phase automation as 'the common theme that has run through my life' (cited in Spector 2000: 16). By first-phase automation, Bezos means 'where you use technology to do the same old ... processes, but just faster and more efficiently'. Within e-commerce, using barcode scanners and point-of-sale systems would be typical examples of first-phase automation. In such cases an e-commerce enterprise would be using the internet to do 'the same process you've always done, but just more efficiently' (ibid.: 16).

First-phase automation did not interest Bezos. He wanted to do more than simply transfer life as it is done in a physical space to the online world of the internet. He preferred to think in terms of second-phase automation. This is 'when you can fundamentally change the underlying ... process' – in his case, a business process – 'and do things in a completely new way'. For Bezos, second-phase information is 'more of a revolution instead of an evolution' (ibid.: 16).

To a large extent, buying a book on Amazon.com *is* a qualitatively different experience from buying a book in a conventional store. For example, Amazon.com invites consumers to reconstitute themselves in certain ways. Each webpage for each book has space for readers to post reviews of the book, an evaluation rating scale for readers to post their rating of the book, and a facility for readers to say whether they found a particular review useful (and the same holds for all other items sold through Amazon.com, such as music CDs, movies, electronic components, kitchenware, etc.). To this extent, consumers are being invited to *also* become critics, reviewers or commentators. The practice of inviting reader/user-consumers to submit reviews can be seen as part of Amazon.com's suite of strategies for encouraging customers to buy maximum product. Amazon.com has gone so far as to offer cash prizes to customers who write the first customer review for certain listed books and other products sold through Amazon.com.

So far as the book side of its operation is concerned, Amazon.com's mission is 'to use the Internet to transform book buying into the fastest, easiest, and most enjoyable shopping experience possible' (Amazon.com 1996–2000: 1). In line with this, the company also supplies a rating for each book based on customer evaluations and a ranking number that indicates how well the book is doing in sales from the website in comparison with other books (this ranking system applies equally to all the other products listed by the company). Amazon.com also recommends books you might like, based on your previous purchases or on information you have provided, and offers an alerting service to let you know when new books are available, using keywords you key into the service sign-up form. This web of services, products and customer participation is distinctively 'new' with respect to what it means to 'shop' online. We will return to Amazon.com a little later.

Meanwhile, we will now look more closely at what we think are some important dimensions along which the two mindsets vary as they play out in everyday life. The dimensions we will explore in more detail in the following section are summarized in Table 2.1. We want to emphasize that these are intended to illustrate in concrete ways how the two mindsets play out in the context of everyday life within typical kinds of routines and social spaces. They do not 'exhaust' the mindsets. Moreover, other people might emphasize different foci. The point is not to try and provide a definitive set of dimensions but, rather, to provide some indicative examples that can be varied and improved upon from case to case and setting to setting. Our main aim is to provide a general sense of how the mindsets play out, recognizing that the kind of dichotomy depicted here is sharper and more 'ideal' than exists in real life. In other words, the construct of mindsets, as spelled out and used here, is more heuristic than tightly *scientific*.

Elaborating the mindsets

Competing 'ontologies': atoms and bits, physical and cyber spaces

The scale of difference that can arise between interpreting and responding to the world from a physical-industrial perspective and a non physical-informational/postindustrial perspective has already been illustrated by reference to Negroponte's anecdote about the monetary value of his laptop computer. It is sobering to reflect on the profundity of the gulf that separates the two valuations, and what this represents in terms of who and where one is in the contemporary world. From a physical-industrial perspective, it is perfectly 'natural' to think of the computer as a material commodity of a particular brand and to estimate its monetary value accordingly. From the perspective of 'being digital', however, the first thing that is likely to spring to mind in terms of value is what is on the hard disk and how much it would 'cost' to lose that (e.g., ask someone who has lost the data set for a doctoral dissertation to a hard disk crash about what a computer is worth).

A similarly wide gulf in perspective is apparent from a very different

Table 2.1 Some dimensions of variation between the mindsets

Mindset 1	Mindset 2
The world is much the same as before, only now it is more technologized, or technologized in more sophisticated ways:	The world is very different from before and largely as a result of the emergence and uptake of digital electronic inter-networked technologies:
• The world is appropriately interpreted, understood and responded to in broadly physical-industrial terms	• The world cannot adequately be interpreted, understand and responded to in physical-industrial terms
• Value is a function of scarcity	• Value is a function of dispersion

• An 'industrial' view of production:
  • products as material artefacts
  • a focus on infrastructure and production units (e.g., a firm or company)
  • tools for producing
	• A 'post-industrial' view of production:
	  • products as enabling services
	  • a focus on leverage and non finite participation
	
	  • tools for mediating and relating

• Focus on individual intelligence	• Focus on collective intelligence
• Expertise and authority 'located' in individuals and institutions	• Expertise and authority are distributed and collective; hybrid experts
• Space as enclosed and purpose-specific	• Space as open, continuous and fluid
• Social relations of 'bookspace'; a stable 'textual order'	• Social relations of emerging 'digital media space'; texts in change

angle in the way Barlow discusses the issue of censorship on the internet and, specifically, in the different kinds of responses he mentions about how to address pornography on the web. There are very different ways of looking at such concerns depending on whether one comes from the physical space mindset or from an alternative mind-set associated with understanding cyberspace.

From the standpoint of the first mindset, 'keeping the internet safe' becomes a matter of imposing blocks and filters in ways that parallel physical world behaviour: road blocks, fences, restraints, and so on. Barlow captures something of the difference between first and second mindset approaches to censoring the internet or keeping it safe by reference to the difference between using filters and adopting educative responses to address pornography. He believes that imposing gross filters to control content ultimately cannot work because internet space cannot be controlled in that way. The more elaborate the filter, the more elaborate will be the search to find ways around it, and the more powerful these resistances become. Barlow advocates more local and individualized filters that work on the principle of people taking responsibility for their choices and deciding what 'noise' they want to filter out. He reasons as follows: 'If you have concerns about your children looking at pornography the answer is not to eliminate pornography from the world, which will never happen; the answer is to raise them to find it as distasteful as you do' (Barlow, in Tunbridge 1995: 5).

The important educational implication of this, as we will see below, is that physical type responses to the use of the internet in schools largely end up either eliminating use of the internet altogether, because safety cannot be assured, or providing such controlled opportunities for using the internet that learners incur a double loss: they get a distorted experience of the internet and, at the same time, lose out on opportunities to learn how to keep themselves safe, which, as research increasingly indicates (e.g., Leander 2005), young people who range widely over the internet learn to do and become disposed to doing. Schools are often trapped here and inevitably go for the safe option, because for teachers to play an educative role that truly assists young people to assume moral responsibility for their internet activity, teachers themselves need to 'know their internet', which, to a large extent, they still do not.

Reflection and discussion

- Taking the case of a school in which you're currently working, or that you attended as a student, how does this school address student 'safety' online?

- To what extent do these 'security measures' enhance or hinder student learning? To what extent do these measures shape how computers and the internet are used at your school, and how does this compare with how you use computers and the internet outside school contexts?

- If you can, examine a school's technology use policy (try searching online for one). Does the statement contain tensions or contradictions between the 'promise' of digital technologies (e.g., the internet will enable students to access experts around the world), and many of the 'rules' written into the policy (e.g., students will be unable to use email at school). If so, what do you think is going on behind the words?

Competing bases of value

Barlow also distinguishes between paradigms of *value* he sees operating in physical space and cyberspace respectively. In physical space, says Barlow, controlled economics increases value by regulating scarcity. To take the case of diamonds, the value of diamonds is not a function of their degree of rarity or actual scarceness but, rather, of the fact that a single corporation owns most of them and, hence, can regulate or control their scarcity. Within this paradigm, scarcity has value. We might note here how schools have traditionally operated to regulate scarcity of credentialled achievement, including allocations of literacy 'success'. This has maintained scarce 'supply' and, to that extent, high value for those achievements that are suitably credentialled. In the economy of cyberspace, however, the opposite holds. Barlow argues that with information it is familiarity, not scarcity that has value. With information, 'it's dispersion that has the value, and it's not a commodity, it's a relationship and as in any relationship, the more that's going back and forth the higher the value of the relationship' (in Tunbridge 1995: 5). The implication here is that people who bring a scarcity model of value with them to cyberspace do not understand the new space and will act in ways that diminish rather than expand its potential. For example, applying certain excluding conditions to the use of information (e.g., copyright restrictions) may constrain the dispersal of that information in ways that undermine its capacity to provide a basis for *relationship*. This would in turn undermine the potential of that information to work as a catalyst for generating creative and productive conversations, the development of fruitful ideas, the emergence of effective networks. The kind of value Barlow sees as appropriate to cyberspace has to do with maximizing relationships, conversations, networks and dispersal. Hence, to bring a model of value that 'belongs' to a different kind of space is inappropriate and creates an impediment to actualizing the new space.

Production, intelligence, authority and expertise: Web 1.0 and Web 2.0 in relation to the mindsets

The idea that within 'information space' value is related to dispersion has been extended in some interesting new directions since the time Barlow was interviewed. Some of these have been nicely captured in recent discussions surrounding a distinction that some influential writers and commentators on matters pertaining to the internet have drawn between 'Web 1.0' and 'Web 2.0' as different sets of design patterns and business models in software development. Tim O'Reilly's (2005) account of Web 2.0 and how its approach and perspective differ from Web 1.0 is a well-known and widely read account of the distinction to date. O'Reilly's key points and illustrative examples apply directly to three important dimensions of difference between the two mindsets that we have tabulated above (see Table 2.1). These are, respectively:

- the difference between an 'industrial' view of production evident within the first mindset and a 'post-industrial' view integral to the second mindset;
- the difference between a focus on intelligence as a quality or possession of individuals and a focus on collective intelligence;
- the difference between seeing expertise and authority as 'located' within individuals and institutions, as in the case of the first mindset, and seeing them as distributed, collective and hybrid.

To elaborate these points we will first provide a brief overview of salient aspects of O'Reilly's account of Web 1.0 and Web 2.0.

O'Reilly traces the origins of the distinction between Web 1.0 and Web 2.0 to discussions that addressed issues and ideas arising from the fall-out of the 2001 dot.com crash, including the observation that the major companies to survive the crash seemed to share some features in common. Parties to the initial discussions began assigning examples of internet applications and approaches to either a Web 1.0 list or a Web 2.0 list. Some of the examples most likely to be familiar to readers were assigned as shown in Figure 2.1.

Participants provided the reasons that inclined them to identify a particular application or approach as belonging to Web 1.0 rather than Web 2.0, or vice versa. Among the many considerations addressed, several are particularly relevant to our account of the two mindsets. We will briefly describe some of the examples O'Reilly covers and show how the features and principles relevant to their assigned status in terms of Web 1.0 or Web 2.0 respectively relate to the mindsets.

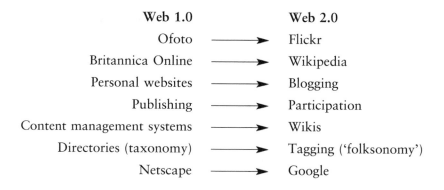

Figure 2.1 Some typical examples of Web 1.0 vs Web 2.0
Source: Adapted from O'Reilly (2005: n.p.)

The examples that fall within the Web 1.0 column take the form of products, artefacts or commodities that are produced at a source and made available to internet users. Britannica Online is a classic example of an internet commodity that subscribers can access at a fee. Ofoto began as a front for Kodak to sell digital photo processing online to users who could post digital photos on the Ofoto server to share with friends. Much like the free e-card that serves as a conduit to buying flowers or greetings cards online, Ofoto's gallery space was an enticement to buy a product rendered by a supplier. As O'Reilly notes, even the free web browser offered by Netscape took the form of an artefact – as a 'piece' of software in the form of a desktop application – that was released in updated versions from time to time that needed to be downloaded. It in fact comprised the centrepiece of Netscape's strategy to 'use their dominance in the browser market to establish a market for high-priced server products' (O'Reilly 2005: n.p.).

The point here is not about *commercial* product delivery so much as the fact that what users receive are readymade artefacts or commodities. O'Reilly speaks here of 'packaged software'. In Web 1.0 the 'webtop' as a platform largely emulates the desktop, with producers and consumers engaged in creating and consuming applications and informational *artefacts*. Users are not positioned as controllers of their own data. What one 'gets' on a website is what web publishers put there. The logic is of use rather than participation; of reception and/or consumption rather than interactivity and agency. Directories and the taxonomies they are based upon or 'enact' are developed at a 'centre' and are made available for users in the form that their creators have designed. They get used because they are presumed to be 'authoritative' and to reflect 'expertise' and 'experience' and 'wisdom' possessed by their designers.

While this oversimplifies things somewhat, there is enough here that is familiar to readers for making a link to the first mindset. The first generation of the web has much in common with an 'industrial' approach to material productive activity. Companies and developers worked to produce artefacts for consumption. There was a strong divide between producer and consumer. Products were developed by finite experts whose reputed credibility and expertise underpinned take-up of their products. Britannica Online stacked up the same authority and expertise – individuals reputed to be experts on their topic and recruited by the company on that basis – as the paper version of yore. Netscape browser development proceeded along similar lines to those of Microsoft, even though the browser constituted free software. Production drew on company infrastructure and labour, albeit highly dispersed rather than bound to a single physical site.

The picture is very different with Web 2.0. Part of the difference has to do with *the kind of products* characteristic of Web 2.0. In contrast to the 'industrial' artefactual nature of Web 1.0 products, Web 2.0 is defined by a 'post-industrial' worldview that focuses much more on 'services' and 'enabling' than on production and sale of material artefacts for private consumption. Production itself is based on 'leverage' 'collective participation', 'collaboration' and distributed expertise and intelligence, much more than on manufacture of finished commodities by individuals and work-teams operating in official production zones and/or drawing on concentrated expertise and intelligence within a shared physical setting.

Google.com, Wikipedia.org, Amazon.com, and Flickr.com provide some representative examples of many of the touchstone differences found in Web 2.0 internet services when compared with Web 1.0 software and internet applications and, by extension, between our two mindsets, as well as between established and 'new' literacies.

In the case of Google, there is no product to be downloaded, no artefact to be consumed. Instead, there is a service we can use in order to search for information, including images, videos, sounds, and the like. If we purchase products sold by companies who advertise on Google we may pay indirectly for using the service. Otherwise, to all intents and purposes the service is free. The service functions as an *enabler* for users – it helps optimize our internet experience by helping us find what we may be looking for. Google does not host the information it provides. That information can be stored anywhere. The search engine simply mediates between users, their internet browsers, and the servers and sites that contain information. As software, the search engine is not a distributed software application (as, say, Netscape was). Rather, the software is located on the internet and storage servers and *performed* by users who key in the URL for accessing the Google interface. Users have to know how to locate and use it. They can use it more or less efficiently. What they get from Google may reflect their degree of efficiency in terms of identifying useful search terms, understanding the role of Boolean logic in an effective search, knowing how to conduct a natural language search, being familiar with the full range of search functions available on Google (e.g., knowing about Scholar.google.com; knowing that entering the following string into Google's search window, enables a particular website or space to be searched: searchterm site: URL. For example, we can search for the references to the term 'affinity', on our own blog by using this string – affinity site: everydayliteracies.blogspot.com).

At the same time, there is an interesting and important *reciprocity* here. The search engine enables users to locate information, but at the same time users contribute to the value of the search engine by enhancing 'the scale and dynamism of the data it helps to manage' (O'Reilly 2005: n.p.). Google is, ultimately, a massive database and data management system, that evolves and improves and becomes more responsive the more it is used. Users *participate* in and through Google. They contribute to building a continuously improved and more dynamic database that is mediated by Google's page rank system. To this extent, the information one user gets as a consequence of doing a particular search is a function of searches that other users have done previously. The database is, so to speak, at any point in time a product of the collective participation and 'intelligence' (as enacted through use of keywords, Boolean logic, natural language, etc.) of all users. To all intents and purposes, Google's 'product' is the database that is *managed* through the software and generated through millions of users performing the software. The users are an integral part of Google's production; integral to developing its product. And the service automatically improves the more that people use it – a principle that O'Reilly identifies as inherently Web 2.0.

Reflection and discussion

The user-driven qualities of Google's page rank system has spawned, among many other things, two related phenomena known as Googlebombing and Googlewhacking.

Googlebombing involves a user deliberately manipulating page ranks by creating multiple links that use a specific phrase or 'anchor text' to click-through to a target site in order to associate the target site with the anchor text more closely in Google's estimation of relevance (the anchor text doesn't have to appear on the target site, only on the hyperlink texts on the referring webpages). This process can be used to make a social statement or a humorous point (see en.wikipedia.org/wiki/Googlebomb). Perhaps the most famous example of Google-bombing is the search phrase, 'miserable failure', which (in early 2006) returns the official biography of current US president, George Bush, at the top of the results list.

Googlewhacking is akin to a game or competition where the goal is to generate a two-word search with just one solitary search result (for more see: googlewhack.com). In this game, the more bizarre the two search words, the better (see http://www.googlewhack.com/tally.pl).

- Why do you think these practices have emerged?
- To what extent are these sorts of user-driven effects worth paying attention to when studying new literacies?

The free, collaboratively produced online encyclopedia, *Wikipedia.org*, likewise reflects the principle of mobilizing collective intelligence by encouraging free and open participation and trusting to the enterprise as a whole functioning as a self-correcting system. Whereas an 'official' encyclopedia is produced on the principle of recognized experts being contracted to write entries on designated topics, and the collected entries being formally published by a company, *Wikipedia* entries are written by anyone who wants to contribute their knowledge and understanding and are edited by anyone else who thinks they can improve on what is already there. In other words, it is an encyclopedia created through *participation* rather than via publishing. While identifiable people are responsible for beginning and overseeing the initiative, the content is generated by anybody willing to do so.

The idea is that as more and more users read and edit entries online, the more the content will improve. At the same time, ideally, the content will reflect multiple perspectives, excesses and blindspots will be edited out, and by countless incremental steps the resource will become increasingly user friendly, useful, reliable, accountable and refined. The logic is one of distributed and collective expertise. Trust is a key operating principle. The ethos is to reach out to all of the web for input, through limitless participation, rather than the more traditional belief that expertise is limited and scarce, and that the right to speak truths is confined to the 'properly credentialled'. The idea is *not* that anyone's opinion is as good as anybody else's but, rather, that anyone's opinion may stand until it is overwritten by someone who believes they have a better line. The right to exercise this belief is not constrained.

We referred earlier in this chapter to the example of Amazon.com and Jeff Bezos' idea of wanting 'to do things [in business] in a completely new way'. We noted that this involved much more than just purchasing a book, or some other product online, and mentioned specifically Amazon's practice of inviting customer reviews and ratings. It is interesting to see how this practice reflects Web 2.0 logic.

O'Reilly makes two salient, related points here. First, he notes that unlike other online booksellers Amazon harnesses user activity to produce better search results than their competitors. Whereas competitors typically lead with the company's own products or with sponsored results, Amazon always leads with the 'most popular' item corresponding to the search terms. The popularity index is a real-time computation based on an amalgam of sales and 'flow' around a product (e.g., how much user attention the book obtains, other books bought by customers who buy the book in question and how these other books are selling and are rated), and so on. Second, he argues that Amazon's database for books has now become the main source for bibliographic data on books. According to O'Reilly, like its competitors Amazon obtained its original database from R.R. Bowker, the ISBN registry provider that publishes *Books in Print*. However, Amazon outstripped and transcended this kind of data. The company

> relentlessly enhanced the data, adding publisher-supplied data such as cover images, table of contents, index, and sample material. Even more importantly, they harnessed their users to annotate the data, such that after ten years, Amazon, not Bowker, is the primary source for bibliographic data on books, a reference source for scholars and librarians as well as consumers ... Amazon 'embraced and extended' their data suppliers.
>
> (O'Reilly 2005: n.p.)

In other words, Amazon leveraged collective intelligence in the form of reader engagement and consumer data into the number one bibliographic data source on books, providing a free service for scholars as much as consumers while simultaneously outstripping competitors in sales. In doing so they turned users into distributed 'experts' and 'authorities' on book data. They also transformed bibliographic data directories from centralized published sources to a collaboratively generated freely available and 'always on' and permanently updated searchable database in multiple languages, serving multiple countries at the disposal of anyone who has internet access.

The highly popular photograph sharing service, Flickr.com, adds an interesting dimension to user annotation by means of 'tagging'. This has generated a 'bottom-up' approach to providing metadata for classifying online content that enables searching, popularly known as 'folksonomy'. The basis of folksonomy is 'tagging'. The principle involved is simple. Flickr is a service that allows people to post photographs to the web after they have signed up for an account. For each photograph or set of photographs account holders upload to their site they can add a number of 'tags'. These are words they think describe their photo and that would lead other people who key the word(s) into the Flickr search engine to their photos (and there are a range of options that determine who a person permits to view their photos). Account holders can also invite or accept other people to be on their list of contacts. Contacts can then add tags to the photos posted by those people who have accepted them as contacts. The account holder, however, has the right to edit tags – their own and/or those added by contacts – as they wish. The millions of photos publicly available on Flickr become a searchable database of photos. Tags provide a basis for patterns of user interests to emerge in ways that enable communities of interest to build and for relationships to develop among members who share common interests, tastes, etc. They have enabled different interest groups to coalesce around shared image projects (e.g., the Tell a Story in Five Frames group, the Secret Life of Toys group).

Reflection and discussion

Open Flickr.com and find the 'Popular Tags' hyperlink or go directly to: http:www.flickr.com/photos/tags. Click on this link, and examine the 'tag' map you'll find there. Click on any tags that appeal to you, then try searching for different tags and see what results:

- What does the tag map or cloud tell you about the Flickr universe?

- In what ways might the tags people place on their photos shape the way viewers look at these photos? Does this matter?

- What, if anything, stops Flickr's tag system from becoming overwhelmingly random?

Return to the Flickr front page, and look for the 'Groups' hyperlink at the top of the page. Click on this link and explore some of the groups listed on the new page. Try searching for possible groups and see what you find (if you're stuck for ideas, try 'secret life of toys', or 'tell a story in five frames').

- Why might a person subscribe to a group?

- To what extent does the complete set of Flickr groups constitute a kind of folksonomy? (See Davies 2006).

The concept of 'folksonomy' was developed in juxtaposition to 'taxonomy'. Taxonomies are centralized, official, expert-based or top-down classification management systems. The operating principle of taxonomies is that people who presume – or are presumed – to understand a domain of phenomena determine how the individual components of that domain shall be organized in order to make a shared sense or meaning of the domain. The Dewey library classification system is a taxonomy of types of texts, according to which a given book is assigned a number on the basis of the kind of book it is deemed to be and where it fits into the system. By contrast, a folksonomy is a 'popular', non-expert, bottom-up classification management system, developed on the basis of how 'authors' (e.g., of photos) decide they want their works to be described or 'catalogued'.

One interesting consequence of folksonomic organization is that the tags people choose say something about *them* as well as about the tagged object (O'Reilly 2005). When a user finds a photo they would not have expected to fall under a particular tag, they might think the tagger's approach to classification is sufficiently interesting to delve further into it; for example, as a pursuit of 'the idiosyncratic', or the 'quirky', or 'of someone who might think a bit like me'. The scope for participants to make their own meanings, find collaborators who share these meanings, and build relationships based on shared perspectives opens up possibilities that are foreclosed by centralized and authoritative regimes that circumscribe norms of correctness, legitimacy or propriety.

Folksonomy presents one angle on the idea of new computing and communications technologies as 'relationship technologies' (see Schrage 2001; Barlow, in Tunbridge 1995). This opens up a theme which is inchoate in the Web 1.0–Web 2.0 distinction, but which is better made by reference to a similar but different discussion. The connection with Web 1.0 and Web 2.0 can be seen in terms of a contingency around software applications. O'Reilly notes that while both Netscape (Web 1.0) and Google (Web 2.0) can be regarded as software companies, they belong to quite different software worlds. He says:

it's clear that Netscape belonged to the same software world as Lotus, Microsoft, Oracle, SAP, and other companies that got their start in the 1980s software revolution, while Google's fellows are other internet applications like eBay, Amazon, Napster . . . DoubleClick and Akamai.

One dimension along which these software worlds can be distinguished is by saying that many of the products – the 'tools' or 'solutions' – of that first software world were designed to be used in the production and transfer of *information*. They were artefacts primarily designed to be used in the production of information artefacts. They belong to the discursive world of the 'Information Revolution', 'Information Technologies', and the 'Information Society'. By contrast, the software applications of Web 2.0 swim in a different sea. It is a sea that, to be sure, generates information and manages information, but does so largely in the course of (and in the name of) facilitating 'other business'. And in each case this 'other business' is heavily *relational* – it brings people into relationship (which is not to say that they need ever meet or even knowingly interact – although in many cases there is direct, even if impersonal interaction, like buyer and seller. These latter applications are often referred to as 'relationship technologies', and in time may be seen as integral to some kind of 'relationship revolution'.

The point we want to emphasize here has been made most persuasively by Michael Schrage (2001; see also Bigum 2002). Schrage argues that viewing the computing and communications technologies of the internet through an information lens is 'dangerously myopic'. The value of the internet and the web is not to be found in 'bits and bytes and bandwidth'. In a justly celebrated comment, Schrage claims that to say the internet 'is about "information" is a bit like saying that "cooking" is about oven temperatures, it's technically accurate but fundamentally untrue' (Schrage 2001: n.p.). Schrage states the point we want to affirm here as follows:

> While it is true that digital technologies have completely transformed the world of information into readily manipulable bits and bytes, it is equally true that the genuine significance of these technologies isn't rooted in the information they process and store.

> A dispassionate assessment of the impact of digital technologies on popular culture, financial markets, health care, telecommunications, transportation and organizational management yields a simple observation: The biggest impact these technologies have had, and will have, is on relationships between people and between organizations.

The so-called 'information revolution' itself is actually, and more accurately, a 'relationship revolution'. Anyone trying to get a handle on the dazzling technologies of today and the impact they'll have tomorrow, would be well advised to re-orient their worldview around relationships.

(ibid.: n.p.; original emphasis)

As we will see in the next chapter, this point has enormous implications for participant priorities so far as popular everyday engagement with new literacies is concerned.

Reflection and discussion

List all the ways in which you use new digital technologies on a given day (e.g., mobile phone for talking, gaming, text messaging, checking email; computer and internet for web searching, gaming, emailing, shopping, instant messaging, webcamming; etc.). To what extent do your own practices bear out Schrage's claims, and why might this be?

Perspectives on space

From the standpoint of the first mindset, space is typically thought of as enclosed, as having borders. In the educational context, learning space is bordered by the classroom walls, lesson space by the hour or 40-minute time signal, and curriculum and timetable space by the grid of subjects to be covered and the time and physical space allocations assigned to them (if this is 9 a.m. Friday in Room A202, it must be 8th grade Math). Space tends to be strongly centred on the teacher and/or architectural features like the chalkboard, electronic whiteboard or set-up of computers, benches, etc. Tasks tend to be singular and defined at a given time, and learners are expected to be on task, which often means all students on the same task at the same time. Being not on that task is seen as being disengaged from learning.

Learners who have grown up on the inside of a cyberspatial mindset often see things very differently, and approach them very differently. The presumption that one will be working on one task at a time or in one 'place' at a time when engaged in learning (or, for that matter, in entertainment or recreation) is foreign to many who approach and respond to their world from the second mindset. A teenage informant (Violetta) provided a classic statement from the standpoint of the second mindset in an online interview with our colleague Angela Thomas (2006). Violetta explained that at the end of the school day she and her friend Sarah return to their homes:

She calls me on the phone when she's ready to log on later. We keep the phone conversations going while we log on and decide where to go. We're always on my talker, but sometimes we go idle there to visit other places. I keep telling dad I need a bigger monitor, because I end up with so many windows open that I can't always follow what's going on in each one. Then we do about six different things at the same time.

We'll have my talker open, our icq on, we have the role-playing MOO we've just joined going to open, we have our homework open (which I am pleased to report, we both get done at the end of the night, and its sooooo much more fun doing it this way!), we have the palace open, we have our own private conversation windows open for different friends, and we have our phone conversation going on at the same time. And that is not to mention having conversations with mom or dad, popping out for drinks and nibbles, and having my music on in the background. Then, depending what's going on, we have hysterics over the phone together as we manage the activities going on in each window.

(from Angela Thomas' interview with 'Violetta':
'I am Violetta today, I am feeling bright yellow and
somewhat creative'; see Thomas 2006)

It appears that Violetta saw this kind of multitasking not simply as some casual kind of *modus operandi* confined to interactions with her closest friends but, rather, as a way of operating more generally across her everyday life. Violetta divulged to her online researcher-interviewer that she was in fact spreading herself across multiple practices and discourses at the very time of interviewing.

I am talking to you but at the same time I am talking to this cool guy Matt who I know from school, and trying to do some homework – an essay, for which I am hunting some info on the web – you know, throw in some jazzy pics from the web and teachers go wild about your 'technological literacy' skills. Big deal. If they ever saw me at my desk right now, ME, the queen of multi-tasking, they'd have no clue what was happening.

(from Angela Thomas' interview with 'Violetta':
'I am Violetta today, I am feeling bright yellow and
somewhat creative'; Thomas 2006 and forthcoming)

A little later we will look at an example of student multitasking in the context of a wireless classroom, and get a glimpse of how this behaviour came into tension with a conception of classroom propriety grounded in conventional views of managing classroom space in accordance with attention to 'the task at hand'.

Textual 'orders'

Integral to the first mindset is the dominance of the book as the text paradigm, social relations of control associated with 'bookspace', and a discernible textual 'order'. By this we mean that during the age of print the book comprised the text paradigm. It shaped conceptions of layout, it was the pinnacle of textual authority, and it played a central role in organizing practices and routines in major social institutions. The book mediated social relations of control and power, as between author and readers, authorial voice as the voice of expert and authority, teacher/expert and student/learner, priest/minister and congregation, etc. Textual forms and formats were relatively stable and were 'policed' to ensure conformity. Certain genres of texts were privileged over others and seen as appropriate within particular (institutional) settings – e.g., school classrooms – whereas others were regarded as more marginal and not appropriate. Books exerted great influence on institutional space, architecture and furniture, as well as on norms for conduct within particular spaces.

The book in no way comprises the text paradigm in the emerging digital media space. Indeed, there is *no* text paradigm. Text types are subject to wholesale experimentation, hybridization, and rule breaking. Conventional social relations associated with roles of author/authority and expert have broken down radically under the move from 'publishing' to participation, from centralized authority to mass collaboration, and the like. The organization of space, architecture and furniture, and control of movement associated with bookspace have become curious aberrations under the sign of new media. While people who grew up under the hegemony of the book and a stable 'generic order' may ponder whether it is 'proper' to write this kind of way in a blog, or to focus on this kind of theme, digital insiders seem much less preoccupied by such concerns. This is not to say there are no norms in the new space, for there are. But they are less fixed, more fluid, and the sheer proliferation of textual types and spaces means there is always somewhere to 'go' where one's 'ways' will be acceptable and there will be freedom to engage them, and where traditional emphases on 'credibility' become utterly subordinated to the pursuit of relationships and the celebration of sociality.

The mindsets at work within educational settings

The standpoint we are adopting here – our working hypothesis – is that the world is now significantly different from how it was two or three decades ago, and that this difference has a lot to do with the emergence of new technologies and changes in social practices associated with these. In part, this is a matter of what we have called the contemporary fracturing of space. Besides living in and reckoning with physical space, we are now increasingly called upon to reckon with cyberspace. Besides a mechanical world there is also a digital electronic world to be reckoned with, at least on the part of those inhabiting the social mainstream. As in any age, one can choose to withdraw from a mainstream. But anyone wanting to attach themselves to the contemporary mainstream will be called upon to reckon with digital-electronic ways and with cyberspatial ways. In addition, the changes are in part a matter of a move from what we have called 'industrial' values and ways of doing things toward an increasing embrace of 'post-industrial' values and ways of doing things.

To repeat, we are not talking about a *displacement* here. Cyberspace has not and will not displace physical space. The mechanical has not been displaced by the digital-electronic, and will not be in any foreseeable future. Industrial ways have not been displaced by post-industrial ways. The *balances*, however, are shifting significantly. To some extent 'industry' has been displaced geographically – from the 'First' world to pockets of the 'Third' world – yet we still find many industrial principles operating in 'First' world sites. It would be a brave person, however, who would maintain that the industrial mode has not lost a very significant amount of ground to the post-industrial throughout the urban 'First' world, and this trend will most likely continue at a strong rate in the decades ahead.

Against this background we have distinguished two mindsets, although we have spoken of them in somewhat mechanical and polemical ways. It is not as if those who approach the world from the first mindset are conscious of doing so, or would necessarily be aware that there is any other way of approaching the world. Likewise, those who have been born into the digital-electronic-post-industrial world might not be aware in the slightest that the world has changed and this change has a lot to do with the emergence of new technologies and evolving social practices associated with them. It is simply the world they have been born into, grown up in, and whose operating logic they have more or less absorbed. So, when we call these mindsets a 'newcomer/outsider' and an 'insider' mindset respectively, our point of reference is the changed world. Ironically, the newcomers to this changed world are those who have been in the world longest. They grew up under one order, became familiar with it – absorbed it – in just the kinds of ways the 'insiders' to the new order have. But their 'default' logic is different from that of the contemporary world. Despite all their age and experience, they have lived 'outside' this world for the most part. They have to be 'reborn' to enter it; they have to approach it as 'newcomers'.

For their part, the 'insiders' to the new world have grown up inside it. This also includes acquiring an approach to the physical world that is conditioned by their simultaneous insider experience of the cyberspatial-digital/electronic-post-industrial world. They have experienced both worlds and both spaces from birth as 'a *complex*'. Their conception of the physical world is conditioned by their experience of the cyberspatial world, and vice versa. Their experience of what is left of the industrial order has been attained from within circumstances that are increasingly shaped by post-industrial logics and values. This is not a simple age split, of course, since other variables are involved. Some young people who are chronologically of the insider generation may be steeped in 'newcomer' perspectives and ways as a consequence of geographic location, home values, and so on. None-theless, as Barlow says, anyone in western urban centres under the age of 35 is more likely to have significant entrée to the insider mindset than are people in those same centres who are older. It is not clear-cut, although the dice are loaded. It is a matter of overcoming circumstances captured in the idea of 'other things being equal'.

So far as education is concerned, to this point in time teachers are pre-dominantly chronologically 'newcomers' or outsiders. Not surprisingly, then, it is very easy to find examples of the newcomer mindset being applied in classroom contexts that are marked by elements of contemporary change and that are increasingly inhabited by insiders. To put it another way, it is very easy to find examples where teachers and administrators approach new technologies in ways that constitute these new technologies as simply more recent forms of established tools, rather than as constitutive elements of new ways of doing things and new ways of being.

Old wine in new bottles: new technologies and the newcomer mindset

A large corpus of literature now exists that describes uses of new ICTs within school settings, including within literacy education specifically. Very little of this literature, however, describes anything that is significantly *new* so far as literacies and social practices are concerned. It does not follow from the fact that so-called new technologies are being used in literacy education that *new literacies* are being engaged with. Still less does it imply that learners are developing, critiquing, analysing, or even becoming technically proficient with new literacies.

In other work (e.g., Lankshear and Snyder 2000: Ch. 5; Goodson *et al.* 2002: Ch. 4; Lankshear and Knobel 2003), we have identified recurring features of new technology-mediated literacy practices found in classrooms in a range of countries. These reflect a strong tendency to perpetuate the old, rather than to engage with and refine or re-invent the new. Many researchers have identified the 'old wine in new bottles' syndrome, whereby long-standing school literacy routines have a new technology tacked on here or there, without in any way changing the substance of the practice. Using computers to produce neat final copies and slideshow presentation software or webpages for retelling stories, are some obvious long-standing examples. Other examples include using Webquests as a learning tool (Bigum 2003a), generating a school website to 'inform the community' (Bigum 2002), and using weblogs to post homework and assignments or to report classroom events (Knobel and Lankshear 2006; see also Merchant 2005, forthcoming).

These examples reflect thinking from the first mindset: schools, classrooms and literacy are the same as before, just now more technologized. The webpage or slide show stands in for paper, pencil and crayon as a medium for presenting stories or recounts. The webquest stands in for the photocopied worksheet where the teacher poses a question or problem and provides a list of resources students are to use in tackling it. The school website stands in for an occasional newsletter or a printed prospectus or parent–teacher information evening. The blog stands in for homework notebooks or other arrangements whereby parents and caregivers provide evidence of having checked homework, as has been common practice in many schools and education systems for decades.

Such accommodations of new technologies to established ways are hardly surprising when we take larger and underlying institutional characteristics of school into account. School routines are highly regular forms of practice that are intimately linked to what we call the 'deep grammar' of schooling. We can begin to see why this is so by considering two key elements of the deep grammar of school, which constructs learning as teacher-directed and 'curricular'. This very construction is bound up with central tenets of the first (newcomer) mindset.

First, schooling operates on the presumption that the teacher is the ultimate authority on matters of knowledge and learning. Hence, whatever is addressed and done in the classroom must fall within the teacher's competence parameters, since he or she is to *direct* learning.

Second, learning as 'curricular' means that classroom learning proceeds in accordance with a formally imposed/officially sanctioned sequenced curriculum that is founded on texts as information sources. Seymour Papert (1993: 9) observes the long-standing pervasive tendency in the education literature 'to assume that reading is the principal access route to knowledge for students'. The world, in other words, is accessed via books and printed texts (i.e., school is *bookspace*, not cyberspace). This imposes a pressing and profoundly instrumental value and significance on the capacity to *read* – as distinct from more directly on forms of participation with the world, including the social world.

The ongoing agenda to technologize learning still encounters a teaching workforce that is largely un(der)prepared for the challenge of *directing* computer-mediated learning in the role of teacher as authority. That is, most teachers (let alone teacher educators) still lack insider-like experience and expertise with new technologies and contemporary social practices associated with their technical and social evolution as cultural tools and processes. Not surprisingly, teachers often look for ways of fitting new technologies into classroom 'business as usual'. Since educational ends are directed by curriculum, and technologies are often regarded by teachers as 'mere' tools, the task of integrating new technologies into learning is often realized by adapting them to, or adding them onto, familiar routines. One corollary of this is that making learners 'technologically literate' is still largely reduced to teaching them how to 'operate' the new technologies. Beyond that, 'operating' computers is then largely confined to learners doing with computers what they would previously have done with the conventional learning technologies of print and bookspace.

In like manner, teachers who are encouraged to adopt new gadgets are often 'won over' by demonstrations of how new tools can be used to obtain greater efficiencies in managing and controlling physical space and extending their authority and power within the learning process to physical spaces beyond the classroom. For example, using weblogs for administrative purposes becomes a way of reaching directly into the home. Similarly, a popular ruse for getting wireless PDAs into schools has been to demonstrate the ease with which they can be used to keep the roll and, even, to track student movements around the school grounds. With easy taps of the stylus teachers can mark off presence and absence on a class list and send it wirelessly to the school's centralized administrative database.

In short, these ways are wedded to the first mindset: management of physical space; centralized authority and expertise invested in the teacher; fidelity to long-standing conceptions of teaching and learning and their social relations; perpetuation of the book and bookspace, and time-honoured forms of language practice like story telling, recounts, retellings.

This logic can be seen as a specific instance of a much larger phenomenon: the systematic separation of (school) learning from participation in 'mature' (insider) versions of Discourses which are part of our life trajectories (Knobel 1999). School learning is learning for school; school as it always has been. The burgeoning take-up of new technologies simply gives us our latest 'fix' on this phenomenon. It is the 'truth' that underpins many current claims that school learning is at odds with authentic ways of learning to be in the world, and with social practice beyond the school gates. The reason why many school appropriations of new technologies appear 'odd' in relation to 'real-world' practices – with which children are often familiar and comfortable – has to do with this very logic. It is precisely this 'deep grammar' of schooling that cuts schools off from the new (technological) literacies and associated subjectivities that Bill Green and Chris Bigum (1993) say educators are compelled to attend to. To put it another way, new literacies and social practices associated with new technologies 'are being invented on the streets' (Richard Smith, personal communication). These are the new literacies and practices that will (many of them) gradually become embedded in everyday social practice: the literacies against which the validity of school education will be assessed. But the 'deep grammar' of school is in tension here with its quest for legitimation in a high tech world, which is potentially highly problematic for schools.

Reflection and discussion

- To what extent is getting children to retell a story using presentation software like PowerPoint a case of 'old wine in new bottles'? Why?

- Locate online lists of suggested new technology use in classrooms advocated by your federal government (e.g., in the UK, becta. org.uk; in Australia, edna.edu.au; in the US, ed.gov/about/offices/list/os/technology/index.html). Evaluate the extent to which these recommended uses reflect insider and/or newcomer mindsets respectively.

Mindsets, space and tasks: on task, off task, multitask

As part of a recent ethnographic study of young people's ICT practices, Kevin Leander and colleagues observed case study participants in a private girls' school that made extensive use of mobile computing within a wireless environment. Not surprisingly, some students spent considerable time in class engaging in self-selected purposes. This extended to gaming, shopping, and downloading music, as well as including the 'more to be expected' activities like emailing, private chatting and Instant Messaging. Kevin Leander's fieldnotes (see Leander 2005) included vignettes like the following.

[Context: Final exam preparation in a Grade 9 English class; the teacher is focusing on a list of poems they will need to be able to discuss.]

Mia opens her laptop and logs into the network. She accesses Xanga.com – a popular weblog hosting service – and begins reading a weblog. The title of the weblog is, 'Thank God I'm an Atheist,' and Mia laughs while reading the latest entry on this blog.

The teacher asks, 'Is there anybody who doesn't understand imagery?' She walks close by Mia, who quickly opens a blank Word document and keys in 'Imagery' before flipping back to her web browser and reading a different weblog.

Teacher: 'Who can describe an image from "After Apple Picking" by Frost?'

Mia keeps the weblog she was reading open on her laptop, but looks at Richa's book and gives the first answer of the day: 'In the first four lines you get an image of an apple in an apple tree.'

Teacher: 'Good, a very realistic one. Read those lines again because they are interesting lines.'

The blog post lines in front of Mia read: 'There is nothing more foul than dissecting a fetal pig.'

Teacher: 'Frost especially likes to use the seasons of the year.'

Mia opens her own blog and begins working on an entry for that day. She types away, occasionally glancing at the teacher. Most of the other girls in the class are looking in their books.

Teacher: 'What is he doing? Is he looking in the mirror? Frozen water; again, he tries to strengthen that image, of being old, tired, winter, freezing cold.'

Mia continues typing her blog entry.

The teacher asks Richa to read the first five lines of 'After Apple Picking', and asks Mia to read the next line of the poem.

Teacher: 'Is there symbolic value to it?'

Mia: 'I was going to say that it stands for him, but I think it stands for something bigger.'

Teacher: 'Good intuition.'

The teacher calls on Mia at least twice more, and Mia offers her interpretation that the apple picking in the poem stands for death. It is now 22 minutes into the class and Mia is still typing her blog entry. She also changes her blog template to a blue background and the text colour to purple. She stops fiddling with her new set up to read a few lines from the next poem under consideration.

Some of the students, like Mia, who engaged most in pursuing self-selected purposes during class time did not believe they were learning less than they otherwise would as a result of this, and, in fact, even when they were 'drifting' on their screens they demonstrably participated as much if not more in class discussions than their 'on task' peers (proficient 'doers' of school). Two of these students claimed that being able to go to other places during time in class when they already knew about the matters under discussion alleviated boredom. Their capacity for multitasking seemingly allowed them to maintain one eye on task while going about other business.

Contrary to such self-appraisals on the part of students, some teachers soon began to limit the times that students could use their laptops to points in lessons the teachers deemed appropriate. This trend was underway before Leander and colleagues' research was even completed. From the standpoint of literacy education in relation to learning, it is important to note the tension that exists here between newcomer and insider mindsets with respect to multitasking. In formal and non-formal settings beyond the school, including workplaces, the capacity to multitask fluently is often highly valued and sometimes serves as a status marker. Effective multitasking is associated with greater efficiency, as well as with being digitally proficient. From the insider perspective there is no conception of 'disrespect' or of paying insufficient attention to a task if one is multitasking, whereas from the one space–one task perspective of the newcomer mindset, such connotations often apply. Rather, from the insider perspective, the idea is more one of attending to a specific task to the extent needed to perform it adequately or well, but that other things being equal it is better to be able to move fluently between tasks simultaneously, not least because time online is a resource to be used as efficiently as possible. Similarly, under conditions of intensified competition in the world of work, efficient multitasking becomes an important part of competitive edge. It seems very likely that the social, cultural and economic value and esteem associated with multitasking will increase in the years ahead, to the point of becoming the default mode. To this extent, responses like closing down on possibilities for multitasking might well prove in the relatively short term to be on the wrong side of history.

Interestingly also from the standpoint of tensions between the mindsets, the researchers also observed high levels of internet safety consciousness among the study participants. They avoided communication with unknowns and were very careful about what information they gave out about themselves. For students like these there is no legitimate basis for schools to hide behind fears about internet safety as a ground for limiting internet access within formal learning contexts. And so far as Mia is concerned, it appears that even under conditions of extreme multitasking she was able to provide at least as much attention to the tasks specifically associated with the official learning of the classroom to perform them well. That may say something about formal classroom tasks, but it does not provide a basis for pre-emptive strikes against multitasking in class.

Toward 'new' literacies

In the next chapter we will spell out our view of what count as 'new' literacies. Before turning to that, however, we want to consider the implications of our argument about the challenge of mindsets for a viable conception of 'new' literacies.

Briefly, we would argue that the more a literacy practice can be seen to reflect the characteristics of the insider mindset and, in particular, those qualities we have addressed here that internet commentators like Tim O'Reilly have associated with the concept of Web 2.0, the more it is entitled to be regarded as a *new* literacy. That is to say, the more a literacy practice privileges participation over publishing, distributed expertise over centralized expertise, collective intelligence over individual possessive intelligence, collaboration over individuated authorship, dispersion over scarcity, sharing over ownership, experimentation over 'normalization', innovation and evolution over stability and fixity, creative-innovative rule breaking over generic purity and policing, Phase 2 automation over Phase 1 automation, relationship over information broadcast, and so on, the more we should regard it as a 'new' literacy.

This is *not* to say that conventional literacies are not important. It is not to say that from some perspectives and relative to some purposes they may not (still) be *more* important than 'new' literacies. For us to deny the continuing importance of conventional literacies and to otherwise denigrate them would be ingenuous in the extreme. This book and the privileges we enjoy as authors and as academics and researchers owe a vast amount to conventional literacies – including some very 'old' literacies – and we want to make that absolutely clear. Our work as writers and researchers alike draws on literacy practices like 'syllogistic arguing' – presenting information in accordance with norms of reasoning associated with the syllogism as a form of argument. Syllogistic argument dates back to the Ancient Greeks. A lot of the time when we are trying to carve through difficult patches in a chapter, or even in a paragraph, we are *not* multitasking. Rather, we are agonizing over how best to try and state an idea clearly: attending to something that is as specific as whether to put 'not' before or after a particular word. We take as much care as we can to obey the publisher's norms for formatting, and we think in terms of pages, and of trying to maximize the potential of the book to be used in bookspace. Indeed, we write it as a book, and not as a blog, or as a wiki. On the whole we think we perform a bit better as practitioners of conventional academic literacies than we do as 'new' literacy readers and writers. That is not to say that we don't wish we were much better practitioners of 'new' literacies than we are – because we *do* wish that. But we would not wish it at the expense of having to give away any proficiencies we may have as practitioners of conventional literacies. Not yet.

By contrast, vast amounts of perfectly 'proper' engagement in new literacies end up in what O'Reilly calls 'the long tail of the web'. There is not necessarily a lot of kudos in the eyes of the world to be had from, say, making a useful contribution to Wikipedia that might be taken up – for all one would ever know – by many other people. There are no royalties to be had there or, typically, any other public recognition. On the other hand, the riches to be had and enjoyed from membership of online communities and interest groups can be enormous, and there is no questioning the meaning that Violetta – introduced earlier – derives from her online life and its intersection with her face-to-face life. To some extent 'new' literacies bespeak a world of intrinsic satisfactions, whereas the world of conventional literacies – as seen particularly in the fetishized ways literacy is constructed as a personal benefit and a *sine qua non* for social and economic advancement – remains closely tied to considerations of instrumental value.

Here again, it is not all or nothing. Intrinsic values are obviously available within conventional literacy practices, and are commonly pursued; instrumental values can be derived from 'new' literacies and are commonly pursued. Nonetheless, we think that the trend toward massive levels of participation in 'new' literacies, as we will see in later chapters, indicates a growing sense of intrinsic satisfactions to be had there and an equally growing disposition to seek them. It seems likely that schools, with their established grounding in a mindset associated with status and value attaching to scarcity, and with literacy comprising a key instrumentality for unlocking advantage and status through achievements at levels wilfully preserved for the few, will increasingly face a challenge to maintain student engagement in conventional literacies conceived and implemented from the perspective of the newcomer mindset.

Much more could be said here. Sufficient has already been said, however, to clear the way for taking a more focused look at concepts and practices of *new* literacies. We turn to this task in Chapter 3.

'New Literacies':
Concepts and practices

Introduction: How long is 'new'?

This chapter spells out what we mean by new literacies and why we think it is worth taking this idea seriously. We focus first on what we mean by 'literacies' and then on what we mean by 'new'. The chapter also describes some illustrative examples of practices we count as new literacies and maps them in relation to one another. These examples are intended to sample new literacies across a wider range than will be possible in Part 2 of the book, where we focus in depth on Remix practices and Weblogging.

It is easy – indeed, all *too* easy – to make light of 'new literacies' by saying things like: 'Well, there are always newer ones coming along, so that MOO-ing is already an "old" new literacy ...'. Such remarks suggest that new literacies have a similar kind of life trajectory to a new Ford or Toyota car: new in 2006, semi-new in 2007, and old hat by 2008. Against this kind of nanosecond or 'that's so yesterday' perspective, our view is that 'new lit-eracies' are best understood in terms of an historical period of social, cultural, institutional, economic and intellectual change that is likely to span many decades – some of which are already behind us. We associate new literacies with an historical conjuncture and a 'rising' or 'ascending' mindset. From this perspective, the kinds of practices we currently regard as new literacies will cease to be *new* at the point where characteristics and 'ways' associated with the second mindset described in Chapter 2 have been incorporated into mainstream everyday social practice to the point where they are invisible, taken for granted, and lived out as 'normal' – as aspects of what will then be *conventional* literacies.

To repeat an earlier point about 'displacement', this is not to say that the characteristics and 'ways' associated with the 'insider' mindset will be the only game in town. We are not talking about simple or complete displacement of one mindset and *modus operandi* by another, or about a total transition from one 'world' or 'space' to another. How the mix plays out historically, along with what comes next, remains to be seen. But 'new' is not over on an 'instance by instance basis' when, for example, MOOs give way to 3D role-playing worlds or chat palaces, or stand-alone, single player, ascii-interface video gaming gives way to online, massively distributed, three-dimensional, avatar-based, multi-player collaborative gaming that includes real-time text chat, voice chat, and even video/webcam chat. So far as new literacies are concerned, there will be many cameo performances as well as more enduring support roles and lead roles in this evolution. Some specific instances of new literacies may come and go quickly – playing no more than walk-on roles. Despite their short lives, they are nonetheless identifiable as new literacies. They are all historically significant as parts of a larger picture that is not fleeting. To dismiss them as 'old' new literacies bespeaks a failure of historical imagination. Alternatively, to look for what is new in specific instances of 'new' literacies may be a good way of enhancing our perspective on current trends and priorities in our approaches to teaching and learning.

Conceptualizing literacies

We define literacies as 'socially recognized ways of generating, communicating and negotiating meaningful content through the medium of encoded texts within contexts of participation in Discourses (or as members of Discourses)'. As with any definition of a phenomenon whose scope is large and complex, there are a number of key concepts here that need spelling out in more detail.

'Recognized ways'

What we mean by 'recognized ways' can be understood in relation to the concept of 'practice' as it is widely used with reference to literacy. Scribner and Cole (1981) introduced a technical concept of 'practice' to literacy theory based on their research into the relationship between literacy and cognition. This research was undertaken at a time when it was common to think of literacy as a 'tool' or 'technology' – a writing system – that produces valuable outcomes when people apply it. Against this view, Scribner and Cole conceptualized literacy as *practice*.

They define 'practice' in a series of statements. A practice is:

[A] recurrent, goal-directed sequence of activities using a particular technology and a particular system of knowledge...

[It] always refers to socially developed and patterned ways of using technology and knowledge to accomplish tasks...

[T]asks that humans engage in constitute a social practice when they are directed to socially recognized goals and make use of a shared technology and knowledge system.

(ibid.: 236)

According to Scribner and Cole, applying knowledge to accomplish tasks in the presence of technology – where 'technology' isn't confined to the digital, but includes a range of tools and techniques – always involves 'coordinated sets of actions', which they call skills. They identify such skills as part of any practice: 'A practice, then, consists of three components: technology, knowledge and skills' (ibid.: 236).

Rather than simple cause–effect relationships between a technology (e.g., literacy as writing system) and outcomes (e.g., new skills, new kinds of knowledge and thinking processes, economic and social development), a concept and theory of practice sees *all* of these – technologies, knowledges, and skills – as inter-related, dynamically connected to one another, and mutually evolving in conjunction with people's changing ideas about purposes and tasks. Within broad fields or domains of practice – like education, medicine, farming, or cooking – changes in ideas about how something might be done will generate new tasks that call for refinements in knowledge (theory, concepts, etc.), skills and processes, and technologies. These in turn will act back on people's ideas about what else could be done, in what ways, and so on.

Scribner and Cole then apply this concept of practice to literacy. They approach literacy as 'a set of socially organized practices which make use of a symbol system and a technology for producing and disseminating it' (ibid.: 236). They say that literacy is not a matter of knowing how to read and write a particular kind of script but, rather, a matter of 'applying this knowledge for specific purposes in specific contexts of use' (1981: 236). This means that literacy is really like a family of practices – literacies – that will include such 'socially evolved and patterned activities' as letter writing, keeping records and inventories, keeping a diary, writing memos, posting announcements, and so on. These all vary to some extent from one another in terms of the technologies used (pencil, typewriter, pen, font options, the kind of surface 'written' on); the knowledge drawn upon (formatting conventions, use of register, information about the topic), and their skill requirements (hand–eye coordination, using a mouse).

The kinds of literacy practices described by Scribner and Cole on the basis of their research among the Vai people of Liberia constitute so many *recognized ways* of generating, communicating, and negotiating meaningful content through the medium of encoded texts. These ways are 'recurrent' – they are socially recognized as *patterns* of activity – and are engaged in on a regular basis under these socially recognized patterned descriptions. Since Scribner and Cole presented their accounts of practice and literacy practices the concept has been reworked many times (see, for example, Street 1984, 2001; Barton 1991; Prinsloo and Breier 1996; Barton and Hamilton 1998; Hull and Schultz 2001). Subsequent accounts have tended not to focus so explicitly on the technology and skills dimensions Scribner and Cole regard as central to understanding and investigating practice. They tend, rather, to emphasize the social recognition of particular features within given settings. Brian Street (2001: 11), for example, defines literacy practices as 'particular ways of thinking about and doing reading and writing in cultural contexts'. Regardless of such variations, the link between identifiable *literacies* and *recognized ways of engaging* remains intact.

'Meaningful content'

While literacies call us to generate and communicate meanings and to invite others to make meaning from our texts in turn, this can only be done by having something to make meaning *from* – namely, a kind of content that is carried as 'potential' by the text and that is actualized through interaction with the text by its recipients. If there is no text, there is no literacy, and every text, by definition, bears content. Gunther Kress (2003: 37–8) makes this point in relation to alphabetic writing. He talks of readers doing 'semiotic work' when they read a written text. This is 'the work of filling the elements of writing with content' (Kress 2003): that is, the work of making meaning from the writing in the text. Kress argues that meaning involves two kinds of work. One is *articulation*, which is performed in the production of 'the outwardly made sign' (e.g., writing). The other is *interpretation*, which involves producing 'the inwardly made sign' in reading (see also Gee 2004: Ch. 6).

Our idea of 'meaningful content' that is generated and negotiated within literacy practices is, however, wider and looser than many literacy scholars might accept. We think Gee's (1997) Discourse approach to literacies draws attention to the complexity and richness of the relationship between literacies and 'ways of being together in the world' (ibid.: xv). So when we look at somebody's weblog we might well find that much of the meaning to be made has to do with who we think the blog writer *is*: what they are like, how they want to think of themselves, and how they want us to think of them. Likewise, a particular text that someone produces might well be best understood as an expression of wanting to feel 'connected' or 'related' right now. The meaning to be 'filled in' might be much more relational than literal. It might be more about expressing solidarity or affinity with particular people. Our idea of 'meaningful content' is intended to be sufficiently elastic to accommodate these possibilities.

This is an important point when it comes to understanding the internet, online practices and online 'content'. Almost anything available online becomes a resource for diverse kinds of meaning making. In many cases the meanings that are made will not be intelligible to people at large or, in some cases, to many people at all. Some might be shared only by 'insiders' of quite small interest groups or cliques. Consider, for example, the way that eBay has been used to spoof a range of social conventions and to generate diverse kinds of quirky and 'nutty' activity. A man auctioned his soul in 2006 and received a cash payment that came with the condition that he would spend 50 hours in church. In another case an individual auctioned a ten-year-old toasted cheese sandwich the owner said had an imprint of the Virgin Mary in it, and that had not gone mouldy or disintegrated since it was made in 1994. Moreover, she said it had brought her luck at a casino. An internet casino purchased the sandwich for $28,000 and planned to take it on tour to raise money for charity. Other sellers responded with Virgin Mary toasted sandwich makers, T-shirts, etc. (http://news.bbc.co.uk/2/hi/americas/4034787.stm). On 5 May 2006, Yahoo sports reported a Kansas City Royals baseball fan of 25 years finally giving up on the club and auctioning his loyalty (http://sports.yahoo.com/mlb/news;_ylt=AlShQ.C4IOa6BJxsh9YuKJURvLYF?slug=jp-auction050506&prov=yhoo&type=lgns). The meanings of such actions have little to do with established practices of auctioning, and the interpretation of texts describing the items have little or nothing to do with the literal words *per se*. People may be prepared to spend money just to be in solidarity with the spoof: to say 'I get it', thereby signalling their insiderness with the practice, expressing solidarity with the seller, enacting an 'affinity' or, even, trying to save a soul. (See also the 'Hopkin Green Frog Meme' discussed in Chapter 4.)

In similar vein, the Swedish media activist group, Read My Lips, produced a now well-known multimedia commentary on the Bush–Blair alliance in the Iraq war. Read My Lips spliced together fragments of news videos of George Bush and Tony Blair, and synched their lip movements and onscreen actions with the love song, 'Your Eyes', to produce a text suggesting an intimate romance between the two (atmo.se/zino.aspx?articileID=399). The resulting video expresses a strong indictment of the Bush–Blair alliance in the invasion of Iraq and is a popular clip within affinity spaces shaped by people critical of this invasion and/or critical of the militarist alliance between the US and Britain. Having no knowledge of the political and social controversy surrounding the war in Iraq would render this clip more or less meaningless or uninterpretable.

Aside from shared experiences or knowledge of current events, meaningful content within many new literacy practices clearly requires shared interests and pleasures. Remixing anime videos or films makes this point very clearly, as we will see in Chapter 4. This practice involves, for example, splicing together – remixing – very short clips from a range of commercial anime (animated Japanese cartoons) to create an entirely new narrative set to a matching new soundtrack (e.g., tfcog.net). Some remixes include no dialogue, but are instead synchronized, or 'synched', with a deliberately selected music track to create anime music videos (Hatcher 2005). Anime remixes are likely to appeal most to existing fans of all things anime who enjoy other fans' tinkering around with original texts to create new – albeit still recognizable – anime. Popular culture anthropologists like Mimi Ito argue this kind of creative work is driven largely by a push to communicate with and relate to interested others, rather than by the goal of sharing 'information' about specific anime productions or characters (Ito 2006).

'Encoded texts'

By defining literacies in relation to 'encoded texts' we mean texts that have been rendered in a form that allows them to be retrieved, worked with, and made available independently of the physical presence of another person. 'Encoded texts' are texts that have been 'frozen' or 'captured' in ways that free them from their immediate context of production so that they are 'transportable'. From a cultural point of view the most salient point about literacy concerns the scope and scale of cultural production that encoded texts enable (by comparison with 'unencoded' texts that 'expire' at the point and time of production other than in the extent to which they live on in the memories of people who were there at the time). Encoded texts give (semi) permanence, transcendence, and transportability to language that are not available in the immediacy of speech, hand signs, and the like. They can 'travel' without requiring particular people to transport them. They can be replicated independently of needing other human beings to host the replication.

The particular kinds of codes employed in literacy practices are varied and contingent. Literacies can involve any kind of codification system that 'captures' language in the sense we have described. Literacy includes 'letteracy' (i.e., within the English language, recognition and manipulation of alphabetic symbols), but in our view goes far beyond this. Someone who 'freezes' language as a digitally encoded passage of speech and uploads it to the internet as a podcast is engaging in literacy. So, equally, is someone who photoshops an image – whether or not it includes a written text component (see Chapters 4 and 5 for more detailed discussion of this point).

Reflection and discussion

Compare and discuss the literacy knowledges, skills and techniques required to produce or make use of texts found at the following websites:

- Worth1000.org
- BoingBoing.net
- Manganews.net
- Newgrounds.com
- Youaintnopicasso.blogspot.com
- JibJab.com
- Mugglenet.com/mugglecast

The different texts hosted on these websites can be variously copied and pasted into new texts, downloaded and uploaded to listening or viewing devices, burned to a CD-ROM disk for viewing on a different computer, saved to one's hard drive and replayed endlessly, bookmarked in one's web browser for future return visits, emailed to a friend, linked to from one's own webspace.

'Participation in (or as members of) Discourses'

Jim Gee (1997: xvi) speaks of sociocultural approaches to language and literacy as *Discourse* approaches. Discourse can be seen as the underlying principle of meaning and meaningfulness. We 'do life' as individuals and as members of social and cultural groups – always as what Gee calls 'situated selves' – in and through Discourses, which can be understood as meaningful coordinations of human and non-human elements. Besides people themselves, the human elements of coordinations include such things as people's ways of thinking, acting, feeling, moving, dressing, speaking, gesturing, believing, and valuing, and non-human elements include such things as tools, objects, institutions, networks, places, vehicles, machines, physical spaces, buildings.

A person rushing an email message to head office as they hand their boarding pass to the airline attendant at the entrance to the aircraft boarding ramp is recognizable (to others and themselves) as a certain kind of person. In this moment she is part of a *coordination* that includes as its elements such things as the person herself, some way of thinking and feeling (maximizing time to get more done), rules (the phone must be switched off after leaving the gate), institutions (airports and air travel, the company they work for), tools (a phone, a network), accessories (a briefcase and compact travel bag), clothes (a suit, perhaps), language (facility with emailing concisely and accurately). These various elements all get and are got 'in sync' (ibid.). The various elements simultaneously coordinate the others and are coordinated by them (institutional requirements and timetables prompt the particular use of the phone during the last seconds before boarding; the email message makes a demand back on someone in the company; the meeting ahead has influenced choice of clothes – smart but comfortable; etc.). This 'in sync-ness' tells us who and what that person is (like, a business executive in the middle of a three-city day). As Gee puts it: 'Within such coordinations we humans become *recognizable* to ourselves and to others and *recognize* ourselves, other people, and things as meaningful in distinctive ways' (ibid.: xiv).

Humans and non-human elements move in and out of such coordinations all the time. Identities (of humans and non-humans alike) are chronicles of the trajectories of coordinations we move through, over time. Different coordinations call on us to think, act, believe, dress, feel, speak, relate in different ways to a greater or lesser extent. To know how to do this, when to do it, and that we should do it is the 'nature' of living meaningfully. Another way of saying this is to say that we get recruited to Discourses as part of our 'birthright' as social and cultural beings, and that in and through our social engagement with Discourses we each become identifiable as a particular kind of person (a trajectory and amalgam of 'situated selves' that change as our purposes, contexts, and Discourse coordinations change) and learn to be a particular kind of person. A Discourse

> is a way of 'being together in the world' for humans, their ways of thinking and feeling (etc.), and for non-human things, as well, such that coordinations of elements, and elements themselves, take on recognizable identities. 'Discourse' names the patterning of coordinations, their recognizability, as well as that of their elements.
>
> (ibid.: xv)

Discourses are of many kinds – classrooms, sports, friendship networks, church gatherings, clubs, gangs, academic disciplines, discussion lists, chatrooms, types of women, weddings, funerals, families. They are made up by coordinations and they make coordinations and elements recognizable. Discourses are the stuff of meaning and meaningfulness; they constitute the 'shape' and 'order' of the world. We enact them and they enact us. To be in a Discourse is to be able to coordinate elements of that Discourse competently and to be coordinated by them competently.

These ideas provide us with ways of thinking about literacies, as elements of coordinations, and as themselves coordinations that are parts of Discourses, depending on the level of specificity being operated with in a particular case. So, for example, the case of the executive *emailing* a memo or request or reminder to head office while boarding a plane might be seen as an element in the enactment of a particular coordination that constitutes part of being a business executive (working on the run in a way that is recognizable as quintessential business executive *modus operandi*). From this perspective, a literacy is an element in a coordination.

At a different level we might think of a literacy practice in the sense spelled out by Scribner and Cole as a coordination among technology, knowledge and skills. The case of the business person from our earlier example who is being a letter writer, emailer, or memo writer involves coordinating an internetworked telephone with knowledge of email/memo etiquette, format, register and institutional structure (who to send it to in order to get the desired result) and requisite skills (texting on the run with one hand and an eye to luggage and boarding pass with the other, all the while organizing thoughts succinctly . . .).

As constitutive parts of participation in or membership of a Discourse, literacies are always about much more, and involve much more, than just the production of texts. They are (also) contexts or pretexts for enacting and refining memberships of Discourses that include such dimensions as feeding back, providing support, sharing knowledge and expertise, explaining rules, sharing jokes, commiserating, doing one's job, expressing opinions, showing solidarity, enacting an affinity (Gee 2004), and so on.

In short, literacies are 'socially recognized ways of generating, communicating and negotiating meaningful content through the medium of encoded texts within contexts of participating in Discourses (or, as members of Discourses)'. As such, blogging, fanfic writing, manga producing, meme-ing, photoshopping, anime music video (AMV) practices, podcasting, vodcasting, and gaming are *literacies*, along with letter writing, keeping a diary, maintaining records, running a paper-based zine, reading literary novels, note-making during conference presentations or lectures, and reading bus timetables.

Reflection and discussion

Identify two quite different Discourses in your own life. Examples of Discourses to consider include your own family Discourse, dating Discourse, graduate student Discourse, teaching or teacher Discourse, political party Discourse, etc. Analyse key elements of the two selected Discourses in terms of characteristic, distinctive or socially recognized ways of:

- thinking and believing and 'seeing' the world;
- speaking, reading and writing;
- acting, moving, gesturing, etc.;
- dressing;
- feeling (e.g., about something, towards others);
- valuing, etc.

In your analysis, include such non-human elements as:

- tools and technologies;
- objects (including machines and vehicles);
- institutions;
- networks;
- places;
- physical spaces, buildings, etc.

Discuss how such elements are coordinated within each Discourse. Then discuss how your two target Discourses require different social and language 'moves' and the ways in which people learn to move and act effortlessly within these Discourses.

Hint: Thinking about what a 'newcomer' to each Discourse would need to know in order to participate fully in each Discourse can help with identifying key characteristics of each.

So much for literacies in general. What now of *'new'* literacies?

'New': in theory and in practices

At the end of Chapter 1 we spoke of literacies that can be regarded as 'new' in an *ontological* sense of being made of new kind of 'stuff'. We distinguished between new *technical* 'stuff' and new *ethos* 'stuff'. At the heart of the idea of new technical stuff is *digitality*: the growth and ongoing development of digital-electronic technologies and the use of programming languages, source code and binary code for writing programs and storing and retrieving data. At the heart of the idea of new ethos stuff is the emergence of a distinctly contemporary mindset, discussed at length in Chapter 2. In this section we will elaborate briefly on these ideas by focusing on some especially salient aspects of 'new technical stuff' and providing concrete exemplifications of 'new ethos stuff'.

'New technical stuff'

Much of what is important for literacy about the 'new technical stuff' is encapsulated in Mary Kalantzis' idea that 'You click for "A" and you click for "red"' (Cope *et al.* 2005: 200). Basically, programmers write source code that is stored as binary code (combinations of 0s and 1s) and drives different kinds of applications (for text, sound, image, animation, communications functions, etc.) on digital-electronic apparatuses (computers, games hardware, CD and MP3 players, etc.). Someone with access to a fairly standard computer and internet connection, and who has fairly elementary knowledge of standard software applications can create a diverse range of meaningful artefacts using a strictly finite set of physical operations or techniques (keying, clicking, cropping, dragging), in a tiny space, with just one or two (albeit complex) 'tools'. They can, for example, create a multimodal text and send it to a person, a group, or an entire internet community in next to no time and at next to no cost. The text could be a photoshopped image posted to Flickr.com. It could be an animated Valentine's Day card sent to an intimate friend. It could be a short animated film sequence using toys and objects found at home, complete with an original music soundtrack, attached to a blog post. It could be a slide presentation of images of some event with narrated commentary, or remixed clips from a video game that spoof some aspect of popular culture or that retell some obscure literary work in cartoon animations.

The shift from material inscriptions to digital coding, from analogue to digital representations, has unleashed conditions and possibilities that are massively 'new'. In the case of the shift from print to the post-typographic, Bill Cope (Cope *et al.* 2005) describes what this means for the visual rendering of texts. He explains that digital technologies reduce the basic unit of composition from the level of a character to a point below character level. In the case of a text on a screen the unit of composition is reduced to pixels. This has an important implication. It means that text and images can be rendered together seamlessly and relatively easily on the same page and, moreover, that text can be layered into images – both static and moving – (and vice versa) in ways that were very difficult – and in some respects *impossible* – to do physically with the resources of print.

> In an old book there was a section with the plates and a section with the text ... For many hundreds of years ... text and images were quite separated, for very pragmatic reasons ... [I]n the first half of the 20th century ... photographic techniques ... moved away from letter press and plate systems [bringing text and image] together a bit more [with] film and plates, but it was still very difficult. But now the elementary manufacturing unit has changed radically. The raw materials you work with are on a screen. So when you press a key it actually builds a visual representation out of pixels.
>
> ... [Moreover] if you go back one layer ... beyond pixels, the same compositional stuff produces sound as well. So you have got these basic things about human communication – namely, language, visuals and sound – which are all being manufactured in the same raw material on the same plane in the same platform.
>
> (ibid.: 200)

'Podcasting' provides another example 'of the moment' (in early 2006). Let's imagine the case of a hypothetical conference going on at this very minute. Given any necessary permissions being granted, the conference organizers or a delegate can podcast a presentation (it might be a keynote, or simply a regular paper that the person organizing the podcasts believes will be of interest to other people). The podcaster records the presentation on a suitable digital recorder (e.g., an iPod equipped with an iTalk add-on, or a digital voice recorder, such as those made by Olympus). Many of these devices record audio files in a *.wav format, which generates a high-fidelity, easy-to-edit, but very large file. When the talk is finished, the conference delegate transfers the audio file from their recorder to their laptop, converts the file to an mp3 format using software like iTunes or Garageband, which maintains the fidelity of the recording, but reduces the size of the file and makes it more 'playable' on a range of software applications and audio devices. The person podcasting the recorded presentation uploads the digitally encoded audio mp3 file to a server that can be accessed publicly via the internet.

Technically speaking, to podcast means that one posts audio files relatively regularly to the internet, and interested others can subscribe to the podcast and receive new audiofiles automatically. That is, podcasts are 'syndicated' (i.e., the location of the files online is 'pointed to' by 'really simple syndication' code [RSS]), and podcast aggregators can be used to 'subscribe' to all of this podcasters' posted audio files. These aggregators – like Firefox or iTunes, for example – will automatically check for and download newly posted podcasts that then can be transferred to portable listening devices and played when convenient. Posting audio files online doesn't necessarily require RSS feeds and syndication, however. The conference delegate could just as easily upload a single audio file to a server, and then make a post to their weblog that contains a hyperlink to that file. From that moment, anybody who accesses the blog can immediately access the sound file of the presentation by clicking on the appropriate hyperlink. (For more on mediacasting, see Chapter 5.)

Returning to our example, the recorded conference presentation can be augmented in various ways, such as including a short introductory narrative recorded and spliced into the front-end of the file by the podcaster, or by the addition of an accompanying short video sequence filmed during the presentation, or an automated copy of the slideshow presentation used by the presenter to illustrate key points. Alternatively, some digital voice recorders have camera functions that permit photo taking during a presentation. These photos can be 'pegged' to the sound file, so that at the moment in the sound file when a photograph was taken it will pop up as an image on the screen of the person viewing this 'voice album' file. This file can be uploaded to the internet and/or burned to a CD-ROM for ease of sharing, and so on. The same – or elements of the same – binary functions, programming logic, conventions and 'stuff' that encode sound can also be used to encode the images and video, the display interfaces themselves, and any online file hosting and networking services. The net result is a seamless, clean, elegant and rapid production that has global 'reach' at close to 'real' time (for an example of a podcast conference, see: isis.duke.edu/events/ podcasting/casts.html).

The kinds of 'enabling' and 'sharing' reflected in what we have just described are quite revolutionary. Relatively unsophisticated bedroom-based desktop publishing software can generate text and image effects that the best printers often could not manage under typographic conditions, and 'publishing' now is no longer limited to print or images on paper, but can include additional media such as voice recordings, music files, 2D and 3D animation, video, photoshopped images, scanned images of paper-based artworks, etc., as well. Even the concept of 'text' as understood in conventional print terms becomes a hazy concept when considering the enormous array of expressive media now available to everyday folk. Diverse practices of 'remixing' – where a range of original materials are copied, cut, spliced, edited, reworked, and mixed into a new creation – have become highly popular in part because of the quality of product it is possible for 'ordinary people' to achieve.

Machinima animations are a good example of our point here. 'Machinima' is the term used to describe the process by which fans use video game animation 'engines' (i.e., the code that 'drives' or generates all the images in a given video game) and computer-generated imagery (CGI) to render new animated texts on their desktop computers (in the not so distant past, this kind of text production demanded extremely expensive, high-end 3D graphics and animation engines and was found mostly within the realm of professional animators). Creating machinima involves using tools found within the game engine such as camera angle options, script editors, level editors, and the like, along with resources, such as backgrounds, themes, characters, settings etc. available in the game (en.wikipedia.org/wiki/Machinima). According to Machinima.com, a popular how-to website and archive of machinima animations:

> You don't need any special equipment to make Machinima movies. In fact, if you've got a computer capable of playing Half-Life 2, Unreal Tournament 2004 or even Quake [all three are popular video games], you've already got virtually everything you need to set up your own movie studio inside your PC. You can produce films on your own, or you can hook up with a bunch of friends to act out your scripts live over a network. And once you're done, you can upload the films to this site and a potential audience of millions.
>
> (2006: 1)

The term – machinima – is also used to describe the genre of animation generated by this process. These animations may be fanfics and extend a game narrative in some way, or the game may simply provide tools and resources for producing an entirely unrelated text. Machinima need not be amateurish in quality, either. Animations like *Hardly Workin'* and *Red vs Blue* have won film festival awards around the world. It is now possible to download open source software kits developed expressly for designing and editing one's own machinima using content from any video game. Those new to the machinima creation process can also now access online tutorials and interviews with high profile machinima makers for insider tips on how to create one's own high-quality animations.

The popularity of this kind of animation remixing has seen the launch of games that directly and openly encourage remixing, like Lionhead Studios' 'The Movies' (themoviesgame.com). Alessandro Cima, a well-known short film producer, has produced a range of animated texts that retell an often-overlooked piece of classic gothic literature (generally attributed to Bram Stoker), *Dracula's Guest*. Cima has used tools and content resources from 'The Movies' in ways that give little indication that the backgrounds, characters, movements and camera angles were *not* created specifically for his *Dracula's Guest* animations, but were instead selected from a preset menu of tools and resources (see: candlelightstories.com/movies.asp). Increasing numbers of video games are also recognizing the popularity of machinima and are creating games that more easily lend themselves to modification or to remixing (e.g., 'Dark Reign 2').

In a similar vein we find game 'modding'. This involves the use of a video game's image and strategy engines to create fan-driven 'modifications' to the game. These modifications remain 'true' to the game's 'universe' (i.e., how characters can move, act, solve problems and what kinds of challenges are put in place etc. within the world of the game), but add, say, a new mini-adventure or quest for characters to complete. Such additions may expand a level by adding new skills or qualities to the game, or create an entirely new level for players to complete that adds a layer of difficulty or complexity to the game (cf. Squire forthcoming; Steinkuehler forthcoming).

Music can be sampled and remixed using desktop computers and audio editing software. Indeed, the term 'remix' itself grew out of the DJ sampling, scratching and mixing scene that began in the late 1970s and early 1980s (although music remixing itself has a long history as a practice; cf., blues music, ska music from Jamaica). This kind of music remixing now no longer requires an extensive and eclectic vinyl record collection, multiple turntables and bulky and expensive mixing and amplification equipment as it did in the 1970s. Software that comes bundled with most computers is all one needs to convert music files from a CD into an editable format (e.g., *.wav), to edit and splice sections of different songs together and to convert the final music files back into a highly portable format (e.g., *.mp3) and upload them to the internet for others to access, or to use them as a background soundtrack in a larger multimedia project. The popularity of Do-It-Yourself music remixing has also been recognized in the commercial sector, and for the price of a video game it is possible to purchase software packages that run on game-playing machines, like 'MTV Music Generator 3: This Is the Remix' for the Xbox gaming computer. (For more on remixing, see Chapter 4.)

This *enabling* capacity of binary code – the new technical 'stuff' – is integral to most of the new literacies that will concern us here. A lot of this enabling is by now so commonplace that we take it for granted, such as in everyday templates and interfaces. Examples include:

- blog templates and authoring tools that automate the 'look' of one's text (and make it easy to change font style, colour, size, to include images or hyperlinks);
- writing/publishing tools like word processing software that make it easy to change fonts and text layout (e.g., columns, alignment, page orientation), or to insert images or figures or even sound files or live internet links, play with colours, and so on, by simply selecting a menu option;
- being able to open multiple programs – and windows within these programs – at the same time and move content between them via the copy-and-paste function;
- instant messaging interfaces that enable us to include iconic emoticons, attach files and save conversation transcripts;
- email interfaces that make it easy to read and respond to email, keep copies of sent messages, store and manage messages;
- being able to complete and submit forms online due to the development of 'editable' webpage interfaces;
- website interfaces that encode password and username functions that enable authorized access to certain online spaces;
- collaborative interactional spaces mediated by subscribing to email discussion lists using generally standardized subscription processes (e.g., sending an email to a listserv program that includes your full name and the command, 'subscribe');
- online forum interfaces that allow members to post, read and respond directly to comments;

- online real-time text-based chat interfaces that are now embedded into websites and no longer require the downloading and installation of specially-developed 'client software' in order to participate.

Reflection and discussion

The broadcast media run seemingly endless stories about young people reading and writing less and less these days. Yet large and increasing numbers of young people devote much time and energy to projects that involve remixing practices like machinima, photoshopping and music composing, and fan practices like manga drawing and fanfiction writing, etc. These projects very often employ sophisticated and/or complex narrative (and other generic forms, such as composing procedural texts and the like).

- How do you explain all this effort?

- Why do you think such practices aren't considered significant or important by broadcast media accounts of young people's reading and writing habits?

- Do you regard them as significant or important *practices*? If so, why? If not, why not?

- Do you regard them as significant or important *literacy* practices? If so, why? If not, why not?

Finally, there is a major issue associated with a feature of digitally encoded material available on the internet that introduces something profoundly new. The point in question is made by Lawrence Lessig (2004: 141–3). It has to do with copyright and a fundamental difference between physical space (or what Lessig calls 'real space') and cyberspace.

Lessig shows how copyright law in physical space distinguished three categories of use of copyrighted material: unregulated, regulated and fair use. For example, there are various uses of a book that are not subject to copyright law and permissions because they do not involve making a copy of the text (unregulated), or because they involve only copying an amount of the book (whether by photocopying, reproducing in a citation, or whatever) or having a purpose (e.g., scholarly review and critique) that is deemed to fall within the limits of 'fair use'. So A can lend a book to B to read, and B to C and so on, without falling foul of copyright – since no copy of the text is made. A can even resell the book. These fall within the category of unregulated uses, because to borrow and read a book or to sell it does not involve making a copy.

But the 'ontology' of material available on the internet – 'a distributed digital network' (ibid.: 143) – is different in a fundamental respect from material available in physical space. On the internet 'every use of a copyrighted work produces a copy' (ibid.). Without exception. This 'single arbitrary feature of a digital network' carries massive implications:

> Uses that before were presumptively unregulated are now presumptively regulated. No longer is there a set of presumptively unregulated uses that define a freedom associated with a copyrighted work. Instead, each use is now subject to the copyright, because each use also makes a copy – category 1 [unregulated] gets sucked into category 2 [regulated].
>
> (ibid: 143)

We do not have space here to deal with the intricacies of copyright law and permissions. Instead, we urge readers who have not done so to read Lessig's book. An excellent and important book on copyright and literacy, it goes to the heart of some pressing issues related to differences between the mindsets that we have distinguished here and the 'worlds' to which they attach. We will conclude this section with the point Lessig (2005) makes concerning young people and 'creative writing' in the current epoch of new tools.

Lessig describes a range of digital remix practices like AMV (Anime-Music-Video remixing), where people, a very large proportion of them young people, take 'found' artefacts and remix them into something new. In AMV practices, for example, participants record a series of anime cartoons and then video edit these to synchronize them with music tracks (see, for example, animemusicvideos.org). Lessig discusses digital remix as a practice of cultural creativity against the background of a particular kind of approach to creative writing that has traditionally been common in North American schools. In this practice

> you read the book by Hemmingway, *For Whom the Bell Tolls*, you read a book by F. Scott Fitzgerald, *Tender is the Night*, and then you take bits from each of these books and you put them together in an essay. You take and combine, and that's the writing, the creative writing, which constitutes education about writing: to take and to remix as a way of creating something new ... And in this practice of writing we have a very particular way of thinking about how we learn to write. We learn to write in one simple way, by doing it. We have a literacy that comes through the practice of writing, writing meaning taking these different objects and constructing with them.
>
> (Lessig 2005: n.p.)

However, whereas the conventional creative writing practice as remix described by Lessig does not infringe copyright law, digital remix often does – and practitioners face the risk of legal action. Yet, says Lessig (2005: n.p.), digital remix as a practice of cultural creativity is a kind of writing. In fact, new digital media, he says, are changing what it means to write. Digital remix, of whatever kind, involving whatever media, 'is what writing is in the early 21st century' (ibid.). It involves working with a different set of tools from those we have written with in the past, says Lessig, but 'it is the same activity that we did [in the past] with words'. Now, however, 'it is not just words; it is words, sounds, images, video. What our society consumes is the source for this writing' (ibid.).

Lessig makes two further, crucial, points with respect to this new kind of writing. First, he argues that the way today's young people in societies like our own come to know their world is 'by tinkering with the expressions the world gives them in just the way that we [of earlier generations] came to know the world when we tinkered with its words'. To this Lessig adds the claim that this new writing needs the same freedoms as did the writing of the eighteenth, nineteenth and twentieth centuries. To do it well, he says, to understand how it works, to teach it, to develop it and to practise it require freedoms that are currently outlawed. Hence, the kind of enabling potential inherent in digital tools underpinned by the ontology of digital code is a two-edged sword under current legislation conditions. On the one hand, it 'democratises a certain creative process' (Lessig 2005). On the other hand, its very nature means that the exercise of this democratized potential puts practitioners at risk under copyright law. Lessig argues that the law must change, and with that we agree entirely.

Reflection and discussion

While we were writing this book Marvel and DC Comics made a move to copyright the word, 'super-hero'. This unleashed a flurry of diatribes across the internet aimed at the comics conglomerate for presuming that such a term could be 'owned' and 'corralled', so that no-one else could use it without express permission.

- What's going on here? Why might Marvel and DC Comics feel compelled to lay legal claim to the term 'super-hero'?

- What might be some of the implications of Marvel and DC Comics' attempt to copyright 'super-hero' for fan-produced creations, or for future/new super-hero comics?

- What might be some of the implications for everyday citizens of Marvel and DC Comics' copyright manoeuvre? How would you feel about living in a world where certain phrases can only be used with corporate permission? What might this mean for the music industry, for example? What implications might this have for education in general, and for literacy education in particular?

'New ethos stuff'

As we will see in depth in later chapters, large and growing numbers of people are 'joining' literacies (and devoting impressive amounts of time and energy to them) that differ greatly from mainstream cultural models of literacy of the modern era (and, particularly, of literacies as they are constructed and engaged within formal educational settings like schools). Much of the 'nature' of this difference is captured in Jim Gee's accounts of learning within affinity spaces (e.g., Gee 2004). While our interest here is wider than learning *per se*, some of the key features of affinity spaces that enable learning are nonetheless the very 'stuff' of how contemporary literacies are constituted and experienced more generally by people engaging in them. Gee describes affinity spaces as

> specially designed spaces (physical and virtual) constructed to resource people [who are] tied together ... by a shared interest or endeavor ... [For example, the] many websites and publications devoted to [the video game 'Rise of Nations'] create a social space in which people can, to any degree they wish, small or large, affiliate with others to share knowledge and gain knowledge that is distributed and dispersed across many different people, places, Internet sites and modalities (magazines, chat rooms, guides, recordings).
>
> (ibid.: 9, 73)

Affinity spaces instantiate participation, collaboration, distribution and dispersion of expertise, and relatedness (ibid.: Ch. 6). These very features are integral to the 'ethos stuff' of what we identify here as 'new' literacies. In this section we briefly exemplify these features by reference to aspects of blogging, fanfiction writing and collaborative writing in wikis.

Blogging as participation
We take up the theme of blogging as participation at length in Chapter 5. We will briefly anticipate that larger discussion here, by reference to how blogging taps into important aspects of the politics of internet architecture.

O'Reilly (2005: n.p.) observes that some systems are designed to encourage participation (with the corollary that others are not, or are less so). Systems and media based on the logic of 'broadcast' are designs that minimize participation: few get to broadcast, and the traffic is one-way. Systems like conventional publishing allow for limited participation: those (the few) who make it past various editorial gatekeepers get to publish their work, whether as authors of books, magazine articles, newspaper columns or letters to the editor. But again, apart from the very limited opportunities for review and response, this too is essentially one-way traffic. If we take Mitch Kapor's dictum that architecture is politics (cited in O'Reilly 2005), then the architecture of broadcast and publishing is a politics of participation by the few and reception by the many.

On the internet we certainly find examples of system designs that tend more toward broadcast and publishing. But we also, and increasingly, find examples of system designs that encourage large-scale interactive participation – as well as designs at points between these extremes. The architecture of weblogs and the blogosphere can be seen as strongly pro-participation at many different levels. And the uptake in participation has been dramatic, with the number of *active* blogs estimated at 28 million by Technorati.com in mid-February 2006. Given the enormous number of blogs now populating the internet, it is interesting to consider some of the different kinds and levels of participation in blogging and how they are facilitated and sustained.

An obvious starting place is with how the expertise of various agents has been put at the disposal of millions in the form of simple-to-use interfaces that make setting up and maintaining a weblog quite straightforward. Easy to follow instructions are quickly to hand. Most blog templates provide diverse options for degrees of 'interactivity' and 'connectedness to others' that users can set to their personal tastes and modify at will. These include options for enabling or disabling the 'comments' function attached to each blog post, for choosing to password-protect one's blog so that only invited others have access to it, and so on. The ready availability of online blog publishing tutorials and lists of frequently asked questions and answers to these questions (known as FAQ lists) make it as easy as possible for users to 'grow' with their blogs. They can shape the look and feel of their blog, vary its degree of connectedness to other blogs by means of outbound (and inbound) links, and enhance its degree of interactivity around the comments function or by adding a tagboard, and so on.

For example, Blogger.com, a popular weblog publishing service, has recently launched a user-to-user blogging help group (groups.google.com/group/blogger-help) where bloggers can post questions about technical issues (e.g., how do I change font colours? How do I add links to my blog sidebar?), or management issues (e.g., how do I delete my blog?), to troubleshooting queries (e.g., what does it mean when I get a 'permission denied' message when I try and republish my blog?), or problems concerning access, use and participation (e.g., how can I block certain people from commenting on my blog?), and so on. Blogger also posts links to step-by-step online tutorials on inserting hyperlinks into one's posts, hints and tips, such as how to aim for good quality writing in one's posts, and so on.

The most basic blog 'set-up' offers users an array of participation and interactivity options ranging from being a lone blogger and silent reader of other blogs to structural features of the blog that enable one to develop a 'friends' list that creates a tight network of people usually interested in similar things. The 'friends list' function of Livejournal.com blogs, for example, enables a blogger to link directly to up to 750 other LiveJournal accounts. Recent blog posts made by each 'friend' on a blogger's list are automatically collated within the blogger's 'friends' page, making it easy not only to keep up-to-date with other people's doings but which also enables conversations to spill across blogs (Rezak and Alvermann 2005). The 'comments' function available within most blog interfaces also distinguishes blogs from their earlier cousin, the personal website. The comments function means that blogs are not simply one-way publication sites, but that they can become highly interactive as readers comment on a post and as the blogger responds to comments in subsequent posts and perhaps elaborates on ideas, or visits the blogs of people who have left comments and leaves his or her own comments in relation to a post found there (Davies and Merchant 2007).

More elaborate degrees and forms of participation are made possible through the use of services and conventions like syndication software and commands (RSS) and permalinks. O'Reilly (2005: n.p.) describes RSS as 'the most significant [recent] advance in the fundamental architecture of the Web'. The RSS function allows users to *subscribe* to a webpage (whether a conventional website, web news page, wiki, or a blog) and be automatically notified through their browser (e.g., Bloglines.com, Squeet.com) or desktop client (e.g., NetNewsWire, Firefox) each time any page they subscribe to changes (provided that the owner of the website or blog etc. has included the syndication code as part of the 'background' program code that drives their site). In the case of weblogs, this means subscribers can read the most recent post on a blog to which they've subscribed and interact with it (e.g., by leaving a comment, linking to the post from their own blog or website, making a discussion post about it on their own blog), as well as simply participate in the life of that blog by following it actively.

RSS feeds may also be augmented with 'permalinks' (see the next Reflection and discussion box) that point to a specific post on somebody's weblog and that help open it up for discussion – so that when the post is automatically archived and no longer appears on the blog's front page (a further architectural feature of weblogs) it can still be retrieved easily and directly. Tom Coates (2003: n.p.) describes permalinks as 'the device that turned weblogs from an ease-of-publishing phenomenon into a conversational mess of overlapping communities'. Permalinks built the first bridges between blogs, and with this addition 'discussion emerged. Chat emerged. And ... friendships emerged or became more entrenched.' O'Reilly (2005: n.p.) adds that the combination of RSS and permalinks turned the blogosphere into

> a new peer-to-peer equivalent of Usenet and bulletin-boards ... Not only can people subscribe to each other's sites, and easily link to individual comments on a page, but also, by a mechanism known as trackbacks [see the next 'Reflection and discussion' box], they can see when anyone else links to their pages, and can respond, either with reciprocal links, or by adding comments.

Relatedness and deep and active participation are enabled in the blogosphere through collaboration and sharing of expertise and material resources, realized in the form of readily appropriated interfaces, free blog hosting, syndication services, linking and tracking mechanisms, and information and help available at point of need. This spirit of an architectural politics designed to encourage participation has been taken up on a scale unimaginable less than a decade ago. The blogosphere has become a most vibrant dimension of 'the live web'; of 'we the media' – 'a world in which "the former audience," not a few people in a back room, decides what's important' (O'Reilly 2005: n.p.).

Reflection and discussion

Visit BoingBoing.net and locate the *permalink* for any one of the posts appearing on the main page to see how permalinks work.

Next, click on the *blogs' comments* link to see how the 'trackback' function on a blog works. This link will take you to all the blogs that link directly to that particular post. In some cases there may not yet be any links. Try the trackback link on a range of posts spanning a week or longer.

- What do you notice? To what extent does this tally with Coates' and O'Reilly's claims above?

- What do you think might this mean for effective school-based applications of blogs and blogging?

Collaboration, participation and distributed expertise in fanfiction

Fanfiction, which receives more in-depth attention in Chapter 4, has exploded as a popular literacy with the growth of the internet. In fanfiction 'devotees of a TV show, movie, or (less often) book write stories about its characters' (Plotz 2000: 1). Fanfic based on video game plotlines and characters is also growing in popularity. Fan fictions chronicle alternative adventures, mishaps or even invented histories or futures for main characters; relocate main characters from a series or movie to a new universe altogether; create 'prequels' for shows or movies; fill in plot holes; or realize relationships between characters that were only hinted at, if that, within the original text.

David Plotz describes fanfiction as turning writing into a communal art, wherein 'writing and reading become collaborative. We share the characters and work together to make them interesting and funny and sexy' (ibid.). Other fanfic writers are equally forthcoming about the collaborative and shared nature of their writing practices. One of our adolescent informants, Silver Excel Fox, describes how she supplied a character for another online friend's narrative:

> She liked my review for one of her stories, and I was kind of talking about one of her characters [in the review], and she was, so, 'I need another character. Do you want to be it?' And I'm like, 'Sure,' and I gave her a description of what I wanted my character to look like, and she took my character and put it into her story.
>
> (interview, 2005, by Knobel and Lankshear)

Elsewhere, collaboration occurs when reviewers provide feedback on texts posted by authors for comment and review. This kind of dynamic exchange most often occurs via online forums and email discussion lists (see Black 2005a, 2005b; Chandler-Olcott and Mahar 2003a). Authors and reviewers take the role of reviewing very seriously. Many fanfic writers, for example, make use of forums dedicated to 'beta-reading': public pre-publication forums where authors can obtain feedback on new stories before posting them to or publishing them on more formal fanfic sites (Black 2006a, 2006b). Some moderated or filtered fanfic forums expect authors to have their narratives beta-read before submitting them for consideration for publication. *The Force* (fanfic.theforce.net) suggests that a beta reading should look for:

- Grammar and spelling errors. While a few errors are bound to make it through, too many such errors will result in a rejection.
- Plot continuity and technical errors. Your betas should let you know if there are any plot threads left unintentionally unresolved, and note places where there are internal continuity problems (e.g., you had a character leave the room on page four, and she speaks again on page five without re-entering or using a comm-link).
- Character issues. Fanfiction allows much more freedom than professional fiction in terms of character interpretations, but your betas should point it out if your characters suddenly begin to behave very oddly for no appreciable reason.
- Intangible things. Ask your betas to tell you what they got out of your story before you tell him or her what you meant. 'I like this!' is a nice thing to hear, but what you need from a beta reader is to hear, 'I really liked the way you showed Qui-Gon's early dissent from the Jedi Council, because it resonates with the way he behaves in his early scenes with Shmi in TPM' (or whatever). If that's what you meant to convey, it tells you that you've succeeded. If it's not what you meant, it can mean two things. You may decide that you really like it, and want to leave it alone or even expand on it. You might also decide that you absolutely don't want to give that impression, and therefore you want to change the things that gave it.

(fanfic.theforce.net/authors/subguide.asp)

Two points are worth noting here. First, these guidelines for beta readings are a typical example of the kinds of resources users can access in affinity spaces. Other similar kinds of resources that abound on fanfic sites include feedback discussion forums, feedback functions automatically appended to posted narratives within fanfic sites that let reviewers comment directly on a new text, and reviews sent to email discussion lists dedicated to fanfiction writing and/or fan art. Such resources typify the 'ethos' of affinity spaces generally. The beta reading guidelines resemble things available in the games-based affinity spaces discussed by Gee (2004: 84), like 'FAQs that explain various aspects of the game and give players help with the game' and 'strategy guides and walkthroughs for "newbies" [new players]'. Artefacts like *The Force's* beta reading guidelines can be seen as embodying several defining features of affinity spaces as described by Gee. These include: 'Newbies and masters and everyone else share common space'; 'Both individual and distributed knowledge are encouraged'; 'There are lots of different routes to status'; and 'Leadership is porous and leaders are resources' (ibid.: 85–7).

The second point concerns the character of fanfic peer review at the level of lived experience. This, of course, varies from case to case, but an already recurring theme in the as-yet small corpus of literature that exists is of participants approaching peer review in open, non-defensive/non-aggressive, constructive and generously supportive ways. These ways often become communicative and relational in tone and on levels that differ from the circumstances and connotations of peer review within conventional 'zero sum' publishing (academic and non-academic) contexts. Moreover, they may spill over into learning opportunities that extend far beyond immediate fanfic purposes.

Rebecca Black (2005a) presents a case of the social relations of peer review at their most expansive. An adolescent native Chinese speaker, now living in Canada, regularly begins her fanfics with an 'author's note' (which she marks as, 'A/N') that asks for readers' patience with her English while at the same time indicating that she is keen to improve her written English fluency. Her following author note begins with a friendly Japanese greeting ('Konichiwa minna-san'), which translates as, 'Hello, everybody'. This fanfic author also includes manga-fied ASCII emoticons in her message (e.g., ^_^ instead of the traditional :) to indicate a smile):

A/N: Konnichiwa minna-san! This is my new story
^_^. Please excuse my grammar and spelling mistakes.
Because English is my second language. Also,
I'm still trying to improve my writing skills ... so this
story might be really sucks. ...–;;

Black reports that these kinds of author notes 'provide writers with direct access to the reader and enable authors to specifically state those elements of the story (e.g., form or content) on which they would like readers and reviewers to focus' (ibid.: 125). The author in Black's example indicates tangentially that feedback on spelling and grammar would be appreciated. Reviewers have seemingly heeded these author notes and have written encouraging comments, including comments that the author writes much better stories than many native English speakers, or they have made suggestions for addressing grammar and spelling errors in the text (which, according to Black, the fanfic writer always addresses when revisiting and editing her posted narratives). At the same time, reviewer feedback emphasizes that these errors are 'minor and do not interfere with the effectiveness and overall message of the story' (ibid.).

Collaboration, community and collective intelligence in Wikipedia

Wikipedia is an online encyclopedia being produced collaboratively on the web on the basis of broad principles of open source cooperation. It uses open-editing, collaborative writing software – a 'wiki' – that allows users to edit content online as they read. Many readers will be familiar with *Wikipedia* as a free online source of information, without necessarily being aware of how it is produced, and how one can edit the site just as 'freely' as one can access it for the purposes of obtaining information.

A wiki is about as easy to set up as a weblog. There are various free wiki hosting sites where one can register and establish a wiki for the purposes of a collaborative writing project. Bob Godwin-Jones (2003: 15) says the goal of wiki sites is 'to become a shared repository of knowledge, with the knowledge base growing over time'. This goal means that wiki content is 'generally expected to have some degree of seriousness and permanence', and that successful wikis depend on users being 'serious about collaborating and willing to follow the group [those who set up and participate in the wiki] conventions and practices' (ibid.).

Wikis can be established on different bases, around such variables as membership, security, goals, and so on. For example, a research project team might set up a wiki for the purposes of collaboratively writing their research report and/or for generating articles, chapters or books out of their research. They might make the wiki password protected so that only members of the team can read and edit the content. All changes are logged on wikis, so it is possible to know when a change was made to content and who made a particular change (or, at least, the machine from which the change was made). It is also easy to arrange for anyone with access to the wiki to automatically receive information when a change has been made. At the other extreme, a wiki might be established as a maximally 'open' project, where anyone from anywhere can access the content and make any changes they want as well as to read what is there. (For a quick introduction to wikis see, for example, the entries on 'wikis' in *Wikipedia* at en.wikipedia.org/wiki/Wiki; or in *How Stuff Works* at howstuffworks.com/wiki.htm.)

Wikipedia is located at the open end of the continuum. Andrew Lih (2004: 3) explains that with thousands of international contributors, *Wikipedia* is 'the largest example of an *open content* wiki'. The goal is to 'create an encyclopedia that can be shared and copied freely while encouraging people to easily change and improve the content' (ibid.). The origin of the project is interesting. Jimmy Wales, founder and Chair of the Board of Trustees of the Wikimedia Foundation that operates *Wikipedia*, had previously been involved in a project to create a free online encyclopedia – Nupedia – with recognized experts as contributors who, with few exceptions, would have PhD degrees. When resources for the project ran out (with just a tiny proportion of articles written), Wales and his collaborator, Larry Sanger, put the completed material into a wiki and invited netizens at large to edit and add to the material. This new wiki-based project became *Wikipedia*.

Wikipedia was established with an editorial policy and guidelines. The cornerstone of the policy is a concept of maintaining a neutral point of view, which involves trying 'to present ideas and facts in such a fashion that both supporters and opponents can agree' (cf. Lih 2004: 4). Philippe Aigrain (2003) says that this editorial policy, together with a clear vision of what it is trying to achieve, means that *Wikipedia* has, in effect, a constitution.

It is often observed that *Wikipedia* is not the kind of project one might expect to work. Its operating logic seems counterintuitive, and the extent to which it has earned respect and generated content across a wide range of subject areas rather than collapsing into chaos seems surprising. There is no overt upfront gate keeping mechanism to check credentials of contributors, quality of the material contributed, or even the goodwill of contributors. Yet, by February 2004 it had more than 200,000 articles in English at various stages of development. This number exceeded 975,000 in February 2005, at which time the English version had almost 950,000 registered users, and 820 administrators. Administrators have 'SysOp' (systems operator) rights, and anyone who has been an active contributor for a while and is generally a known and trusted member of the [Wikipedia] community can be an administrator, and is actively encouraged to be one (Lih 2004: 9). Total content at this time exceeded 3,400,000 pages, and contributors had made over 40 million edits. Lih (ibid.: 9) reports that by early 2004, *Wikipedia* was being cited increasingly frequently in the commercial press as 'a secondary source for further reading' and also as 'a source on historical facts and figures'.

Commentators explain the success of *Wikipedia* quite simply. Its constitution provides guidelines that are easy enough to operate, such that if enough people are operating diligently on the basis of the constitution it is not difficult to eliminate 'noise' or 'excess' (Aigrain 2003). Felix Stalder and Jesse Hirsh (2002: n.p.) suggest that this condition is met because *Wikipedia* 'has a "community" character to it, so there seems to be a certain shared feeling that it is a valuable source and needs to be maintained properly'. This is enabled by an 'advanced versioning system' (Aigrain 2003: n.p.) that makes it easy to revert to an earlier version of an entry. It actually takes much more effort and time to 'mess with a page' or 'enter noise' than it does to revert to an earlier version (a single click). Stalder and Hirsh (2002: n.p.) mention two further factors contributing to the workability of *Wikipedia*. One is that contributors who have devoted time and effort to making an entry have a vested interest in maintaining and improving it. Hence, they will return to it and tend it regularly. This is abetted by an RSS function that sends alerts to people who request them when a particular entry has been amended. Participation can be at any level from correcting a minor glitch, to being 'an author who maintains a lengthy entry', to being an editor 'who continuously improves other people's entries' (ibid.).

An interesting case occurred in January 2006 when it was found that staff in the offices of some politicians in the US House of Representatives had modified material in the *Wikipedia* entries on these politicians that risked reflecting badly on them. More than 1000 edits in total were involved. When Wikipedia members examined the server addresses of people who had made changes to these particular entries, they traced a significant number of them directly to politicians' offices in Washington. The selective editing and revision were first reported in a Massachusetts newspaper by Evan Lehmann (2006). News of the sleuthing spread rapidly through the blogosphere and into the broadcast media. An independently re-written *Wikipedia* entry for one of the politicians involved now contains references to staff interference in the original *Wikipedia* entry. There is also a new separate entry in *Wikipedia* on 'Wikipedia: Congressional Staffer Edits' that documents the scandal and lists politicians implicated in it.

O'Reilly (2005: n.p.) identifies *Wikipedia* as a Web 2.0 initiative that 'embraces the power of the web to harness collective intelligence'. This is the principle of maximizing user activity to generate more valuable outcomes. Just as Amazon.com's architecture for information management and its suite of user activities end up producing a fantastic bibliographic data base, so *Wikipedia's* architecture and user 'brief' are producing an impressive informational resource. O'Reilly is one of several commentators who associates *Wikipedia* with the open source software principle coined by Eric Raymond that 'with enough eyeballs all bugs [or glitches] are shallow'. In the context of writing code, this means that the more people with some knowledge of programming – and they don't have to be *experts* and most of them aren't – who apply that knowledge in the act of peering at code, the more likely and easy it is that 'bugs' in programs will be identified and fixed. In addition, however, it is also more likely that many small contributions will be made (not simply bug elimination) that positively *enhance* the elegance and functionality of the program. In the context of *Wikipedia* we can see these two sides to harnessing collective intelligence.

One side enhances the quality of what is already there, by adding cumulative positive improvements (40 million edits). The other side maintains quality by removing value-subtracting material, whether malicious or simply low quality fare ('noise').

This all adds up to a distinctive 'stuff' of social practice, particularly when we relate it to regimes of literacies with which we are familiar: where competence is presumed to be a private possession (hence, we test it): where expertise is the preserve of authorities (teachers, academics) who ladle it out (often ineffectually) as curriculum, remediation, instruction; where correct or successful performance is governed by 'one size fits all' sets of rules (which, among other things, means that legions of learners born on the wrong side of standardized grammars, lexicons, and semiotics spend their school lives actively reproducing their own failure); where commodification is normal practice (an author wants to publish a novel, so hires an agent who makes suggestions for improvements, pitches to publishers, greases wheels, etc.); where, more often than not, the rules and criteria are vague, hidden, inaccessible; where status is individualized because achievements are individualized; and so on.

In terms of 'ethos', the ontology of literacies like blogging, writing fanfiction and collaborating in *Wikipedia* promotes and celebrates the values of inclusion (everyone in), mass participation, distributed expertise, valid and rewardable roles for all who pitch in, free support and advice, building the practice, collective benefit, cooperation before competition, everyone a winner rather than a zero-sum game, and transparent rules and procedures. There is more. Within a few hours of completing this section we were checking the news from an Australian perspective online, using the News.com.au service. Beginning here: news.com.au, we selected the 'Week in review' link which took us to: news.com.au/story/0,10117,18176795–421,00.html (link now defunct). At this page we selected a hyperlink for 'Bali Nine verdicts'. This took us directly to a *Wikipedia* entry: en.wikipedia.org/wiki/Bali_nine. From News Corp to *Wikipedia* in two degrees of separation. Current news being reported in an online newspaper was drawing on an *Wikipedia* entry with no author byline, and which, in all likelihood, was produced by multiple authors and editors whose only connection to each other may be that their efforts ended up on the same webpage.

Reflection and discussion

- What implications for 'knowledge' and 'news reporting' do phenomena like blogs and *Wikipedia* have?

- What becomes of 'experts' within these practices?

- To what extent do you agree that practices like contributing to *Wikipedia*, fan-fiction writing, blogging, and remixing are new literacies? What reasons support your position?

'New' literacies: paradigm and peripheral cases

We see the 'technical stuff' and the 'ethos stuff' that for us constitutes what is *new* about new literacies as being closely related to one another. A certain kind of technical stuff – digitality – facilitates the kinds and qualities of collaboration, participation, distributedness that we have described. Equally, however, a certain kind of ethos stuff – an insider mindset/a Web 2.0 orientation – will shape the take-up and development of technical stuff in some directions (e.g., relational, interactive, collaboratory) more than in others. Hence, computers have become telephones and telephones have become computers. The kinds of practices we regard as *paradigm* cases of new literacies are characterized by both the new technical stuff of digitization and the new ethos stuff of the second mindset and, more specifically, a Web 2.0 orientation.

As O'Reilly (2005) affirms, you can have new technical stuff without having new ethos stuff. As he also argues, however, the direction of shift at the technological 'leading edge' appears to be increasingly toward architectures supporting practices that are forging stronger and deeper realizations of the second mindset. We think this is an historical trend. It supports our view that where literacies participate in the second mindset but are not (necessarily) mediated by digital technologies, we can nonetheless plausibly regard them as 'new' literacies – albeit as more *peripheral* cases of new literacies than cases that *also* involve new technical stuff. In other words, having new ethos stuff is a sufficient condition for being a new literacy. By contrast, having new technical stuff is neither a necessary nor a sufficient condition for being a new literacy. It might just amount to a digitized way of doing 'the same old same old'. In the final analysis, being on the inside of 'the new' has to do with mindset. Technical stuff can amplify and more fully realize that insiderness. Merely having access to the technical stuff, however, is no guarantee of insider status.

To conclude this chapter we will describe two new literacies and relate these to key points in our account of new literacies. One of these – Flickr photo sharing – is a *paradigm* case of a new literacy. The example we begin with, however, is a *peripheral* new literacy. This is scenario planning, a chronologically recent literacy, increasingly popular from the 1970s. It has no necessary link to the use of new technologies, although computers can play very useful roles in the scenario planning process and are now often used by scenario planners for a range of purposes (from maintaining archives to modelling data).

Scenario planning

Scenario planning has emerged as a generic technique to stimulate thinking about the future in the context of strategic planning (Cowan *et al.* 1998). It was initially used in military planning, and was subsequently adapted for use in business environments (Wack 1985a, 1985b; Schwartz 1991; van der Heijden 1996) and, more recently, for planning political futures in post-apartheid South Africa, Colombia, Japan, Canada and Cyprus (Cowan *et al.* 1998), as well as in technology futures planning in Europe and elsewhere (Börjesson 2005). While scenario planning can be undertaken on behalf of very large units (European Union, individual countries, global corporations), with expert guidance by paid consultants, much smaller concerns like schools, community organizations, faculties within a university, and clubs engage in this form of narrating possible futures.

Scenarios are succinct narratives describing possible futures and alternative paths toward the future, based on plausible hypotheses and assumptions. The idea behind scenarios is to start thinking about the future now in order to be better prepared for what comes later; to facilitate conversation about what is going on and what might occur in the world around us, so that we might 'make better decisions about what we ought to do or avoid doing'. Developing scenarios that perceive possible futures in the present can help us 'avoid situations in which events take us by surprise' (Cowan *et al.* 1998: 8).

Proponents of scenario planning insist that scenarios are *not* predictions. Rather, they aim to perceive futures in the present (Rowan and Bigum 1997). Peter Schwartz (1991) provides the analogy of an experienced actor who has been given three very different plays to read and practise during the preceding weeks, but on opening night does not know which one s/he will be performing. Schwartz says the good actor will have learned all three plays and will immediately look at the set. The surroundings reveal which play the actor is in. Being prepared for all three underwrites a successful performance. In this sense, scenario planning is like writing and rehearsing plays now for some future performance. The trick is to write plays of such a nature that our rehearsing them *now* means that we can perform well in that future time.

Within typical approaches to scenario planning a key goal is to aim to make policies and decisions *now* that are likely to prove sufficiently robust if played out across several possible futures. Rather than trying to predict the future, scenario planners imaginatively construct a range of possible futures. In light of these, which may be very different from one another, policies and decisions can be framed at each point in the ongoing 'present' that will optimize options regardless of which anticipated future is closest to the one that eventually plays out in reality.

Scenarios must narrate particular and credible worlds in the light of forces and influences currently evident and known to us and that seem likely to steer the future in one direction or another according to how they play out. A popular way of doing this is to bring together participants in a policy or decision-making exercise and have them frame a focusing question or theme relevant to the area they are concerned with. If, for instance, our concern is with designing courses in literacy education and technology for inservice teachers presently in training, we might frame the question of what learning and teaching of literacy and technology might look like within educational settings for elementary school-age children 10 years hence.

Once the question is framed, participants try to identify 'driving forces' – social, technological, economic, political, etc. – they see as operating and as being important in terms of their question or theme. When these have been thought through, participants identify those forces or influences that seem more or less 'pre-determined': that 'will play out in more or less known ways in any credible story that is told about the future' (Rowan and Bigum 1997: 81). Participants then identify *less predictable* influences, or uncertainties: key variables in shaping the future which could play out in quite different ways, but where we genuinely can't be confident one way or another about how they will play out. From this latter set, one or two are developed as 'critical uncertainties'. These are forces or influences that seem especially important in terms of the focusing question or theme but which are genuinely 'up for grabs' and unpredictable.

The 'critical uncertainties' are then 'dimensionalized' by plotting credible poles: between possibilities that, at one pole are 'not too bland' and, at the other, not too 'off the wall'. These become raw materials for building scenarios: stories about which we can think in ways that suggest decisions and policy directions *now*. In one scenario planning exercise in which we were involved, concerning the future of technology and literacy teaching in elementary or primary school learning, the critical uncertainties were identified as the nature and use of new computing and communications technologies and the nature of schooling as related to work and play. This yielded two axes. One ranged between 'schooling is highly regulated, controlled and work-directed' and 'schooling is based on personal fulfilment, individualistic, anarchic'. The other ranged similarly between 'new technologies used to liberate: a technosociety that is anarchic and democratic' and 'new technologies controlling and regulating all aspects of life' (Rowan and Bigum 1997: 81–2). Making one of these the X axis and the other the Y axis gave four quadrants, each of which was developed as a scenario ('Surface Paradise', 'Newtopia', 'Bill@the_world', and 'Space-haus') in the light of all the prior discussion and knowledge searching done to elaborate the 'driving forces' (for examples from other contexts, see Börjesson 2005; Cowan *et al.* 1998).

In terms of our account of literacies, scenario planning generates and communicates meaningful content of different kinds at multiple levels of interest and engagement – from identifying and describing 'drivers' and 'critical uncertainties' (and what *makes* them uncertain but extremely important) through to the narratives themselves. Planning scenarios may be an aspect of participating in Discourses as various as those of policy developer, curriculum planner, club committee member, corporate executive, curriculum planner, etc. At the level of socially recognized ways of doing the text production and exchange, scenario planning can be understood as practice in terms of its *technological* components (participants might use blackboards, whiteboards, butcher's paper, word processors, networked computers, etc.), some kind of *knowledge system or systems* (e.g., about narration, strategic planning, policy) and a range of *skills* (how to distill critical uncertainties, identify drivers, frame punchy motifs for crafting scenario narratives).

Scenario planning emerged before the advent of personal computers and long before personal and networked computing became popular. It developed in contexts of face-to-face interaction and the use of conventional print resources. Much scenario planning work is still best conducted around a board, using small groups and charting ideas on paper. Nonetheless, it is easy to discern much of what we regard as 'new' about new literacies in scenario planning. Successful scenario planning positively depends on distributed expertise, as well as upon dispersed knowledge. In collaborative activity the participants bring different perspectives and knowledge to bear on a theme and progress is made through interactivity, feedback, and sharing ideas and expertise around. Indeed, the very subject matter – possible futures, and 'what if X happened?' – resists and transcends individualized expertise. There is much of the second mindset in scenario planning as a practice. It is more service than product oriented, and the process benefits from maximum dispersion. Scenarios are often made widely available because their true value comes from engagement with them, and feedback, and improvement on policy thinking that can come from this engagement. The benefits of good scenario planning are collective, not private, which presupposes dispersion. Mobilizing collective intelligence enhances outcomes and adds value.

Flickr

Flickr (flickr.com), now part of Yahoo.com, is a website established for archiving and sharing digital photographs and for providing related web services. Use is free, and anyone can browse photos that are designated 'public' regardless of whether or not one is a member. Signing up is a straightforward matter of clicking on the sign-up button on the Flickr homepage. There appear to be two main ways that people come to join Flickr. They may hear of it by word of mouth (or page or screen), locate the Flickr website and join up. Alternatively, they may receive an invitation by email from an existing member inviting them to join. Anyone can browse photos that are available for public viewing (rather than designated 'private' or only for the user's chosen contacts to view). Only account holders, however, can actually post and comment on photos. There are two types of accounts. One is free. The other requires a yearly subscription fee and grants access to a range of added features. To save space and complication we will focus here on participation as a member (or account holder) holding a free account.

Members can use Flickr in different ways and to different degrees. One extreme is wholly private use, where the space is used simply for storage: to archive one's photos and, perhaps, as a base for uploading photos to one's blog. At the other extreme members invite others to view their photos, join groups based on a theme or interest, establish groups and recruit others to them, comment on their own and other people's photographs, participate in Flickr forums (ask/respond to questions, suggest features, report a bug) and activities, and build special relationships that can spill over into offsite spaces (and, even, into physical space) with other members who share an interest (Davies 2006).

The catalyst or stimulus for participation in Flickr is the digital image and, especially, the digital photograph. Images uploaded to Flickr can include scanned hand-done drawings or paintings, paintshop-generated cartoons, scanned collages, and so on. But the most prevalent image-type within this space, by a large margin, is the digital photo. Posting photos involves making various kinds of written contributions. When users upload photos to their Flickr account the on-screen display template provides a space for keying a title for each photo. A second space for keying a short description appears beneath the photo. There is also space to write words to serve as 'tags' or keywords for the photo (see Chapter 2 for more on the use of tags). In addition, a function in a menu bar above the photo enables the user to write notes that will appear directly on the image when s/he scrolls the cursor over each 'note' icon. The display template also provides a space for comments, similarly to a weblog. Other users can comment here on each photo and users can comment on their own photos.

The free version of Flickr also has provision for users to establish up to three 'sets' of 'like' photos. This serves several enabling purposes. It helps with managing viewer access to images, with joining groups that are organized around a subject, interest, or endeavour (e.g., Flickr members who take pictures of bins, or fire hydrants, toy and doll shots, storytelling projects), with bookmarking 'favourite' images posted by other members, with designating who can access each photo (e.g., everyone, or only those users marked as 'friends') and what rights others are assigned with regard to using the photo in other venues. It also helps with inviting other people to join Flickr and to become a contact (friend or family) of the user. As discussed in Chapter 2, users designated as 'contacts' can add 'tags' to the user's photos.

There are many other aspects of posting photos that we cannot go into here (e.g., monthly image uploading limits, procedures for starting a new Flickr 'group', etc). We will confine further discussion here to a typical example of participation on Flicker.com. It involves the Flickr group 'Tell a Story in Five Frames' (flickr.com/groups/visualstory). The group page describes the purpose of the group and how to participate. Participation has two 'sides'. One is to present a story in five or less photographs, with the only admissible text being the story title. The other is responding to stories that are presented. Response 'can take many forms, such as a poetic or prose rendering of the visualization, a critique on the structure of the story, comments on the photograph, or other constructive forms' (ibid.). The group page provides the rules of the game (e.g., 'A title is the only words that can be used. Rely on the photographs to bring the story to life'), quasi-technical instructions on how to submit a story, and some guidelines for telling a story. The guidelines distinguish different ways of telling a story – 'journalistic reporting, sequential photos that reveal a moment, photographic poetry and narrative' – and provide some guidelines for narrative, including a sequence of suggested 'roles' for a set of five photos (e.g., '1st photo: establish characters and location ... 5th photo: have a logical but surprising end').

Flickr presents a tricky case so far as identifying it as *a literacy* is concerned. From conventional standpoints it might look like a *smorgasbord* of literacies from which different participants select their particular 'mixes'.

Some may spend almost all their time simply uploading photos and adding tags, titles and descriptions and, perhaps, responding to any comments they receive. Their main purpose might be to contribute to a global image archive in the public domain. Others, by contrast, might devote most of their energies to commenting on other people's photos. Others again may limit their activity purely to 'telling a story in five frames'. At the same time, they all fall under a general description of meaning making activity that we might call photo sharing. It is arguable that this is no more 'multiple' or 'hybridized' than letter writing or, even, a particular kind of letter writing like informal letter writing to friends and intimates. When we bundle three photographic prints into an envelope with a Post-it sticker that reads 'pix from the concert XXXXOOOO (kisses and hugs)' and mail it, we are *letter writing* as much as when we spend an entire letter responding to a friend's description of their new romance.

Part of the issue here has to do with what one takes as the 'unit of analysis' for literacy. The nearer one is to a view of literacy that is exhausted by *text*, or some *mode* of text, the less plausible it is to regard photo sharing as a literacy. The nearer one is, however, to holding a full-fledged 'sociocultural practice' view of literacy, the less implausible it seems. Participants recognize themselves engaging in the practice as a *whole*, without compartmentalizing it along the lines of 'Now I am commenting; ah, but now I am uploading an image; now I am tagging; now I am ... . Whatever we are doing at any point in time within this practice we are generating, communicating or negotiating meaningful content in recognized ways through the medium of encoded texts within contexts of participation in Discourses (or, as members of Discourses). That is, photo sharing is a literacy.

The 'technical stuff' of digital literacies like photo sharing checks in here, in the sense that we *click* for 'A' and we *click* for Red. We experience the practice holistically and seamlessly – moving in and out of different facets and functions – because it basically *is* holistic and seamless. The website itself and the templates involved – the technical stuff – make it so: click here and read a comment, and click here and add a comment, and click here and add a tag. With a set-up like Flickr there are not even any multimodal complications around design choices for displaying photos: it is template governed. There are no layout issues or options to consider (Flickr even resizes one's photos automatically to fit the template as the photos are being uploaded). Decisions are limited to tags (not insignificant, but not exactly a science either at the level of folksonomic engagement), titles, and descriptions. In addition, of course, when conceived as a literacy in this way we can also readily see photosharing as a *coordination* or as an *element* in a coordination of identity. Who are you? (In part) 'I'm a Flickr person; I do Flickr.'

Flickr instantiates some other important facets of new literacies as we have discussed them here. For example, the points we made in relation to blogging about the sharing of expertise in the form of interfaces and templates that radically democratize participation and enable people with minimal knowledge, expertise, and confidence to join, apply equally to Flickr. So also do points about distributed expertise and having help and guidance at hand (cf., the guidelines for creating a story in five frames).

A further aspect concerns the fact that reading any internet text involves making a copy and, to that extent, raises potential copyright issues. The technical stuff and the ethos stuff of new literacies converge here. The second mindset relates the value of information to dispersal, and asserts the need to treat information differently from physical stuff as appropriate (cf. Lessig 2004). The work of people in 'open source' and 'creative commons' movements is vital for keeping some spaces free from proprietary constraints. Flickr has a potentially valuable role to play in the area of images, since it provides a way to build a massive database of images in the public domain free from restrictions upon use and permissions constraints. For people plagued by such concerns, including educators, authors and researchers, the participatory and collaborative spirit manifested in the public dimension of the Flickr community assumes great significance. When Flickr members designate their photos 'public' they are (consciously or unconsciously) participating in a progressive politics of information. They contribute to building a practice and a space steeped in values associated with the second (insider) mindset and, to that extent, opposed to the politics of proprietary information.

Finally, tagging is also part of what is new about photosharing on Flickr as a literacy. The meanings that participants assign to images through their selection of tags collectively become a 'folksonomy' (Davies 2006; also Chapter 2 above). Folksonomy is a collaborative categorization of content (images) that gives a fluid quality to meanings within a field, rather than classifying the components of that field into clear-cut, rigid categories. This kind of 'fluidity' resists centrally imposed classifications – it privileges 'folk' over 'experts', is bottom-up rather than top-down, and is answerable to everyday ways of making sense and assigning meanings. As O'Reilly (2005: n.p.) puts it, folksonomies allow for 'retrieval [of content, information] along natural axes generated by user activity'.

Flickr's data management procedures generate this evolving folksonomy as a 'network effect from user contributions' (ibid.). The network effect generated by Flickr's tag-based folksonomy is *semantic*. This is potentially very important to the development of a 'semantic web', in which searching and information retrieval are facilitated through the assignment of machine-readable meaning to the content of material on the web. Whether folksonomic meanings will serve users well and what range of user interests they serve well, remains to be seen. At present there is no reason to believe they will not serve 'folk' interests well. And in a world where folk interests have for so long been subordinated to those most served by expert-generated meaning, that certainly represents something 'new'.

In Part 2 we present detailed discussions of some *paradigm* cases of new literacies.

New Literacies in Everyday Practice

CHAPTER 4

New Literacies as Remix

Introduction

Until recently the idea of 'remix' as a practice of taking cultural artefacts and combining and manipulating them into a new kind of creative blend was associated almost entirely with recorded music. In March 2006, the *Wikipedia* definition of a remix was in terms of using audio editing techniques to produce an alternative mix of a recorded song that differed from the original. This is remix in the sense described on a University of California, Riverside, ethnomusicology webpage on the history of remix as the idea 'of taking apart the various instruments and components that make up a recording and remixing them into something that sounds completely different' (ethnomus.ucr.edu/remix_culture/remix_history.htm). As such, remixing became very popular during the 1990s across a range of musical genres – notably, in hip hop, house and jungle music, but also in mainstream pop, and rhythm and blues, and even in heavy metal music (ibid.).

In this vein, discussions of remix soon fan out into retrospective reconstructions of remix in the world of recorded music, especially from the 1940s and the introduction of 'readily editable magnetic tape' (*Wikipedia*: Remix). Most accounts date modern remixing to Jamaican dance hall culture in the late 1960s, and the interventions of DJs and music recording producers who, for example, used twin turntables with different versions of the same song to be played together while controlling for speed (beats to the minute), or edited tapes to produce versions of songs suited to different kinds of audiences. Remixes sometimes simply provided a speedier version of a song, or a leaner, more stripped back sound, or an elongated song to keep people dancing longer. Once digital sound became the norm, however, all manner of 'sampling' techniques were applied using different kinds of hardware devices or software on a computer (Hawkins 2004).

While this remains the dominant conception of remix, its conceptual life has expanded recently in important and interesting ways within the context of increasing activism directed at copyright and intellectual property legislation. This conceptual expansion is particularly interesting from the standpoint of new literacies. In short, and beginning with music remix, *digital* remixing has been the object of high profile and highly punitive legal action based on copyright law. The legal backlash against popular practices of remix has helped fuel an organized oppositional response to what is seen as unacceptable levels of constraint against the public use of cultural material. And within one very important arm of this organized oppositional response – namely in the arguments developed by Lawrence Lessig (e.g., Koman 2002) for the need to establish a Creative Commons – the idea of remix and remixing has become a key rallying point. We referred briefly to Lessig's work in the previous chapter with respect to the 'technical stuff' of new literacies. It was argued in that context that 'the technical stuff' of new literacies intersects with copyright laws to create issues that do not arise in bookspace. The ideas addressed below are drawn from the same work. This time, however, we focus specifically on Lessig's thesis that digital remix constitutes a contemporary form of writing.

Lawrence Lessig on digital remix as writing

As noted in Chapter 3, Lessig (2005) refers to a particular practice of creative writing within the school curriculum in parts of the US. In this practice students read texts by multiple authors, take bits from each of them, and put them together in a single text. This is a process of taking and remixing 'as a way of creating something new' (ibid.: n.p.). Until recently this kind of remixing was done with paper, pencil, typewriter and the like. These same tools were used for learning to write in the most general sense, which, it can be argued, is also a practice of remix. Learners take words that are presented as text in one place or another and they use these words and texts and the tools of pen and pencil to make new texts, or to remix text. Lessig says that we learn to write 'in one simple way, by doing it' (ibid.). Hence, there is a literacy 'that comes through the practice of writing; writing [means] taking these different objects and constructing with them' (ibid.).

This kind of writing, says Lessig, may be seen as an instance of a much more general practice that we can call 'remix'. Remix in this general sense is quite simply the idea 'of someone mixing things together and then someone else coming along and remixing that thing they have created' (ibid.). When seen in those terms, we can say that 'culture is remix'. Indeed, remix is evident in every domain of cultural practice: Lessig claims that politics is remix, just as knowledge is remix. Everyone engages in remix in this general sense of the idea, and remix is everywhere. Still thinking at this general level of remix, Lessig explains:

> You go see a movie by [Michael Moore] and then you whine to your friends about how it is the best movie you have ever seen or the worst movie ever made. What you are doing is taking Michael Moore's creativity and remixing it in your life. You are using it to either extend your own views or criticize his views. You are taking culture and practising this act of remixing. Indeed, every single act of reading and choosing and criticizing and praising culture is in this sense remix. And it is through this general practice that cultures get made.
>
> (ibid.)

At the broadest level, then, remix is the general condition of cultures: no remix, no culture. We remix language every time we draw on it, and we remix meanings every time we take an idea or an artefact or a word and integrate it into what we are saying and doing at the time.

At a more specific level we now have *digital* remix enabled by computers. This includes, but goes far beyond simply mixing music. It involves mixing digital images, texts, sounds and animation; in short, all manner of found artefacts. Young people are picking this up on a massive scale and it is becoming increasingly central to their practices of making meaning and expressing ideas. Lessig argues that these practices constitute remix as *writing* for these legions of digital youth:

> When you say the word *writing*, for those of us over the age of 15, our conception of writing is writing with text ... But if you think about the ways kids under 15 using digital technology think about writing – you know, writing with text is just one way to write, and not even the most

interesting way to write. The more interesting ways are increasingly to use images and sound and video to express ideas.

(in Koman 2005: n.p.)

Lessig (2005) provides a range of examples of the kinds of digital remix practices that in his view constitute 'the more interesting ways [to write]' for young people. These include remixing clips from movies to create 'faux' trailers for hypothetical movies; setting remixed movie trailers to remixed music of choice that is synchronized to the visual action; recording a series of anime cartoons and then video-editing them in synchrony with a popular music track; mixing 'found' images with original images in order to express a theme or idea (with or without text added); and mixing images, animations and texts to create cartoons (including political cartoons and animations), to name just a few types.

Reflection and discussion

- Do you accept Lessig's extension of the concept of 'writing' to include practices like digital remix? If so, what are your reasons? If not, what are your reasons?

- Try to locate in the literature examples of literacy scholars who take a different view (e.g., Kress 2003). If you adopt the standpoint of Lessig, what arguments and evidence would you present against the opposing view? What arguments and evidence from the opposing view would you bring against Lessig?

We accept this conceptual extension of 'writing' to include practices of producing, exchanging and negotiating digitally remixed texts, which may employ a single medium or may be multimedia remixes. At the same time we also recognize as forms of remix various practices that do not necessarily involve digitally remixing sound, image and animation, such as fanfiction writing and producing manga comics (whether on paper or on the screen). This accords with Lessig's point that remix is not necessarily *digital* remix (see also Latterell 2006). The important point for our purposes, however, is that the kinds of remixing practices identified by Lessig as instances of an extended contemporary concept of writing all conform with our definition of 'literacies' as 'socially recognized ways of generating, communicating and negotiating meaningful content through the medium of encoded texts within contexts of participation in Discourses (or, as members of Discourses).' This will become evident in the remainder of this chapter where we discuss four very popular kinds of remixing practices. These are fanfiction, manga, adbusting and photoshopping, and anime and anime music videos (AMV), respectively.

Remix 1: Fanfiction – remixing words and content

Fanfiction – or 'fanfic' to its aficionados – is the name given to the practice where devotees of some media or literary phenomenon like a TV show, movie, or book write stories based on its characters (Plotz 2000: 1). In addition to the three categories of catalyst for fanfic, fan narratives based on video game plotlines and characters are also increasing in popularity. Most fanfic is written as narrative, although songfic and poetryfic are also popular forms and some fanfictions are carried as manga drawings and animations. 'Costume play' or cosplay – dressing up as favourite manga and anime characters – and live action role plays based on a favourite popular culture text are also gaining in popularity (for still more categories, see en.wikipedia.org/wiki/Fan_fiction).

Some commentators recognize forebears to contemporary fan fiction dating far back into the past; for example, to the 1400s with Robert Henryson's sequels to some of Geoffrey Chaucer's poetry (Pugh 2004). The phenomenon as we know it today, however, is most usually related to the advent of serialized television shows. In particular, the *Star Trek* television series, which first aired in 1966 and rapidly gained a cult following, is credited with helping to establish fan fiction as a distinct genre and social practice (Jenkins 1988). From the first episode, fans began writing their own stories set within the *Star Trek* universe and using key *Star Trek* characters. These fanfic writers mimeographed and bound their stories into handmade books or magazines and distributed them at *Star Trek* fan conventions, fan club meetings, or via mail. Since then, fanfic has become an established genre and the subject of academic study (see, for example, Black 2006; Jenkins 1992; Somogyi 2002; Thomas 2005; fanfiction-studies.net).

Fanfic writers now innovate on myriad screen and book texts. The various *Star Trek* series remain hugely popular. Other television shows or animations currently attracting large numbers of fanfic writers include *Card Captor Sakura, House, M.D., Scarecrow and Mrs. King, Angel, Battlestar Galactica: 2003, Stargate: Atlantis, Law & Order: SVU, Lizzie McGuire, Gilmore Girls*, and *Xena: Warrior Princess*. Popular movies include *Star Wars, Lion King, The Matrix, Moulin Rouge, X-Men* and *Pirates of the Caribbean*. Books include *Harry Potter, Phantom of the Opera, A Series of Unfortunate Events*, and the Bible, among many others.

Fanfic writing can be classified into a number of different types. The most common of these include 'in-canon writing', 'alternative universe stories', 'cross-overs', 'relationshipper (or shipper) narratives', and 'self-insert' fanfic:

- In-canon writing maintains the settings, characters and types of plotlines found in the original media text as far as is possible, and simply adds new 'episodes' or events to the original text (e.g., a new 'episode' of the television show, *Xena: Warrior Princess*, that maintains the characters and setting as faithfully as possible and that builds directly on the narratives and character histories and adventures already developed within the series itself). Pre-sequels and sequels are popular versions of in-canon writing.
- In alternative universe stories characters from an original media text are transposed into an entirely new or different 'world' (e.g., placing key characters from the *Star Wars* movies into a *Lord of the Rings* universe, or an entirely new, invented universe).
- Cross-overs bring characters from two different original media texts together in a new story (e.g., Spiderman brought together with the characters from the sci-fi television series, *Stargate SG–1*).
- Relationshipper (or 'shipper') narratives focus on establishing an intimate relationship between two (often minor) characters where none existed or was downplayed in the original text. These texts can focus on heterosexual relations (e.g., between *Star Trek*'s Admiral Kathryn Janeway and Chakotay characters), or homoerotic/homosexual relations between characters (e.g., between *Star Trek*'s Captain Kirk and Mr Spock). The latter kind of fanfics are also referred to as 'slash fiction'.
- In self-insert fanfic writers insert themselves as recognizable characters directly into a narrative (e.g., many young female fanfic writers write themselves into the Harry Potter series in place of Hermione, one of Harry's closest friends; many writers invent a character that is a mix of themselves and attributes from popular culture characters and insert this hybrid character into their text).

Fan fiction was a well-established practice before the development of the internet and a lot of fanfic activity still goes on outside of online environments. Nonetheless, the explosion of the internet has had a massive impact on the scale and culture of fanfic. It has enabled almost infinitely more people to actively participate in contributing and critiquing fanfic than was previously possible. Prior to the internet becoming a mass medium, fanfic was circulated person to person among relatively small circles of aficionados and subjected to sustained critique. Authors received peer comments and suggestions for improving their stories usually in face-to-face encounters or, perhaps, via snail mail. Today, however, fanfic narratives in the tens of thousands are posted in open public forums on the internet, to be read and reviewed online by anyone who cares to do so. A Google.com search early in April 2006 for the term, 'fan fiction', returned 13,900,000 hits, while a search using 'fanfic' as a keyword returned 2,730,000 hits, indicating a powerful online presence.

The internet 'geography' of fanfic is complex. A good place to start is with Fanfiction.net, a pre-eminent online fan fiction site founded in 1998. This website has a searchable archive-plus-discussion board format. Fanfiction.net hosts tens of thousands of fanfics, organized by categories. The front page provides an 'at a glance' sense of the site. Most of the page is taken up with news about recent developments on the site (e.g., news that forums can now have moderators, or that a software glitch has been fixed). There is a simple menu bar across the top of the page. Users can use this menu to find works that are just in, to access different fanfic communities, to search the site (by author pen name, story title or summary), to go to discussion forums associated with each category of fanfic (in March 2006 there were more than 150 forums for anime alone), to use the site directory (organized by pen names and categories of fanfic and communities), and to use the site's online dictionary and thesaurus.

The specific categories of fanfic on this site are: Anime, Cartoon, Game, Movie, Book, Comic, TV Show and Miscellaneous. Clicking on the 'Book' link, for example, takes users to a hyperlinked listing of the various books that have spawned fanfic works. In March 2006, there were around 220 links under Books. Each link has a number after it, referring to the number of distinct items of fanfic writing currently published on the site for the work or author in question (with each item often running to multiple chapters in length). Clicking on the link for George Orwell's book, *1984*, for example, revealed 73 items of fanfic writing in early March 2006. Clicking on each fanfic link reveals three 'sub' links: one for accessing the written fanfic text itself, one for accessing details about the author, and one for reading or posting reviews of that particular piece of fanfic writing.

On 28 August 2004, a writer using the pen name, 'Johnnycakesdepp', published a fic based on the cult movie classic, *Pirates of the Caribbean*. 'Eternity in bliss' runs to 1800 or so words. It relates an imagined future scene in which Captain Jack Sparrow's beloved Anamaria has died while giving birth to their daughter, Maria Victoria (in the movie, there is no actual long-term relationship between Jack and Anamaria). Jack has taken the baby to the home of Will Turner, his trusted shipmate, and Will's wife, Elizabeth, to raise as their own on Jack's behalf. The grief-stricken Jack then turns himself in to the bumbling Commodore Norrington to be hanged for his pirately ways. Will, hearing of this 'capture' visits Jack, who explains he only wants to be with Anamaria, but cannot take his own life. The fic ends with Jack's earthly demise on the gallows and his entry into eternal bliss with Anamaria. His last words are to Will and Elizabeth.

'Take care of Maria! She's your daughter now, Maria Turner.'

'We'll tell her all about you and Ana, Jack! And the Pearl too!' Elizabeth said shakily, looking back at the little dark-skinned girl in her arms. Yes, Maria was lovely and every day Elizabeth and Will would be reminded of the brave, witty pirate that was doomed on this day.

'Fer that I thank you!' He said, once again happy and back into his usual pirate talk. 'Tell Maria that I loved 'er,' he grinned back at the couple before nodding at the soldier who pulled the lever. There was no rushing through the crowd this time or sword to stand on. This was what Jack wanted.

He didn't struggle, or rather he tried not to, feeling his lungs burn, hungry for air. And then he suddenly gave up.

'Coz I'm broken, when I'm open
And I don't feel like I am strong enough.

She was there before him surrounded in a white almost blinding light. She opened her arms ready to embrace him as he came running towards her. He swept her up in his arms and spun her around. *To hold her again*. They smiled at each other happy to be together again, before embracing in a deep kiss. They walked together into the light holding hands, her dark skin contrasting with his tanned light skin. A few months of being broken was worth the eternity in bliss.

You've gone away, you don't feel me anymore.

(From 'Eternity in Bliss', accessed 3 March 2006,
at fanfiction.net/s/2033837/1/)

Woven through the narrative are lightly modified lines from the song 'Broken' by Seether (see: members.shaw.ca/sevylanglois/lyrics/broken.htm). Johnnycakesdepp acknowledges the song and the 'edit' – 'This is *Broken* but it has obviously been rewritten and hopefully for the better' – and explains in response to a review that the lyrics had been added to convey 'those parts like after a person talks when the author adds stuff about the person or whatever'. Remix.

Freak and Proud's review is encouraging:

thats really sweet but sad. i kind of have a hard time believing anyone would be so stupid, but thats coz i dont do romantic so well. kind of like romeo and juliet. that annoyed me. oh well. nice fic. i like 'oh well' it fits so many emotions. enjoyin your work.

(fanfiction.net/r/2033837/0/1/)

In general, fanfic readers, writers and reviewers value good quality writing, including the development of satisfying characters, engaging plotline, logical story and character developments within the story, and good grammar and spelling. With respect to character development, for example, fan-produced online writing guides to good fanfic stories warn writers about falling victim to the 'Mary Sue' syndrome. 'Mary Sue' is a character who in many ways embodies the author's perfect alter-ego, and as such, tends to dominate the entire story and squeeze the lifeblood out of it. As one style guidester put it:

[Mary Sue] is usually young, extremely beautiful, and skilled at many things. She becomes the main focus of the story, and everyone else [is] reduced to cardboard support of her (and her relationship with the main handsome young male). She is prone to be extremely skilled at rescuing the characters from whatever problems befall them. She is described in honeyed terms, because she has no equal. All the males in the game – particularly the handsome young ones – cannot resist her charm. She is either paired up with the main handsome male, or she dies, leaving everyone grief-stricken at her passing, and disconsolate. When you meet a story where an original character completely dom-inates the scene, watch out: she is bound to be a Mary Sue.

(M.P. 2005: 1; see also, Hale 2005)

One strategy sometimes used by novice writers in search of credible char-acters involves borrowing (with permission) an original character from another fanfic author. One young (16 years) fanfic writer known to us has written an Inuyasha-based (anime) story currently running at 11 short chapters. A prolific and popular writer online, at school Silver Excel Fox is not doing all that well in her English classes. She begins Chapter 4 of her story, 'Runaways', by acknowledging that a character developed by someone else has been 'borrowed' for this story:

Okey-Dokey peoples this is chapter 4! I want to thank Shan-Chan (hey that rhymes!) for letting me borrow Shaoran for my story ... Shaoran belongs to Shan-Chan so if you want to use him talk with Shan[-Chan]. Alrighty on with the story.

(fanfiction.net/s/1527062/4/, accessed 3 March 2006)

Besides 'borrowed character acknowledgments', other kinds of disclaimers often appear at the start of each fanfic, signalling the writer's awareness of having no copyright claims to the original characters or story on which the narrative builds. Hence, Silver Excel Fox's explanatory note at the start of Chapter 4 also includes the line, 'Anyway, I don't own Inuyasha, Yugi-oh, or Rorouni Kenshin [all commercial manga or anime characters] or Shaoran' (ibid.).

Fanfiction.net's forums provide aficionados of particular works and/or authors with a space to raise topics for discussion with other users sharing similar interests. The forums are often moderated by volunteers and have specific participation rules, including the requirement that all discussion, content and language be suitable for teens. Forums are text-specific; that is, they are organized around the popular text that fan writers are remixing. So, for example, within the movie-focused forums, there were 26 separate discussion forums associated with the movie, *Pirates of the Caribbean*, in early March 2006. Topics and purposes addressed within these forums are still rather wide-ranging, and include discussion of the original movie and its forthcoming sequels; speculations on the development of the romantic relationship begun in earnest only at the end of the first movie between two of the central characters, Will and Elizabeth; forums dedicated to pirate lore in general; a forum for role playing *Pirates of the Caribbean* fanfic; plot bunny topics (e.g., speculations on storylines should Jack Sparrow – the pirate at the heart of the movie – have a son or daughter); discussion of historical accuracy within the movie itself, as well as within relevant fanfics; listings of people willing to act as 'beta' readers who provide feedback on narratives prior to them being posted publicly for review, and so on. Similar discussion thread purposes and uses can be found across all the forums hosted by fanfiction.net

Moving away from sites like Fanfiction.net, Fictionalley.org, Fanfics.org, and Bitchnmoan.net into other resources within fanfic affinity space takes us to sites like *The Force* (fanfic.theforce.net, see p. 87), *Plot Bunny 101* (plotbunny101.tvheaven.com) and *How to Write Almost Readable Fan Fiction* (littlecalamity.tripod.com/HowTo2.html). These are all spaces that help resource fanfic writers. As we saw in Chapter 3, *The Force* provides guidelines for beta readings of works prior to final publication. It also offers writing tips posted by members, random writing contest-type events that specify story parameters to which fanfic authors must adhere, a fanfic lexicon, a submissions style guide for members, and links to email-based discussion lists, among other services. *Plot Bunny 101* is a site for fanfic writers to use to share 'plot bunnies': ideas for narratives that someone makes freely available to others for developing into their own stories. Plot bunnies can range from a 'story-starter' idea through to a full-blown plot line and set of characters for a story. Like Plot Bunny 101, Plot Bunny Adoption Center (sg1hc.com/pbac) is an online archive of story starters and plotline sketches. How to Write Almost Readable Fan Fiction offers a guide to writing that includes advice on character development, guides to grammar and punctuation conventions, and general advice concerning spell-checking and proof-reading, how to avoid repetition and redundancy in stories, and so on.

The character of fanfic as remix is often most richly apparent in the writing of younger authors as they move across an array of media and cultural genres to combine their own stories and characters with existing ones in new narratives that may be complex and require the reader to have read widely and/or viewed or played a range of anime-related shows or games in order to fully appreciate the warp and weft of each story. In interviews, Silver Excel Fox (S.E.F.) talked about some of the direct influences on her own story writing, which include Greek mythology, the Harry Potter stories, the Bible, romance stories, hacker culture, thriller/adventure movies, and a range of anime and manga texts like *Inuyushu, Yu Yu Hakusho*, and *Sailor Moon*, among others:

S.E.F:	Like in Greek mythology. They have the River Styx and they have the ferry man who will take you down to the underworld, or wherever you're going. And–
Michele:	Have you done that at school?
S.E.F:	I don't know. I just like Greek mythology. She [points to her mother] got me into it, and I kind of stuck with it.
Michele:	It sounds like it's helped you out in terms of–
S.E.F:	It has because the girl in my story – in the original myth it would be a guy – it's a girl, and she's pretty. It's like the person who is taking you to your death is a girl, and she's ((laughs))- like, I'm dying and *you're* taking me ((laughs)) And she rides an oar, which kind of makes sense because she's on the River Styx. You're gonna need something to get up that river! ((laughs)) And Yusukai [a character from *Yu Yu Hakusho*] goes and he meets kind of the Japanese version of Jesus.

(interview, 2005 by Knobel and Lankshear)

The kinds of remixing practices engaged in by fanfic writers produce unmistakably creative texts that draw on a range of content and resources. This includes deliberate, albeit eclectic if not idiosyncratic, selections regarding what texts to draw on and in what ways (e.g., Johnnycakesdepp taking key characters from a movie, like *Pirates of the Caribbean*, and creating a possible future for them and then weaving in song lyrics to help convey mood and emotions, or Silver Excel Fox drawing on a range of classical epic texts, adolescent literature, and modern manga to create new narratives). These practices speak directly to O'Reilly's claim that cultural 'creativity is rooted in re-use' and reinvention (in interview with McManus 2004: n.p.). Ian McDonald, himself a celebrated science fiction writer, discusses how remixing practices are very much in keeping with current times, and argues that the strong trend towards using material from a range of literary and non-literary sources is 'a product of our technological ability to surf, sample and mix' (in interview with Gevers 2001: n.p.). He goes even so far as to claim that, '[a]nyone with an eye on the zeitgeist would agree that the art of the edit will be the cultural skill of the new century' (ibid.).

With respect to fanfic as a 'new' literacy, we considered some aspects of collaboration, participation and distributed expertise in Chapter 3 (see pp. 86–88). It is interesting to get a sense of this from the standpoint of everyday participants like our young informant, who describes the reviews that her work receives as helpful and, especially, affirming:

Michele:	The reviews that you get. Do you pay attention to them?
S.E.F:	Oh, yes, I always read my reviews. I have 24 and most are for one story. And I was so happy 'cause the first time I posted it, I got two.
Michele:	Perfect.
S.E.F:	That was the thing. These were the people that I knew and they were complimenting my story, and I was sitting there ((her eyes widen in an expression of delighted surprise)). I had to be bounced down the stairs! Oh my God, I got reviews! Oh my God! Oh my God! Oh my God! And then I got even more reviews. Oh my God, this is cool! They're reading what I wrote. They read my stuff. Yes!
Michele:	I know reviewers sometimes make suggestions about what you should do. Do you make any changes based on what they say?
S.E.F:	Yes, because there was one person who kind of commented on my spelling of somebody's name.
Michele:	Ahhh.
S.E.F:	Because there are two different types of Rikus in video games. There's the Riku from *King of Hearts*, and that's r-i-k-u. And there's the girl Rikku from *Final Fantasy*.

> Now, *King of Hearts* is kind of like a merge between Disney and *Final Fantasy* all by itself. That's how they kind of distinguish the material; Rikku as a girl is r-i-k-k-u, and a guy is r-i-k-u.
>
> (interview, 2005 by Knobel and Lankshear; for more on learning from fanfiction reviews see Chatelain 2003).

Of course, the ordinariness of a lot of fan fiction does not suit everyone's tastes. At least one site – albeit one not for the faint of heart, the politically correct, or the 'morally conservative' – has emerged for the purposes of identifying the 'worst' of fan fiction and exhorting (would-be) practitioners to 'try not to write like this'. The Godawful Fan Fiction site can be found at www.godawful.net, self-billed as 'Your guide to the absolute worst fan fiction on the Web. Read them and weep'. For a sample of the site's material that is approved for general audiences, check out the *Star Trek TNG* sample site at www.Sciencefictionbuzz.com/TNG-Sample.html.

Reflection and discussion

Search the Fanfiction.net (http://www.fanfiction.net) archives to find a book, television show, a movie, a manga comic or an anime, etc. with which you are familiar and browse a number of fanfics associated with your choice before settling on one in particular in order to respond to the questions below:

- What did the author keep intact with respect to the original text(s) on which they drew and what did the author change in this story?

- What would a reader need to know in order to truly appreciate your selected fanfic? What assumptions about audience knowledge does the author appear to make, and how do you know?

- Reviews play a large role in fanfic writing – what kind of a social practice does reviewing appear to be within this space? How does this compare with the ways in which student writing typically is reviewed in classroom settings?

Remix 2: Fan manga and fan anime – remixing words and graphics

Manga (usually pronounced as 'mahngah') is a stylized graphic genre generally referred to as 'Japanese comics' that can be dated back to the often humorous outline drawings done by sixth-century Shintoist monks to illustrate calendar scrolls (Sanchez 2003). The term 'manga' itself (which translates roughly into 'whimsical pictures' in English) was first used to describe a particular style of illustration until the late eighteenth century. Manga emerged as a popular cultural form in the late 1940s and early 1950s and the work of Osamu Tezuko, who is perhaps best known to English audiences for the animated television series, *Astro Boy*. By 1999 manga – whether serialized or collected together in graphic novel form – comprised 40 per cent of Japan's book and magazine sales (Allen and Ingulsrud 2003).

English translations of manga began in the late 1980s, and quickly caught on as popular reading texts for young English-speaking people (e.g., especially the *Yu-Gi-Oh!* and *Dragon Ball Z* serialized novels, and the *Shonen Jump* serial collections). In English-speaking countries, manga fans (known as *otaku*) are mainly adolescents and young adults. Females are a sizable proportion of manga readers (Lent 2003). The US is the largest market for manga outside Japan, with around $100 million spent on manga in 2002, and while book sales overall 'are growing 1–2 percent yearly, manga sales show triple-digit increases' (ibid.: 40).

Manga are complex texts requiring English-language readers to learn to read comic frames from right-to-left and to recognize the significance of different sized-frames. For example, a narrow, page-length frame can denote time passing or direction in a journey, a thin frame spanning the width of the page is often used as a space in which to convey emotion, while a two-page single frame can signal something momentous is about to happen, or is in the process of happening, etc. The illustrator can also shift the reader's point of view or stance from that of 'outsider, looking in' to 'viewing the scene from the perspective of the different characters in the story' and the reader needs to be able to keep up with changing points of view within the story itself as the author moves among 'showing' the story through the eyes of different characters (Allen and Ingulsrud 2003: 679).

Manga comics are published primarily in black and white. Drawing styles include the highly stylized (e.g., *Hikaru No Go*, a contemporary manga focused on the game of go and a medieval go-playing ghost), the 'super-cute' (e.g., *Pokémon*, a series about characters that evolve), and the cartoonish or sketchy (e.g., *One Piece*, a pirate fantasy manga). Showcase collections like Taschen's *Manga* (Amano 2004) provide an excellent overview of a range of extremely diverse, but instantly recognizable, manga drawing styles. Recognizable in-common dimensions of diverse styles tend to include characters with very large eyes, sculpted hair, and minimal facial lines, although facial expressions are often exaggerated to convey emotion and overall mood.

Anime (usually pronounced as 'ah-ni-may') can be equated roughly with 'animated manga', since a lot of anime is influenced by artistic styles and storylines found in manga comics. Like manga, anime artistic styles are highly diverse yet immediately recognizable. Anime come as TV cartoon series as well as in the form of video games and computer games and, in diverse movie genres including science fiction, adventure stories, medieval fantasy, action, and the like. Popular topics and themes in manga and anime include:

- Transformer or 'mecha' manga and anime, comprising stories about giant robots that can change shape, or characters that morph back and forth between shapes or genus types (e.g., *Mazinger Z*, *Cutie Honey*).
- Doll, toy or animal/creature manga and anime (e.g., *Hello, Kitty!* and *Pokémon*).
- Science fiction manga and anime, beginning with Osamu Tezuka's *Astro Boy* series in the 1960s, and including Nightow Yasuhiro's *Trigun* series and Hagio Moto's *Star Red* series.
- Game-based manga and anime, which includes some sort of game playing as a key component of each installment (e.g., *Yu-Gi-Oh!*, *Hikaru No Go*).
- Hero or battle manga, which includes stories that centre around fights or battles (e.g., *Dragon Ball Z*).
- Magical, mythic or paranormal manga centring on reincarnation, being possessed by ghosts, becoming vampires, or concerning magical beings with superhuman powers (e.g., *Ceres, Celestial Legend, Sailor Moon, DNAngel, Shaman King*).
- Hetero romance manga and anime (e.g., Shinobu Nishimura's *Third Girl* or Hana Yori Dango's *Boys Over Flowers*). This type of manga also includes what is described as 'magical girlfriend' stories, where the main male protagonist has a magical girlfriend.
- Gay and lesbian romance manga and anime (e.g., Haruka Minami's *Forbidden Sweet Fruit*).
- Office or school day manga and anime focusing on the everyday lives of ordinary people (e.g., *Section Manager Kosaku Shima*).
- Erotic manga and anime (e.g., Naoki Yamamoto's *Dance*).
- Historical manga and anime (e.g., Tatsuya Terada's violent adaptation of the classical Chinese folklore, *Saiyuki*; Yoshikazu Yasuhiko's *Namuji*, set in medieval Japan; WWII fighter pilot manga).

Reflection and discussion

Visit a book shop and browse their manga titles:

- What do you notice? What does this tell you about the store's assumptions regarding their target audience(s) for these texts?

- Why might many parents and teachers take issue with manga comics as reading materials?

- What important things, if any, might they overlook by taking this position?

- Why do you think manga are so popular with young readers? What research evidence can you find for your response?

Not surprisingly, popular manga and anime have generated a great deal of fan (*otaku*) activity. Three forms are common. The first takes the form of fanfic narratives (also poetry and screenplays) based on anime series or movies that follow the general conventions and forms of fanfiction writing described in the previous section (see, for example, simplyscripts.com/ unpro_anime.html; neko-machi.com/misc/tft; see also Black 2005b). The second is 'amateur manga' in the form of fan art: individual images, or entire comics created by fans (and known as '*dōjinshi*'). Third, some *otaku* also produce what is known as fansub or digisub anime, where they insert English-language subtitles into original Japanese anime. Another popular practice among *otaku* is to re-mix clips from a range of commercial anime to create an entirely new narrative (e.g., tfcog.net). We will look at examples of the first two types here and will consider the third type at the end of this chapter in conjunction with anime music videos, or AMV, remixes.

As with other forms of fanfiction, manga–anime fan fiction takes characters, storylines, and other resources and mixes them into new adventures or new universes altogether. In 'Digital resources: English language learners and reader reviews in online fan fiction', Black (2005b) analyses a corpus of data from a case study she made of a 16-year-old native Mandarin Chinese speaker who began writing fan fiction narratives based on the manga (which, from 1998, was also an anime), *Card Captor Sakura*. Black's case study subject was an extremely successful writer of anime-based fan fiction, and her *Love Letters* fic, first published in December 2002, had received 2261 reviews by March 2006. This provided Black with an appropriate research context for using Gee's (2004: 97) proposition that there are 'three types of design that reap large rewards in the New Capitalism: the ability to design new *identities, affinity spaces*, and *networks*' as a lens 'through which to view the interactions and activities taking place on fanfiction.net' (Black 2005b: 3). Using a form of discourse analysis, Black examined examples of salient types of reader reviews and, particularly, reviews the author responded to in her author notes, fictions, and thank you notes, to address three research questions. These questions were concerned with the kind of linguistic work the author's texts and reader reviews are doing, the ways the texts represent successful design with respect to identities, affinity spaces and networks, and how the texts index the author's identity as a successful writer of fanfic and the readers' identities as knowledgeable peers, thereby enabling all parties to accrue cultural capital within that context (ibid.). Black's findings speak powerfully to education from the standpoint of new literacies.

In this section we want to briefly suggest a related angle to looking at manga–anime fanfic, although we will not have space to develop it in detail here. Immediately following the sentence cited above by Black, Gee (2004: 97) goes on to say: 'In turn, people who are adept at taking on new identities, adept at using and interacting within affinity spaces, and are well connected in networks will flourish.' We will focus here just on being adept at taking on new identities and look at this in terms of Gee's (ibid.: 111–14) account of 'virtual', 'real world' and 'projective' identities that he develops in relation to role-playing video games. This will involve taking some small liberties with Gee's idea but, hopefully, none that distort.

In the context of a role-playing game, one's virtual identity is the character one has taken up (and, in some cases modified by allocating one's allotment of 'qualities' to the 'off the shelf' character). This is the character one acts through in the game, building up his or her history and trajectory as a distinct identity as the game proceeds. One's real-world identity in the game is that combination of identities and subjectivities one brings to the game and, in a sense, 'plays out of'. 'This me' has the game character do X, whereas 'that me' might have the game character do Y. One may play out of various 'me's at different points in the game. One's projective identity is the identity one projects onto the virtual character while making this character into an identity that will be realized through the playing of the game. Gee gives a powerful example of how in one game he had his virtual character do something that gave her a 'bit' in her history he (the real-world Jim) did not want her to have.

This kind of 'play' is identity work. It provides a context and a medium for reflection, for imagination, for accountability, for experimentation; that is, for contemplating how 'one' could be different, for trying out various 'ones' that one could potentially be. This is the kind of 'training' we would expect to be useful for becoming adept at taking on new identities.

While writing fanfic is not the same as participating in a role-playing game, it nonetheless has some significant structural similarities with Gee's role-playing scenario. We have a situation of remix, not a blank slate. The characters the fanfic author can develop are to some extent circumscribed by what has come before. There are, for example, limits to what one can do with Astro Boy and Livian and Atlas before they are out of character. Even if one is mixing a character from a video game into an Astro Boy fanfic, that character has to operate within certain limits to maintain plausibility. The situations being built in the fiction have their limits as well. And these in turn circumscribe what an author's own character or characters can do and be. In short, the manga–anime fanfic space, like any fanfic space, sets up possibilities for an author's real-world identity to 'play' a virtual identity in ways that may cumulatively realize a projective identity and that amount to doing identity 'work' that is more than random, casual, or unreflective.

We want to look at these ideas by reference to a pretty typical example of fan manga–anime fiction: *Eternal Bond* written by Alexia Winters, based broadly on the Astro Boy anime series. Framing motifs are provided by characters from popular video games, such as Yuna and Paine from *Final Fantasy X–2*, Auron from *Fatal Fantasy X*, and Mayu Amakura from *Fatal Frame II: Crimson Butterfly*). The fic can be found at <fanfiction.net/s/1890965/1/> and the plotline is easy to follow, even for readers unfamiliar with *Astro Boy*. We will briefly describe what we see as four 'moments' of the character Livian. Livian, in the original series, is a young blonde female human character in the *Astro Boy* series whose closest friends and associates include androids and robots; she is also the companion of Atlas, Astro Boy's brother and arch enemy. In Alexia Winters' fanfic, the larger context for her story is animosity between the humans and the androids and robots, with danger of a full-on battle always in the air. In this fanfic, Livian is leading a gang in the absence of Daichi (aka Atlas), with whom she is in love, but who is currently absent and who has been 'twisted' by an evil mentor to contemplate waging war on the humans. The four 'moments' that follow present in embryonic form our analysis of different Livians as represented across the chapters of Alexia's narrative.

Four moments of Livian

1 Livian and Saburou (male android) do some 'Clockwork Orange-like' violence on the last member of a rival gang to surrender the gang's turf:

They kicked him back to the ground, his face impacting with the hard concrete ground, his nose now broken in several different places. He looked up in time to be kicked in the face by both Saburou's and the girl's [Livian] foot. They laughed at him as he tried to get back up, his movements slow and wobbly. They then turned, standing back to back to each other, still holding hands.

2   Livian and two android friends come upon three male humans monstering Astro Boy:

Livian took two long steps towards them, a glint of murder in her sapphire eyes. The boys could see that there was something different about her and knew right then that the fat one had said the wrong thing. They quickly took a few steps back, now fearing for their lives, watching in silent horror as Livian spoke again . . .

3   Livian refusing to expel Keri Anna, who is Daichi's girlfriend and Livian's sworn and open enemy, from the gang: a power that Livian has:

'Damn it, Liv, kick her out already!' Jace cried, glaring at her friend, 'You hate her just as much as everyone else here does and she treats you like shit! She should be showing you the respect you deserve; you've known Daichi a hell of a lot longer than her! You have the power, Liv! Use it!'

'Trust me, it's more than tempting, but I can't. Like she said, she's Daichi's girlfriend and I can't do that to him. I may not get along with her, but that doesn't give me the right to take away something that makes Daichi happy.'

4   In the midst of a moment of intense focus on a job at hand, Livian remembers she had told her twin sister she would get takeout Greek food for dinner, and asks Saburou if he would do that for her:

'I promised Lucy I'd pick up some dinner for tonight, but something just came up, so I can't. Can ya do it for me, just tell her I'm stuck in traffic or something? I got a menu with the stuff she likes highlighted up in my room. I know it's a lot to ask after what you did for my motorcycle, but could you do this one little thing for me?'

These four moments may not necessarily bespeak deep and sophisticated character development, but there are enough different identities and crossings between different discursive 'selves' to indicate that in each such episode Livian could have responded differently from how she 'in fact' did respond. There is no telling where Livian could 'go' as an identity project, all the while moving about her worlds within the plausible range of the virtual character hand she has been 'dealt' by the original anime. The person penning as Alexia Winters is doing identity work of a kind that is absolutely consistent with Gee's idea of people who are adept at taking on different identities 'flourishing' under contemporary and foreseeable conditions.

There is an important point to make here about the dimensions of 'flourishing'. Because Gee has raised the point in the context of the New Capitalism, there is the possibility of thinking that the flourishing in question is economic flourishing: that 'shape shifting portfolio people' (Gee 2004) will flourish economically. Some will, and that is part of it. But a larger concept of flourishing and, even, a larger concept of 'economy' than in the simple sense of 'dinero' is operating here. We are talking about a world – it may even be a world in the making that prefigures a 'post-scarcity condition' – in which the *real* economy increasingly trades in symbols and concepts, and where people who do this well are more likely (other things being equal) to prevail in terms of economic power. On the other hand, this 'real' economy involves people in doing more and more of a certain kind of work. Not (just) in the *workplace* but in their everyday worlds, period. Doing symbolic conceptual work – including of the kind that Alexia Winters is doing in *Eternal Bond* – is participating in the cultural arm of this economy. The cultural and the economic converge. Once we made our leisure meanings in sports and viewing. Now more and more of us make our leisure in doing symbolic conceptual 'work' (Gee 2003; Johnson 2005). Spaces blur. And people who do good effective work (build up a readership, get reviewed and *thrill* to this as Silver Excel Fox does) FLOURISH.

We can push this argument further by turning to the fan art dimension. The resulting argument takes us to uneasy places so far as schooled literacy – and, we would want to add, what might be called *modernist* literacy more generally – is concerned.

Let's take some typical examples of manga–anime websites and pages featuring fan art, such as:

- Toriyama's World (toriyamaworld.com/fans/manga.html)
- Temple O'Trunks (templeotrunks.com/images/fan_manga/index.html)

- Fragraham Lincon's Home for Unwanted Fanfic (hfuff.stalo.com).

The images page at *Temple O'Trunks* (templeotrunks.com/images/index.html) is a good place to start, before one moves to download entire fan manga at pages like those archived at *Toriyama's World*. On the Temple O'Trunks site one will find selected scans of commercial manga art found in books, and on cards, stickers, posters etc. (e.g., at templeotrunks.com/images/trunks_scans/trunks_celestrian_scan1.jpg), alongside drawings done by fans (e.g., templeotrunks.com/images/fan_art/FUTRUNKS.jpg and templeotrunks.com/images/fan_art/DBZPIC.jpg). Fans scan manga, draw manga, send manga off to sites that archive it for public viewing and reviewing, establish email-based discussion lists for critiquing fan art, and set up and administer websites that are dedicated to showcasing remixes. Even a scan is part of a remix when a character is taken out of context and manipulated and set alongside or inside other like works.

The question we pose is 'What is going on here?' In terms of literacies, what meanings are being produced and exchanged? After all, a scan – albeit a remix of one order or another (text added or not, the same as the original or not, resized or not) – is pretty much just a scan. Where and what is the meaning being exchanged. One obvious answer is that some kind of semiotic meaning is being produced and exchanged. Trunks is frowning. What does this *mean*? Do we focus on the frown? Is it a frown? Is it a well-represented frown? Might it be a glare? Or do we focus on a different kind of meaning, such as, 'Hey, if you're doing a Trunks fic and you're looking for a good frown in a hurry, you can have this one'? Or do we move to the ultimate statement of meaning from the standpoint of a fan?: 'This stuff ROCKS, I am lost to it, let's build the movement, feed our obsessions, recruit and build the fandom, CELEBRATE.'

Our immediate interest here is in remix as the medium that *carries* fandom: the medium through which enacting one's identity as a fan is accomplished. End of story – at least, this part of the story. It is about understanding non-functional, non-instrumental literacy. Literacy for its own sake, as an end in itself. We do this literacy because *this literacy is us*. It is an act of devotion in which you are called to share with me if you want to. The value is in dispersion because that which is being dispersed is valuable in itself. Lawrence Eng provides a supreme statement of fandom and fan meaning in *The Sasami Appreciation Society* (syste.ms/jurai/sasami/story102.html). In the mid-1990s Eng, studying at Cornell University in the US and a member of the university's Japanese Animation Society, became captivated by the 'cutest, blue-haired anime girl I had ever seen' (ibid.). This was Sasami from the *Tenchi Muyo* anime. 'I eagerly waited for each instalment of TM and was never disappointed. Through all of this my devotion to Sasami only increased', says Eng.

He found a kindred spirit online and they began to build the Sasami Appreciation Society, with the mission 'to spread Sasami fandom in all ways possible, on the Net and otherwise'. Why? It's simple, 'it's our devotion to Sasami ... We're dedicated to bringing her the fandom that she deserves'. Mizuko Ito (2005a), who led us to Eng, identifies this spirit as the very heart of *otaku* culture.

The point we want to make here is about the power of and significance within human life of valuing some things intrinsically: of valuing them as good or worthwhile in themselves rather than simply as a means to something else. This was integral to the idea of a liberal education: activities and pursuits people engaged in for their own sake – simply because they were good to do in themselves, with no further end in view. There was always a strong element of this within the study of subjects like English literature and, indeed, in the very idea of reading itself. Although reading undoubtedly has instrumental and functional value, it was widely believed that reading was good in itself and needed no further justification. Moreover, it was widely believed that teaching reading needs no justification beyond making it possible for people to read. Until relatively recently this viewpoint was very common among educators.

We are now dangerously close in literacy education – not to mention in other areas of the curriculum – to losing this idea altogether. And when the idea gets lost, the practice gets lost as well. In many places the bottom line for getting literacy research funding is to demonstrate how this research will meet national priorities. This bottom line is often the top line too. Studying young people's everyday cultural practices becomes a matter of looking for clues about how to improve professional development for teachers, or how to develop approaches to teaching and learning that will contribute to a more competitive workforce, and so on. But when researchers are on a constant vigil for such clues, it is easy to miss so much of what is going on in the practices – and to lose sight of what is most impressive about them: the joy of engagement in them as worthwhile things to be doing. Who is going to fund research for educationists to study *otaku* obsession for the sake simply of recognizing and articulating it? Who is going to find space in their classroom in between high-stakes testing periods and student progress reporting requirements for enthusiasts like Fragraham Lincon to grow their handmade manga fan art to post, along with that of other enthusiasts, on their 'Home for Unwanted Fanfic' sites?

Yet the world is full of paradoxes and some of them are worth careful consideration. We continue to be struck by our experience of reading an account of a computer programmer, Will Crowther who, in the early 1970s, combined his programming knowledge, his enjoyment of the role-playing game *Dungeons and Dragons*, and his love of exploring caves to produce what was perhaps the world's first role-playing computer game. He created it for his two daughters to play. The game Crowther created, *Adventure*, soon passed from friend to friend, computer to computer, and went on to make a massive contribution to one of the biggest industries that currently exists. His interest was intrinsic. He built the game as an expression of his love for his children. Could such a game be built? What would it look like? How would his daughters respond to it? He didn't set out to create a new commercial product and establish a whole new domain of business opportunities, or to get a patent that would make him rich. He was just building a game for his daughters as an end in itself. What happened, of course, is that building the game successfully showed that it could be done. Paradoxically, something created as an end in itself became a pioneer of a massive industry. Something created as an intrinsic value became a source of great instrumental value.

Some similar kind of lesson could be waiting to be learned from the enthusiasm of fans engaging in practices of remix. It will not likely be a lesson about the next big industry. On the other hand, it could be a paradoxical lesson about some good ways to unleash high quality learning, and about the extent to which current education policies and priorities may be looking for learning in lots of wrong places.

Remix 3: Photoshopping – remixing images for fun, solidarity and politics

Adobe's famous digital image editing software, *Photoshop*, has been appropriated as a verb for diverse practices of image editing, many of which constitute forms of remix. The simple sophistication of image editing software makes photoshopping a relatively easy art to acquire at the operational level of techniques, at least to a level that meets the 'average eye'. Of course, photographic artists or professional image workers with strong technical knowledge of the finer aspects of photography and image editing software functions and techniques will always outperform proficient novices on image quality, seamlessness, and so on. Nevertheless, affordable image editing software and enhanced online storage capacities and image-friendly website interfaces and hosting services mean that photoshopping is fast becoming a significant practice online and is one that engages a wide range of contributors and levels of artistic and technical proficiency.

Image remixing can take various forms. These include adding text to images, creating photo montages (including prankster type remixes that place the head of a famous person on a nude body, or the body of an animal), changing image properties (e.g., changing the colours or image focus, fiddling with brightness levels or shading, etc.). Some of the most common uses of image remixing include for fun (including hoaxes), for expressing solidarity or affinity, and for making political points. Images of all three kinds are often propagated as 'memes' (see Chapter 7 for a detailed discussion).

Memes (pronounced 'meems') are contagious patterns of cultural information that are passed from mind to mind and that directly shape and propagate key actions and mindsets of a social group. Memes include popular tunes, catch-phrases, clothing fashions, architectural styles, ways of doing things, and so on. The concept of the meme was first developed in a systematic way by geneticist Richard Dawkins (1976, 1999). Dawkins proposed an evolutionary model of cultural development and change involving the replication of ideas, knowledge, and other cultural information through imitation and transfer. Subsequently, a range of researchers interested in memetics – the study of memes – have argued that electronic networks along with personal predilections and interests provide ideal conditions for propagating and dispersing memes (e.g., Brodie 1996; Blackmore 1999; Adar *et al.* 2004). Although meme-ing – the practice of generating and/or passing on memes – has always been a part of human practice (Blackmore 1999), 'meme-ing' that makes use of relatively well-defined affinity spaces and electronic networks can be seen as a new literacy practice.

For fun: the shark and the helicopter

This old internet favourite (urbanlegends.about.com/library/blsharkattack. htm) began circulating the internet in August 2001 as an attachment to an email message. The attachment was a Word document that began with an invitation to readers to compare their workday to one that could be considerably worse. The message contained a photo of a person on a rope ladder dangling from a helicopter just metres from the jaws of an enormous white shark leaping from the water. The text accompanying this image insisted the image was real and claimed the photo had been nominated by *National Geographic Magazine* (some versions named a German magazine, *Geo*, as the nominator) for a photo of the year award. Notwithstanding the visible presence of a section of the Golden Gate Bridge (San Francisco, USA) in the photo, the claim that the picture was taken during a British army exercise off the coast of South Africa was seemingly swallowed by many who went to the *National Geographic* website in search of more photos. Internet hoaxing is a long-standing affinity practice that often produces mutations of memes as remix aficionados express solidarity with the perpetrator of the initial hoax. Mutations of this particular hoax include, for example, a large vending machine in place of the shark.

Affinity: The 'Him Name is Hopkin Green Frog' Meme – a mutating visual remix meme

The 'lost frog' meme – introduced briefly in Chapter 3 – was sparked by a child's hand-produced flier announcing a lost pet and posted in Seattle streets (see Figure 4.1). The flier included detailed front and side images of the lost frog, and childlike, heartfelt text declaring the owner's

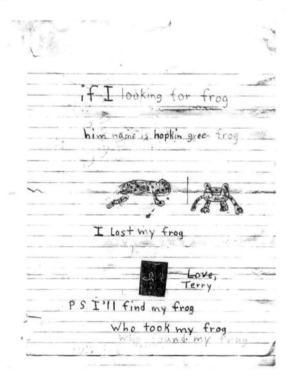

Figure 4.1 Terry's lost frog flier
Source: lostfrog.org

determination to find his frog (e.g., 'Who took my frog' and 'P.S. I'll find my frog'). During September 2004, a scanned image of this flier was posted to an online image-sharing community, where the child's resolute search for his pet struck a chord. Members of this photoshopping group edited and mixed new versions of the flier that lent epic proportions to the child's search for his lost pet. These new images are often playful and humorous, while at the same time, many are also deeply compassionate and empathetic.

These meme mutations were gathered together by Harold Ikes and archived on lostfrog.org. The archive captured widespread attention and quickly became a popular hyperlink in blog posts and discussion forums. Late in September, 2004, Mike Whybark, a resident of Seattle, began researching the background story to the original flier and reported his findings in *The Nation* (see Whybark 2004). The flier was produced by Terry, a 16-year-old autistic boy who had lost a toy frog that had been very special to him. Despite the 'mystery' of Terry and his lost pet being to all intents and purposes solved, photoshoppers continue to contribute to the archive, and lostfrog.org currently hosts over 100 mutations of the original flier. The meme has spilled over into meatspace as well; many of its hosts did their own independent background research and purchased replacement frogs on eBay to send to Terry. Businesses are cashing in on the meme as well, with a 'lost frog' t-shirt and a postcard available for purchase online (store.northshore shirts.com/ilomyfrhisna.html; cafepress.com/hopkin.15679312).

The photoshopped images archived on lostfrog.org remain highly faithful to the 'searching for lost pet' meme generated by Terry with his original flier. However, photoshoppers have liberally reinterpreted his flier, using it more as a 'jumping-off point' (Doctorow 2004: 1) than as a static text to pass on to others. In general, key features from the original flier remain, and, in particular, include the image of the frog drawn by Terry and some of the language he used on the flier (especially, 'him name is hopkin green frog' and 'P.S. I'll find my frog'). The archived images variously make use of typical 'missing persons' announcement vehicles (e.g., broadcast media news reports, milk cartons, road signs), crowd scenes seemingly devoted to spreading the news about the lost frog (e.g., a 'lost frog' banner at a crowded soccer match), attention-grabbing announcement vehicles (e.g., an aeroplane pulling a banner announcement, Prime Minister Tony Blair carrying lost frog fliers and wearing a lost frog badge), and a host of other 'remember Hopkin' scenarios (e.g., lost frog video games, lost frog scratch-it lottery tickets, Hopkin's ID on someone's instant message buddy list, Hopkin as a 'not found' internet file image). Some of the photoshopped images offer explanations as to what happened to Hopkin, including being caught up in one of the *Raiders of the Lost Ark* movies, joining Osama bin Laden, and/or being abducted by aliens.

It seems that the pathos of a child's pet being lost and the child's determination to find him proved highly memorable and contagious. The meme's infection rate was helped by reports on high traffic blogs like BoingBoing.net and discussion forums like Metafilter. Photoshoppers took up Terry's cause – for better or for worse. Many online comments attached to blog posts about lostfrog.org, such as on Metafilter, a premier online discussion forum (see metafilter.com/mefi/36801), described how different forum commentators find the original flier 'heartbreaking', and that it 'tears [them] up inside'. Comments also reveal that many people find the subsequent mutations of this image 'touching', and some even admitted to crying while they viewed the archive. Judging from weblog posts and comments, Terry's lost frog meme seems to have tapped into widely shared childhood experiences of lost pets.

Not everyone infected with this meme found the mutated images sufficiently empathetic or respectful. Nonetheless, even those people who do not understand this set of remixed images or its popularity, or feel the archive is a cruel joke at the expense of an autistic young man and voice their concerns on their blogs or elsewhere online serve to ensure that news about the archive is passed on. Indeed, the longevity of this meme seems assured while the website archive remains online.

This lost pet remix meme seems to have attracted a fairly high coolness quotient as well, with contributors to the image bank described in a number of venues as 'hipsters' (cf. Doctorow 2004). Even knowing about the meme during its early stages is regarded by some as cool, as the following comment in response to a blog post about lostfrog.org suggests: 'Slow poke, this originated on FipiLele about two weeks back. Posted by: riffola at November 7, 2004 04:23 PM' (on blog.filmgoerjuan.com/archives/2004/11/07/000256.php). Needless to say, the spread of remixed visual memes like 'lost frog' are assisted greatly by internet-mediated networks and 'cool hunters'.

We will return at length to the practice of meme production in Chapter 7 and consider some of its possible significance for literacy education.

Photoshopping remixes as politics # *1: Culture jamming with adbusters.org*

At Adbusters' Culture Jamming Headquarters (adbusters.org), a series of elegantly designed and technically polished pages present information about the organization and its purposes, describe an array of culture jamming campaigns, alert readers to new issues of the Adbusters paper-based magazine, and target worthy media events and advertising, cultural practices, and overbloated corporate globalization with knife-sharp critiques in the form of parodies that act as exposés of corporate wheelings and dealings, and/or online information tours focusing on social issues. By turning media images in upon themselves through deft remixing, the Adbusters' culture jamming campaigns show how photoshop remixes can be socially-aware new literacy practices for everyone. One of the best known Adbusters spoof ads has reduced the '*United* Colors of Benetton' to the '*true*' colors of Benetton by photoshopping a mouthful of greenbacks (US dollars) onto an image of a business man, and matching the colour of his shirt and tie to the colour of the money (see Figure 4.2).

The nature of culture jamming and the philosophy that underlies it, together with many practical examples of how to enact culture jamming literacies, are described in a recent book. *Culture Jam: How to Reverse America's Suicidal Consumer Binge – And Why We Must*, is written by Kalle Lasn, publisher of *Adbusters* magazine and founder of the Adbuster Media Foundation. The potential effectiveness of culture jamming was clearly demonstrated in the latter months of 2001. An email posting in January 2002 to the Culture Jammers Network informed recipients that

Figure 4.2   The True Colors of Benetton. Adbusters spoof advertisement
Source: adbusters.org/spoofads/fashion/benetton

Adbusters' activities had come under increased scrutiny following the events of September 11, 2001. According to the posting,

> Recently, our Corporate America Flag billboard in Times Square, New York, attracted the attention of the Federal Department of Defense, and a visit by an agent who asked a lot of pointed questions about our motivations and intent. We wondered: What gives? 'Just following up a lead from a tip line,' the agent admitted.
>
> (Adbusters 2002: 1; for the image, see web.archive.org/web/20030801232645/www.adbusters.org/campaigns/flag/nyc)

Adbusters were clearly worrying people in high places. They observed that any campaign daring to question 'U.S. economic, military or foreign policy in these delicate times', or any negative evaluation of how the US is handling its 'War on terrorism', runs the risk of being cast as 'a kind of enemy of the state, if not an outright terrorist' (Adbusters 2002: 1).

Adbusters' response was to mobilize internet space to engage in a classic act of cyberactivist literacy. The posting asked other Culture Jammers whether their activities had received similar attention, noting that they had received messages from other activist organizations that had found themselves under investigation 'in a political climate that's starting to take on shades of McCarthyism' (Adbusters 2002: 1). Noting that they could live with vigilance, but that intimidation amounting to persecution is 'another bucket of fish', Adbusters established its own 'rat line' and invited others to publicize instances of state persecution within a medium which has immediate global reach: 'If you know of social marketing campaigns or protest actions that are being suppressed, or if you come across any other story of overzealous government "information management," please tell us your story' (Adbusters 2002: 1).

Shortly after this occurred, Adbusters was contacted by Miramax, a Disney corporation, and informed that the corporate US flag billboard was hindering filming sequences in Times Square. Miramax requested Adbusters to either take the billboard down for a few weeks, cover it up, or replace the corporate logos Adbusters had inserted in place of stars on the flag with the original stars. Adbusters decided to reject all three options. Instead, they invited internet users to photoshop their own spoofs on the corporate flag theme. The result was a series of high quality spoofs which Adbusters published on their website, together with their own commentary on Miramax's intervention. In the context of the US war on (other nations') terrorism, the corporate flag campaign lifted remixing as a new literacy to a new plane.

Photoshopping remixes as politics #2: Micah Wright's Propaganda Remix Project

Micah Wright's web biography (micahwright.com/bio.htm) describes him as a writer who 'has worked in television animation, comic books, graphic novels, videogames and film'. Following a 'successful career in animation' Wright developed an interest in the work of First and Second World War poster artists. He remixed these images, adding text within the image, to produce a series of anti-war posters directed at the Bush Administration's foreign policy. His work has been widely featured in leading US and British newspapers and to date has yielded three books: *YOU Back the Attack: WE'LL Bomb Who We Want!* (2003), *If You're Not a Terrorist ... Stop Asking Questions* (2005), and *Surveillance Means Security* (2006). More than 400 posters can be viewed on Wright's propaganda remix site at: www.antiwarposters.com. Figure 4.3 is taken from this site and provides a typical example of Wright's political remix.

Figure 4.3 Sorry We're Late, New Orleans!
Source: Micah Wright, www.antiwarposters.com.

Remix 4: Anime and AMV – remixing animation, voice, and music

Besides producing fanfiction and fan art, manga and anime aficionados also use the multimedia capacities of today's computers – anything from an old iMac up, as Lessig (2005) observes – to produce fan anime (e.g., tfcog.net; newgrounds.com/collection/dragonballz.html) and Anime Music Video artefacts (e.g., newgrounds.com, animesuki.com; animemusicvideos.org).

The TFCog.net site is a portal for Transformers fans. The two fans operating the site hope to expand their content and make the portal 'one of the most entertaining and satisfying websites on Transformers' (tfcog.net). The links in the bottom half of the left-hand side-bar on the front page of the fansite lead to works that fans have produced themselves by taking original Transformer anime material and using a cast of voices to create a new script and soundtrack for each video. Information is provided about auditions for being in an episode along with full details of the cast for each published episode (character and the person doing the voice). The resulting anime takes some time to download, but is well worth it. Original material is cut and spliced into a new adventure narrated–performed by the cast in a decidedly fresh and innovative alternative to conventional classroom practices like Readers' Theatre that involve students reading character parts from novels.

The Newgrounds portal for AMV contains material like Chuck Gaffney's mash-up of clips from several anime shows like *Inuyusha, Dragon Ball-Z*, and *Sailor Moon*, among others, to the chorus of Alphaville's song 'Big in Japan' (newgrounds.com/portal/view/136982); and Brandon Blackburn's 'A Place for my Head', set to Linkin Park's song of the same name and featuring what looks like original anime (newgrounds.com/portal/view/ 34620). This site requires no subscription or registered membership and is a quick way to get a sense of AMV fanwork. Sites like animemusicvideos.org and animesuki.com require membership, which is free, but donations and pledges are welcomed. They provide very high quality AMV fare along with an impressive array of discussion forums and member services.

Ito (2005) pays homage to anime fandom in terms that encapsulate the key themes of this chapter and explain why we believe remix practices of the kinds described above need to be taken very seriously as paradigm cases of new literacies. She identifies anime *otaku* living outside of Japan as media connoisseurs who organize their social lives around activities of locating, viewing, interpreting, remixing and sharing esoteric media works from an often distant and different culture:

Otaku translate and subtitle all major anime works, they create web sites with hundreds and thousands of members, stay in touch 24/7 on hundreds of IRC [chat] channels, and create fan fiction, fan art, and anime music videos that rework the original works into sometimes brilliantly creative and often subversive alternative frames of reference.

(Ito 2005a: n.p.)

These are people who spend much time and energy getting up to speed with challenging language skills and media production arts: 'scripting, editing, animating, drawing and writing'. More than this, they create communities of interest by mobilizing socially and working collaboratively to produce and distribute media. They craft their identities through their practices of remix and the wider social and cultural work that sustains these practices, this new literacy. While such fan activity is decried by many as ' "merely" derivative', Ito observes the importance of this work for where the future – literacy futures, no less – is headed. She sees otaku culture as a prototype 'for emergent forms of literacy' (Ito 2005a: n.p.).

And this is why we want to take it seriously, not simply and generally as some form of 'cultural practice' but, rather, as *literacy*.

Reflection and discussion

Access Michael Goldhaber's paper 'The attention economy and the net' at firstmonday.dk/issues/issue2_4/goldhaber and read it carefully:

- To what extent do you see a relationship between Goldhaber's theory and Ito's claim that *otaku* culture is a prototype for 'emergent forms of literacy'?

- If you see a relationship, what is the basis of this relationship?

- Do you participate in any fan practices? If so, what are they? How important are they for how you think of yourself and want to be seen as a particular kind of person?

- To what extent do you think literacy education should pay attention to the kinds of literacy practices that are associated with being a *fan*? Why?

- To what extent do you think literacy education should pay attention to the kinds of literacy practices that are associated with being a *star*? Why?

- To what extent should literacy education pay attention to neither? Why?

CHAPTER 5

News, Views, and Baby's Got the Blues: Weblogging and Mediacasting as Participation

Introduction

This chapter will discuss blogging and mediacasting from the perspective of new literacies as participatory practices. We aim to describe these literacies in enough detail for readers who are not already familiar with them to get a good sense of what they involve. Beyond that, our aim is to explore them as typical forms of participatory engagement that pack additional meaning into Dan Gillmor's (2004) idea of 'we, the media' (see: wethemedia. oreilly.com). Gillmor focuses on the challenge posed to broadcast news media conglomerates by bloggers, internet discussion and chat groups and the like that enable us to 'roll to our own news'. Beyond this, however, we can extend the idea to people rolling more generally to their own worlds of media that extend far beyond 'the news' – even if we take a broad sense of 'news'. 'We, the media' becomes 'we, the collective and interactive creators and publishers of opinion, news, fictional works, soap operas of our everyday lives, photo galleries, life histories, magazines, book reviews, travelogues, handy hints, any and everything that can be mediated'.

Blogging (weblogging)

Blogs: What are they and how have they evolved?

A weblog (hereafter 'blog') is most easily described as 'a website that is up-dated frequently, with new material posted at the top of the page' (Blood 2002a: 12). Blog entries ('posts') are 'arranged in reverse chronological order so the most recent post appears first' (Walker 2005: 45). For a rich phenomenological description, which captures the ongoing, evolving nature of blogs as 'unfinished business' (Lunenfeld 1999: 7, cited in Mortensen forthcoming), it is hard to best Torill Mortensen's portrayal (Mortensen forthcoming):

> A true-born child of the computer medium, the weblog may have its roots in the research journal, the ship's log, the private diary and the newspapers, all at the same time. But like a mongrel hunting the dark alleys of the digital city, the weblog is nothing if not adaptive and unique at the same time. No fancy thoroughbred this ... but a bastard child of all personal writing, breeding wildly as it meets others of its ilk online.

Forerunners to today's blogs began in the early 1990s as websites listing annotated hyperlinks to other websites. When someone with a website found other sites they thought contained interesting, curious, hilarious and/or generally newsworthy content, they would create a link to that material, annotate it briefly, and publish it on their website. Readers could decide on the basis of the description whether it was worth a click to check the link out. It was an early form of insider generosity: 'I've found this stuff that I think is interesting and you might like it too. Here is a brief description. If it sounds interesting just click here and see if you like it.'

These early 'bloggers' tended to be computing insiders, for at least two reasons. First, you needed some knowledge of webpage and hyperlink coding in order to be able to post material to the internet. Second, you needed a certain kind of cultural understanding of the web to see it as a place where you could actually publish information relatively painlessly, rather than just 'surfing' to see what you could find, or searching to try and locate specific kinds of information. Well-known early blogs of this original kind include *Camworld* (camworld.com), *ScriptingNews* (scripting.com), and the now-defunct *Infosift* (jjg.net/retired/infosift) (Blood 2002b).

In 1999, however, weblog publishing tools and blog hosting services became available on a large scale through Pitas.com and Blogger.com. This made it relatively easy for internet users who were unfamiliar or uncomfortable with using hypertext markup language and the principles of web design for coding and designing their own weblogs. Setting up a blog now simply involved going to a website, signing up for a blog account, following a few fairly straightforward instructions, and in less than 30 minutes one would have some 'copy' up on the web that was automatically formatted and laid out to the tune of your choice by means of whichever off-the-shelf template you had chosen (e.g., our own blog, every-dayliteracies.blogspot.com, uses the 'Jellyfish' template created by Jason Sutter and available through Blogger. We could just as easily use a template from this site: blogger-templates.blogspot.com. Changing the template on a blog is a simple point-and-click process).

This quantum simplification of web publishing spawned a new mass generation of bloggers in a very short time. This new generation was much more diverse than the original blogging generation. Many began using weblogs as a medium more like regularly updated journals than indices of hyperlinks, and posts could document anything and everything from what the blogger had for lunch that day; to movie, book and music reviews; to descriptions of shopping trips; through to latest illustrations completed by the blogger for offline texts and all manner of draft texts made available for commenting upon; and the like.

Most – although not all – weblogs now are *hybrids* of journal entries and annotations or indices of links, or some mix of reflections, musings, anecdotes and the like with embedded hyperlinks to related websites. Rebecca Blood describes this second-wave use of weblogs as concerned most with creating 'social alliances' (Blood 2002b: x). Weblogs are largely interest-driven and intended to attract readers who have the same or similar interests and allegiances as the bloggers. This does not mean having the same point of view but, rather, sharing a sense of what is significant so far as spending time in the blogosphere is concerned. 'Significance' is compatible with 'lowbrow' and the mundane every bit as much as with 'highbrow' and the 'effete', and the myriad points between. That is to say, people find their meaning – their significance – where they find it, and there is no shortage of range and options in the universe of blogs. For example, Technorati.com, a popular blog search service, was tracking around 30 million blogs in the first week of March 2006 (up from 2.7 million blogs in June 2004, and 24.2 million in December 2005). That represents a lot of 'significance'.

New kinds of purposes for blogs are emerging all the time, building on the expansive qualities of blogging software and support services, which are readily accessible, continually improving, and make it easy to publish and update one's content. A notable trend since around 2004 has been the rise of various kinds of fictional blogs. These are discussed later in this chapter.

Blogistics: some nuts and bolts of blogs

Typically, and regardless of a particular blog's purpose, most weblog front pages are similar in terms of general layout. Front pages typically contain at least two columns (although Livejournal.com offers bloggers a single column format, too). One column – the wider one – houses each weblog post, ordered chronologically from the most recent entry to the least recent entry. Individual posts are accompanied by the date (and sometimes the time) they were posted in order to alert readers to the 'currency' or 'timeliness' of the blog. Some bloggers choose to update several times a day, while others may update every few days or once a week or so. Entries are archived automatically after a given period (e.g., a few days, a week, a month). The second column usually serves multiple functions. It may provide an index of hyperlinks to directly related alternative media (e.g., the blogger's Flickr photo site, their personal or institutional website, etc.), and/or to other people's weblogs and websites that the blogger likes, recommends, or otherwise sees as related in some pertinent way to their own blog (see Figure 5.1). This index is often divided into sub-categories that can be topic-based, interest-based, and so on. This second column can also contain an index to archived previous posts. Some bloggers also include a photo or logo in this second column to represent them.

Figure 5.1 Screen grab of Lawrence Lessig's blog

Blog posts – other than fiction blog posts and some journal blog posts – are usually quite short, often just a few lines for each post. Posts are of three main types: (1) posts that include hyperlinks to other blogs, websites, or non-text media (e.g., audio or video files); (2) posts that do not (i.e., are just text); and (3) posts that include a captioned image. Posts that include hyperlinks to other internet sources may begin with a link followed by a brief commentary beneath it, in a form very similar to an annotated bibliographic entry, or the link may be embedded within the annotation itself. Hyperlinked posts may also include quotes from the information or text to which the blogger is linking – in the manner of a 'sound bite' – to give readers a sense of what they will find when they follow the link. An effective example of this type of post is found in the widely-read blog, BoingBoing.net.

Bloggers can fine tune and vary the 'look' of their blog by tinkering with the template text font and size, headings, colours, layout, background images or wallpaper, overall style or theme, and suchlike. As mentioned earlier, Blogger.com allows bloggers to choose from templates supplied by the service or created by other bloggers (e.g., blogger-templates. blogspot.com). If they wish, bloggers can code their blogs to present readers with options for different 'skins' that do not change the layout of a page *per se*, but only the surface appearance. For example, Littleyellowdifferent.com offers its readers a choice between two 'skins' – one blue-based, the other olive green-based – in case they have an ambience preference. Additional features on many weblogs include a banner title, a tag line, a blog or web search function, a calendar that shows the current date and which can be used to access previous, archived weblog entries, links to the blogger's instant messaging ID(s), links that let the reader 'subscribe' to the blog and receive updates on new posts via email or a subscription service (discussed in more detail later in this chapter and mentioned in Chapter 3), and the like.

Reflection and discussion

Visit some of the following popular blog spaces and examine people's template and layout choices with respect to how these choices help convey something about the blogger himself or herself:

- Xanga.com

- Livejournal.com

- Blogger.com

- Typepad.com

- Wordpress.com

- Blogsome.com

- Blogware.com

Why is it considered important to have some control over the 'look' of one's blog?

How important is the concept of 'design' when discussing new literacy practices like blogging?

Some cultural dimensions of blogs

Blogging has evolved into multiple forms reflecting diverse social purposes. Some of this diversity is captured in Figure 5.2, which offers a provisional typology of blogs based on the compositional character of posts. The categories and assignments to categories are intended to be indicative only, not absolute. The typology is a heuristic device for getting us to think about the blogosphere as complex and multiple rather than monolithic and singular. Different categories and assignments from those provided here are entirely possible and may well be more useful. For example, a typology might be developed around dimensions of content rather than the composition of posts. We have chosen to build our typology around types of posts because the number of types can be kept to a minimum. Trying to develop a typology based on content would be difficult because content is so diverse, and many blogs carry multiple types of content. The same would hold for trying to develop a typology based on genres of blogs.

This typology distinguishes four broad types of blog at the top level. We will briefly consider each type:

1 'Links with commentary' blogs.
2 'Meta-blog services'.
3 Journaling.
4 Hybrids.

'Links with commentary' blogs
These are what we identified earlier as the 'original' kinds of blogs. They have a high ratio of links to words in each post. Dave Winer's entry for 8 March 2006, on *Scripting News* provides a good example (each underlined word is a hyperlink to elsewhere on the internet).

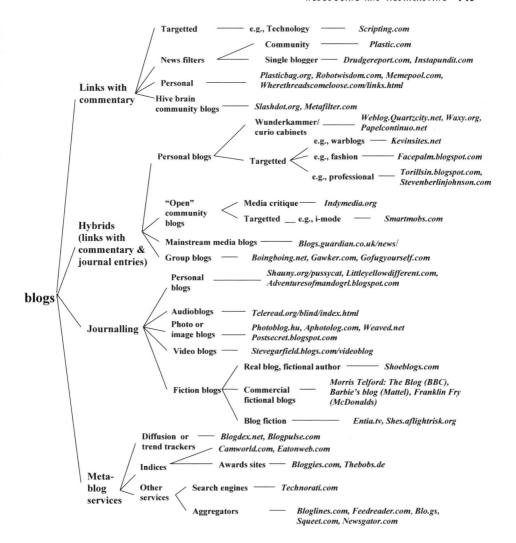

Figure 5.2 A provisional taxonomy of weblogs

I'm at <u>Skobee</u> headquarters at <u>604 Mission,</u> in downtown San Francisco where I'm leading a discussion among engineering-oriented entrepreneurs called <u>106 Miles.</u>

Squash: <u>Poor Web 2.0 fools</u>. 'This VC is a complete and utter twit.'

A few simple ideas I call <u>A Busy Developer's Guide to RSS 2.0</u>. Comments and suggestions are welcome.

Nick Bradbury's <u>BDG for RSS</u>.

Apple is <u>patenting</u> our <u>inventions</u>, again. *Oy.*
(Source: scripting.com/2006/03/08.html)

This sample post contains one link for every eight words. It is pitched at people with an interest in things technological, and anyone who is not a tech head will make little sense of the post. This is a very high links to words ratio by any measure, yet anyone in the space that Winer is pitching to will get extraordinary value for the time it takes them to scan those lines (which is little time at all). Glance, click, note, bookmark, and move on. We describe Winer's blog as a 'targeted' blog since it targets a quite specific interest area: internet technology and service development.

Targeted blogs are one sub-type of the 'links with commentary' category of blogs. We suggest three other common sub-types that can be found in the blogosphere: personal blogs, single blogger news filters, and community blogs. Personal blogs of this type focus on personal interests or other, often esoteric, dimensions of life. For example, *Incoming Signals* (where-threadscomeloose.com/links.html) is a wonderfully quirky, curio cabinet type of blog kept by Christopher Bahn that is heavy on links and light on text, and which clearly embodies Bahn's interests in history, politics, and popular culture, as well as his penchant for the bizarre and/or humorous.

News filters filter news generally in the way that Winer filters information about technology more specifically. We have sub-divided this category of blogs into single blogger filters and community filters. This is to differentiate news filters that target a particular interest community from those that address news more generally, as well as to differentiate between new filters that operate from a single point of view on an event or topic from those that offer multiple points of view. In the case of single bloggers, individuals select events and other items they consider newsworthy and blog these for their readers. These blogs often are written from some political perspective, which further serves to filter and shape what is reported and how. Community news filter blogs are a conglomeration of links with annotations created each day by community members. They open up spaces for discussion that include room for multiple (including opposing) viewpoints on any news item. The community blog *Plastic.com* filters news by having members post items they find newsworthy to one of five categories: Etcetera, Filmtv, Politics, Scitech, and Work. Each item then becomes a forum wherein other members can post comments that add to, or critique, the content or implications of the original news post. The US-based Instapundit.com, by contrast, is written by Glenn Reynolds, who blogs international news events from the (self-described) perspective of 'a libertarian-leaning small-government Republican' focusing on news about developments in business, technology, and government activity, policies and related themes.

Hive brain community blogs, another sub-category of the 'heavy on links' branch of our typology, serve identifiable interest communities. They use a 'heavy on links and light on text' approach to pool resources for such purposes as helping their readership keep up-to-date with technology developments, as is the case with Slashdot.org, or simply to share interesting, weird, curious, perplexing, and sundry other kinds of things with like-minded others, as is the case with Metafilter.com.

All of these blogs, however, have a similar look and feel to Winer's *Scripting News* in that they operate on an 'iceberg principle'. The relatively few words and the relatively many links bring together a lot of reading, analysis and synthesis that goes on, as it were, below water level. Insiders to the interest areas and communities at which these blogs are pitching have the necessary contextual knowledge to make use of the point of view encapsulated in these annotated links. Readers may not agree with the point of view offered in a blog, but they know what this point of view relates to because they are reading out of shared interest space.

Reflection and discussion

Spend some time on the following 'heavy on links' blogs and categorize each according to whether it is (1) a targeted blog; (2) a news filter blog; (3) a personal blog; (4) a hive brain community blog; or (5) none of the above:

- Memeorandum.com

- Infosthetics.com

- *A Welsh View* (xo.typepad.com/blog)

- We-make-money-not-art.com

- Gizmodo.com

- Linkfilter.net

- Memepool.com

> * Plasticbag.org
>
> What criteria or key features did you use to make distinctions between these blogs?
>
> To what extent is a typology of blogs useful in terms of understanding blogging practices and the blogosphere?

'Meta-blog services'

At the opposite pole of our typology from the 'Links with commentary' blogs are at what are known as 'Meta-blog services'. Strictly speaking, 'meta-blog services' aren't blogs *per se*, but are certainly in the service of the blogosphere. Meta-blog services are resources that help people find their way around the blogosphere, that document developments within the blogosphere (e.g., most blogged about topic on a given day, most popular tag on blog posts on a given day). They provide important information on weblogging as social practice and/or provide various kinds of blog-relevant resources useful to bloggers. The various meta-blog services identified here have been integral to the development of our sense of the blogosphere as represented in our typology. Bloggers can find their way around the blogosphere using search engines and other tools provided by their hosting service (e.g., Blogger.com, Livejournal.com), but a more comprehensive view is obtained, and obtained more quickly, by using services like Technorati.com, or subscription services supplied by Bloglines.com.

We have distinguished three main sub-categories of meta-blog services: Aggregators, Indices (or portals), and other services. We will look at some aspects of meta-blog services later in the chapter when we discuss the participatory nature of blogs. The point we wish to focus on immediately is the value of meta-blog services to enable bloggers to get an understanding of the overall space of the blogosphere – which is huge – as well as a sense of what 'counts' on some views as *successful* blogging practices within this space.

Diffusion or trend trackers provide information about trends within the blogosphere by 'trawling' all the blogs included under their 'jurisdiction' on a regular basis and identifying most-linked-to posts, most reported information on a given day or in a given hour, and so on. At one level, a trend tracker service, like Blogpulse.com, tracks all the updates made on blogs as new posts are made, and can keep information about all these blogs current almost on an hourly basis in some cases (e.g., Blogpulse was surveying over 26,400,000 blogs each hour in April 2006). At another level, many trend trackers can provide measures of 'significance' or 'importance' of individual blogs based on the extent to which other blogs link to them. This provides a basis to filter information for online searches. For example, each day Blogpulse ranks the most popular linked-to items within the blogosphere, and lists the 40 most popular hyperlinks used within posts, the 40 most popular posts, and the 40 most popular blogs, all calculated according to the number of times a certain URL is used, or by calculating the number of in-bound links to a specific blog post or blog. In other words, trend trackers operate on the principle that the significance of a blog or a blog post can be measured by the number of 'inbound links' it has: that is, by the number of blogs that link directly to that blog, or to a particular post within that blog.

Blog-specific search engines like Technorati.com or Blogdigger (blog-digger.com) are also useful for finding out what blogs are saying about a topic in which we're interested. The process is as straightforward as feeding a search query or keyword into Technorati's search window, just as one would in, say, Google.com. Search returns are based on chronology; that is, the most recent post appears first, which helps readers to judge the relative 'freshness' of the topic as well as to trace how the topic has been taken up within the blogosphere by working backwards in time through the list of search returns. For example, a search for 'Dick Cheney', the current US Vice president, shows a huge spike in blogging activity associated with him in mid-February 2006, which coincides with when he was involved directly in a shooting incident.

Meta-blog services can also be used to locate which blogs are most popular on any given day. The more inbound links a blog has, the higher it will rank in the league tables of 'important' or 'influential' blogs. This does not mean that high-ranked blogs have the 'best' or most 'accurate' information. It simply means that this is a blog that is taken very seriously by other bloggers. As a result, anyone new to blogging can quickly get a sense of what the blogs taken most seriously are blogging about, and how to locate them simply by going to a large-scale meta-blog service like Blogdex, Blo.gs or Technorati. Blo.gs indexes popularity based on how many times a blog appears in a 'favourites' list or 'blogroll' inside other bloggers' template sidebar. Technorati indexes popularity based on inbound links or the number of times a blog is linked to by other bloggers. A simple click on Technorati's Top 100 Blogs page (technorati.com/pop/blogs) told us that on 8 March 2006, *Boing Boing* was the top rated blog, followed by *Post-Secret* and *Daily Kos*.

On Technorati one can also search by means of tags or via 'blogfinder'. A blogfinder search lets a reader search the 'keywords' a blogger has used to capture the 'heart' or intent of their blog or each blog post (e.g., in March 2006 a Blogfinder.com search for 'knitting' returned the very popular *Yarn*

Harlot at the top of the list). The tag search function of Technorati provides a ranked list of the most popular tags bloggers are using that day and that the reader can then pick and choose from. Tags are very much like key-words attached to a post or uploaded image by the blogger, but are not drawn from a special search engine thesaurus or such like – and bloggers are free to choose whatever tags they want to use to describe their blog or blog posts (cf. tags used in Flickr.com discussed in Chapter 3). For example, on 14 March 2006, the five most popular tags on Technorati were: weblog, diary, entertainment, música and news. At the same time, the five 'hottest' or most used tags for the hour in which these figures were gathered were: Bush, Microsoft, Web 2.0, iTunes and scientology.

An index like Eatonweb.com covers a smaller number of blogs than the aggregators do. Indices act as portals or gateways to other blogs, and generally organize indexed blogs according to different categories. In the case of Eatonweb, blogs are organized in three ways: (1) according to category or topic; (2) according to the language in which the blog is written; and (3) according to the country of origin of the blog. Within the 'Category' index of Eatonweb, blogs are arranged by topic (e.g., academic, acting, advice, animals, anime) and then by alphabetical order within each topic. Clicking on a topic brings up a list of associated blogs. Rankings regarding popularity of a blog or blog post are not part of an index or portal service.

Annual blog awards, like the Bloggies (e.g., 2006.bloggies.com) or the Bobs (Thebobs.de), are another kind of meta-blog service and provide another kind of index of blog popularity. In general, recognized blog award events call on bloggers to nominate and vote for their favourite blogs in accordance with various categories. Blogs receiving the most votes in a category are declared the winners of that category. Nomination and voting categories used in the 2006 Bloggies included: Best Australian or New Zealand Blog, Best Asian Blog, Best Podcast of a Weblog, Best Craft Weblog, and Best Teen Weblog, among many others.

Reflection and discussion

Spend some time online exploring the functions of the following meta-blog services:

- Technorati.com

- Globalvoices.com

- Blogdex.com

- Squeet.com

- Bloggies.com

- Photoblogs.org

- Inform.com

- WhoLinksToMe.com

- QueerFilter.com

- Digg.com

- Blo.gs

- Bloglet.com

- Blogtree.com

- Blogstreet.com

- Feedster.com (choose 'blogs' option)

- Daypop.com (choose 'weblogs' option)

- Pubsub.com (choose 'weblogs' option)

- Weblogs Compendium (lights.com/weblogs; use menu bar on the left to explore this site).

To what extent do these meta-blog services help you to understand the scope and nature of the blogosphere?

To what extent is it important for educators to understand blogging at a meta level? Why? Does the same apply to students as well? Why/why not?

Journaling (including blog fictions)
Journaling is another main branch of our blog typology. Our concept of journaling is of presenting matters of personal significance or personal interest on the basis of what one is thinking or feeling. This is mostly done by means of prose writing, although using photographs and audio and video files is also quite common. In photoblogging, for example, the photos are presented as a log. The emphasis is on the photograph as an expression of thought, feeling and point of view. Text might be used to complement the photo, but the photo is the medium. Where images are used to illustrate a text, rather than the other way round, this may be journaling but not of the photoblogging variety (en.wikipedia.org/wiki/Photoblog). Likewise, we would classify a blog focused on the art of photography as a targeted

personal hybrid blog (cf., photojunkie.ca), rather than as a photoblog. A good example of photoblogging can be found at *Weaved* (weaved.net). In many of the photos logged here, the photographer's thought is partly conveyed by a caption that appears when the cursor passes over the photo. Audioblogging and videoblogging will be discussed later in the chapter under the heading of Mediacasting.

Classic journaling has the author at the centre of the day-to-day matters being written about. Journaling content ranges from the very homely and mundane to the highly esoteric, 'philosophical' and sophisticated. Wherever along this spectrum a particular blog might be, the author is writing 'out of' themselves. While this kind of writing is compatible with linking to blogs and annotating content found elsewhere, journaling in the sense that we intend here will typically be light on links. Moreover, where links are involved, they are likely to be to sites of sociality, such as to a friend's blog or, perhaps, to popular cultural sites or icons (e.g., a restaurant recently visited, Disneyland, Johnny Depp).

Paradigm cases of journaling can be found on the LiveJournal site. For present illustrative purposes we searched LiveJournal using 'urban living' and 'migrant living' as search terms. The searches yielded *Because; We are Ordinary People* (users.livejournal.com/encaustic_) and *Leerona* (zero-2-sixty. livejournal.com) respectively, among numerous others. While these are not necessarily typical of journaling overall, they are good examples of what we're on about here. During the first week of March 2006, at least one of Technorati's top ten rated blogs, *Beppe Grillo's Blog*, (beppegrillo.it/english.php) involved a form of journaling in the form of hard-bitten social critique.

A straight prose composition format of the type that typifies journaling is integral to the burgeoning corpus of fictional blogs (or blog fiction). Tim Wright (2004: n.p.) suggests that if bloggers can be 'independent, authentic voices' who can directly report things that happen in everyday language close to our own and, moreover, provide us with space to add our own voices, 'it would seem natural for the world of the blog to become a fertile ground for new forms of digital storytelling and the development of new independent authentic fictional voices' (ibid.). There seems to be an increasing and diversifying interest in experimenting with the weblog as a medium for writing fiction or personal narratives.

Some narrative blogging follows quite familiar formats, such as the widely reported *Belle de Jour*, which began in October 2003, and more recently outed itself as the diary of a London prostitute. This seems to have done well enough to get Belle published as a book author (with a second book apparently on the way), and work as a book reviewer, including for the *London Times* (women.timesonline.co.uk/article/0,,17909-2021934,00.html).

A long-running and very different format is evident in Paul Ford's *FTrain* (ftrain.com). This personal narrative blog has been running since 1997. Ford is an editor for *Harper's Magazine* and has organized his blog in the form of a complex online magazine (Wikipedia entry for Blog fiction, accessed 10 March 2006) that takes the form of a network.

> Each entry is a node in a network, connected to other nodes at the whim of the author. The result is a branching structure based on semantics rather than a linear chrononology.
> (baboonpalace.blogspot.com/2004/10/blog-fiction.html)

Both these examples involve a single author, as does the widely subscribed-to and fictional, *She's A Flight Risk* (shes.aflightrisk.org), written by a blogger assuming the character of an international fugitive. Each short episode is self-contained in a single post and gives enough of a sense of character for readers to respond as they would to a friend. The downcast tone of the post of 14 September 2005, 'The Politics of Control', elicited comments like 'Isabella, are you OK?', 'hoping all is ok in your world', and 'where did you go?'

Commenting in 2004, Jill Walker remarked that 'what's genuinely new about blog fictions is their use of the network' but that at the time this potential had not really been tested. Walker invited readers to 'imagine a fictional blogger who left comments in other people's blogs, chatted with people, and responded to reader comments as the story unfolded' (cited in McClellan 2004: n.p.). While Walker's hankering for the very real presence online of a fictional blogger has not been fully realized in any widespread way to date, Angela Thomas usefully traces the development of blog fiction as a distinct literary genre that does make the most of blog affordances in the form of hyperlinks, image capabilities, and comment functions, rather than simply as a publication medium for serialized stories (Thomas 2005: n.p.). Thomas argues that the most popular form of blog fiction is 'a chronicle of the adventures of one or more people told in first person diary style' (ibid.), and she identifies *The Glass House* (invisiblejames.com; currently on hiatus) as a good example of this type. The author, Steve Eley (with one female character's part written by his wife, Anna), used the comments function of the blog to leave comments made by the fictional friends of James, the main character in the story. According to Thomas,

> this not only exploits the potential of blogging ... to its fullest, but it cleverly adds another layer to the narrative. Each of the fictional

comment makers adopts a particular style also, and the repetition of this style constructs an image of their personae. And when real people leave comments or questions about the story or apparent incongruence in the story, James weaves the answer or explanation into a later post.

(Thomas 2005: n.p.)

As the story unfolds, James also makes good use of hyperlinks and links to 'songs, wikipedia, poetry, books he is reading, news items and even to the posts of other bloggers' (ibid.).

Overall, fiction blogs cover a wide range. These include blogs about real things but written by fictional characters, blogs written by assumed characters taken from real life (e.g., the faux Harriet Miers blog at harrietmiers.blogspot.com, that spoofed the real-life judge almost elected to the US Supreme Court), or blogs written by finely-honed alter-egos (e.g., Manolo's shoeblogs.com). Other forms include commercial story blogs used to promote products or television series (e.g., the BBC's Morris Telford blog or Mattel's Barbie blog), narrative blogs that make use of all the features of the blog (e.g., chronologically ordered postings, hyperlinks, images) to publish a story. These stories may be wholly contained within a single blog – sometimes called 'blovels' (e.g., *Entia* at www.entia.tv) – or distributed across blogs and other media. Other examples include Spanish-language telenovelas in the form of written and illustrated blogs (mujer-gorda.bitacoras.com), and fanfiction posts in the form of a target character's fictional diary, or in the form of narrative role playing (cf., Thomas 2005; Wright 2004).

Reflection and discussion

Spend some time reading different types of fiction blogs, such as:

- Shes.aflightrisk.org/mt-archives/000002.html (narrative)

- www.entia.tv (narrative)

- Invisiblejames.com (narrative; click on 'the beginning' or 'December 2004' in the right-hand column to start)

- Shoeblogs.com (fictional author, real-world blog)

- Mujergorda.bitacoras.com (telenovela-type)

- Harrietmiers.blogspot.com (fictional spoof)

- Morris Telford's blog (bbc.co.uk/shropshire/features/blog)

- And others listed at: Fictionblogs2.blogspot.com

To what extent do these different fictions reflect Web 1.0 or Web 2.0 emphases? What tells you this?

Why might fiction blogs be growing in popularity, both in terms of more and more people writing them, as well as reading them?

What implications might these approaches to fiction have for teaching at the various grade levels?

Hybrids

In hybrid blogs, posts involve a combination of links plus commentary with content that is more like journaling. This category of blogs is extremely diverse and many of Technorati's top ranked blogs (March 2006) are of this kind (e.g., BoingBoing.net, Michellemalkin.com, Dailykos.com, and Thoughtmechanics.com).

Steven Johnson's blog (stevenberlinjohnson.com) is a good example of a hybrid personal blog and we have followed it quite regularly since it began. Johnson is an influential internet commentator and author who co-founded and edited the legendary online magazine *Feed* in the late 1990s. He might, perhaps, best be described as an internet public intellectual. A semiotics major from Brown University and author of books on interface culture, brain theory, and popular culture, Johnson commenced his weblog on 11 November 2002. It has become a popular source of opinion on matters relating to internet culture, politics, cognition, urban development in New York, hi tech news, landscape architecture, design in general, contemporary media and everyday popular cultural practices. His recent book, *Everything Bad is Good for You: How Today's Popular Culture is Actually Making Us Smarter*, has been a best seller. Johnson is very well connected throughout the internet world, and his articles are published in a range of magazines and journals, including *Discover* (discover.com), for which he writes a regular column, and *Wired*, a well-known geek-chic magazine.

Johnson's blog emphasizes economy and clarity in its design, is rich in hyperlinks on topics covered in the regular posts (typically 3–4 posts per week), and keeps Johnson's work and personal profile strongly in the foreground. At the time of writing, the right-hand column featured a small colour photo of Johnson, a brief bioblurb, short promotional descriptions for his books and accompanying links to Amazon.com, a short list of links to some of his recent published essays, a list of topics covered in his recent postings, and hyperlinks to his blog archives back to June 2005.

After just a short time exploring Johnson's blog a 'savvy' reader will have a good sense of such things as:

- How Johnson wants to be seen publicly – the blog does important identity construction and portrayal work.
- Why Johnson operates a blog – reasons range from promoting his work to taking a position on current issues he sees as important (for example, freakonomics).
- Some potentially powerful 'affinity maps', e.g., constellations of influential people in the blogosphere who take positions on issues Johnson regards as important.
- A perspective on a range of technological innovations and issues.

Readers will find they can glean information quickly and easily because of the blog's 'clean' and 'lean' layout, and the coherence of its hyperlinks. Moreover, it will be apparent that Johnson's sources are ones that many people regard as credible – even if one personally disagrees with their perspectives. We rarely come away from the blog feeling it was not a good use of time. Moreover, Johnson's blog exemplifies what we will shortly describe as the things we most look for in a blog.

The quality of blogs

The question of what makes for a good quality blog is vexed. A cynic might say there is no accounting for taste. From the perspective of self-appointed peer reviewers of quality, the cardinal blogging sin is to be boring. The sometimes annual Anti-Bloggie Awards (see leiascofield.com/antibloggies) are unrelentingly severe about the 'cheese sandwich effect' – where blogs have nothing to say beyond the level of describing what their writers had for lunch that day. From other perspectives this might be seen as elitist, and the point could be argued that the relevant criterion here is that a blog should be interesting. If the mundane can be presented in interesting ways this would, to that extent, be a point in favour of its quality – at least in the eyes of those who find it interesting.

Besides the self-evident criterion of being interesting, there are three further criteria we think characterize effective blogs. These are: (1) evidence of a clear and strong sense of purpose; (2) a recognizable and well-informed point of view; and (3) a good standard of presentation.

Purpose
Unless its creator has an authentic purpose – however whimsical this might be – a blog is unlikely to survive the demands on time, energy,

resourcefulness, affiliation and other forms of identity work inherent in maintaining an enduring and effective blog. Aggregation services that differentiate between active and inactive or 'one-time' blogs and calculate the proportions of each provide, in effect, an index to the relative degree of motivation or purpose among bloggers (see, for example, Blogcount.com). Such aggregation services tend only to count as blogs those that qualify as active – which usually means blogs updated with at least one post within a certain amount of time (e.g., two weeks, one month). For example, on 14 March 2006, Livejournal.com was hosting 9,761,877 blog accounts, and listed 1,995,445 as 'active in some way' (livejournal.com/stats). It also lists 6,628,623 blogs as having been created but never once updated. While purposes driving blogs can be of any kind, they need to be sufficiently motivating to keep the blog active, and sufficiently well defined and contained for the author to be able to generate posts and links that keep readers interested and believing in the blogger's credibility or seriousness.

In many cases a strong and committed sense of purpose may be almost enough on its own to maintain a readership if they share a similar purpose or value orientation. At the least, this is likely to lend coherence to a blog and enhance readers' sense of its identity. It is likely also to contribute to the blog having spirit. A good, if rather extreme, case of a blog being blessed with a strong and clear sense of purpose can be found in *A Family in Baghdad* (afamilyinbaghdad.blogspot.com), which documents one family's experiences of the war in Iraq and its effects on their daily lives in the country's capital city. Written mostly by the mother of the family, the blog makes for powerful reading and has generated some interesting outcomes. For example, the post for 9 March 2006 said:

Good morning...

still in Washington to meet people and Congress staff to talk about Iraq. our days are busy and long, we are very tired, but telling ourselves we have to tolerate all of this for the sake of Iraqi people who are suffering or dying every day since three years of war.

yesterday ... we were in our marching towards the White House, with about 200 women, asking the Bush Administration to stop the war on Iraq, and pull out the troops, and help Iraqis to rebuild their country by their hands...

A Technorati search using the URL for this blog as the search term returns links to this site from 150 other blogs, indicating a very real, widespread presence within the blogosphere for this blog.

The longevity of a blog suggests that it retains a compelling purpose for its author. Blogs like *Scripting News* (scripting.com), *Rebecca's Pocket* (rebeccablood.com), and *Kottke* (kottke.org) all began during or before the year 2000 and retain strong followings.

Reflection and discussion

Examine three blogs – *Scripting News*, *Rebecca's Pocket* and *Kottke.org* – that are all remarkable for their longevity and wide readership (indeed, Jason Kottke of Kottke.org earns a living from his blog):

- What appears to the the *purpose* of each of these blogs? How do you know? Has the purpose of each changed over time or not?

- What is it about their purpose that seems to keep these three bloggers blogging?

- What do you think can be learned from this by people new to blogging?

Point of view

Our second criterion for a good quality blog is that it has a recognizable and well-informed point of view. This is widely seen as central to what blogging is about. Julian Dibbell (Dibbell 2002) remarks that a blog without a point of view is practically a contradiction in terms.

Blood (rebeccablood.com), an early-adopter and chronicler of blogging as mentioned in the previous section, reflects on her awareness of the importance of point of view for her own blogging practices and explains:

> Shortly after I began producing Rebecca's Pocket [her blog] I noticed two side effects I had not expected. First, I discovered my own interests. I thought I knew what I was interested in, but after linking stories for a few months I could see that I was much more interested in science, archaeology, and issues of injustice than I had realized. More importantly, I began to value more highly my own point of view. In composing my link text every day I carefully considered my own opinions and ideas, and I began to feel that my perspective was unique and important.
>
> (Blood 2002b: 12)

The tagline of a blog will often signal state the blogger's point of view (e.g., the tagline for the award-winning blog, *Queerty.com*, reads: 'Free of an agenda. Except that gay one'). The 'profile' section of a blog can also include an explicit statement of a blogger's point of view. Perhaps less directly, a blogger's blogroll, list of favourites, or friends list can also say a lot about their point of view. For example, part of the blogroll for Baghdad Burning (riverbendblog.blogspot.com), an eye-witness account written by a young woman, and whose blog summary reads: 'Girl Blog from Iraq … let's talk war, politics and occupation', includes links to websites like: Iraq Occupation Watch, Iraq Body Count, International Action Center and to blogs written by Iraqi bloggers who offer eye-witness accounts of the ongoing occupation that are often at odds with US media claims concerning the progress of the war. Baghdad Burning won the 2006 Bloggies for 'Best Middle Eastern or African blog'.

Reflection and discussion

What is the difference between purpose and point of view with respect to blogging?

Use the portal, Educational.blogs.com, to locate and examine a number of school and classroom blogs (although not teachers' personal blogs):

- To what extent do the school blogs you've examined present an identifiable point of view to readers?

- What do your findings tell you?

Quality of presentation
Serious bloggers are committed to carefully crafted, well-informed posts. Advice to novice bloggers usually emphasizes the need for good quality, accessible writing. Jennifer Garrett's (c. 2005: n.p.) advice for newbies on the Blogger.com blog publishing website includes the observation that 'a well-written blog indicates respect both for the medium and for the reader'. Jane Perrone, a reporter with *The Guardian*, draws readers' attention to the writing style used by Tom Reynolds (randomreality.blogware.com), a popular English blogger who writes about his worklife as an emergency medical technician for the ambulance service. Perrone writes,

> It's not only the life-and-death subject matter that has kept readers hungry for updates; despite claiming that he is 'absolutely rubbish at writing', Reynolds has a deft turn of phrase coupled with a black sense of humour.

> (2004: n.p.)

Aspects of design and style of writing and overall presentation are interwoven. Having a consistent style in terms of font type, text layout and the like 'helps in [drawing] readers' attention to a specific area' and having a distinctive style of writing 'helps in getting regular readers' (Shanmuga-sundaram 2002: 143). Other bloggers choose to emphasize the importance of relevant comments on pieces they post in order to promote a cohesive and well-informed community of readers and commentators. For example, each blog entry at Plasticbag.org is accompanied by a gentle prompt: 'Please remember to try and keep your comments on-topic, informative and polite. Unpopular viewpoints are welcome as long as they're pertinent.'

Many better-known bloggers adopt clean and lean formats, using crisp prose and drawing on existing online resources (via hyperlinks) to convey information or ideas rather than re-hashing content already available to the judicious searcher (cf., BoingBoing.com or Kottke.org), or to focus reader attention on the content of the post (e.g., Littleyellowdifferent.com or Joshuaink.com). Effective blogs are easy to navigate and follow long-established and readily recognized navigation practices (e.g., underlined blue text signals a hyperlink). In addition, of course, blogs must be accessible in order to be effective. This translates into practices like avoiding unnecessary use of images and other media (like animations) that are heavy on bandwidth in order to facilitate fast loading times, and ensuring that one uses template layouts and the like that can be read by a range of internet browsers (e.g., Safari, Mozilla, Firefox, Netscape Communicator, Internet Explorer).

Weblogging as participatory practice

A concept of participation
Participation means involvement in some kind of shared purpose or activity – taking part in some kind of endeavour in which others are involved. The kinds of activities one might participate in may be things that are already more or less established, with more or less recognized norms and criteria. Alternatively, they might be things that are evolving and being developed, such that one's participation becomes part of building a practice or an affinity or community that may continue to evolve. Or again, they might be things that suddenly emerge and around which people mobilize. The mobilization might just be for a short time, if the purpose or end works itself out and the reason for participation no longer exists. The participation could be over before there is really even time for a practice to take shape. In such cases, participants bring with them to a situation various procedures and understandings they have acquired elsewhere, and operate

on the basis of these until the participation purpose is met. This is one broad dimension along which forms of participation within the blogosphere may vary.

With respect to more or less established purposes and routines, we might think of practices like participating in formal discussions of issues or in friendship networks. An example of participation in building a practice or affinity that may continue to evolve can be found in efforts to build blog fiction – just how *might* the dynamism and interactivity and globality of the net be mobilized within creative endeavours to build new cultural forms of expression? With respect to event-driven participation, as we will describe below, bloggers also can mobilize massively at short notice to challenge an opinion or state of affairs and achieve a result – as in the case involving a televised report by US television reporter and commentator, Dan Rather, that was based on what proved to be (unknown to Rather) a forged and bogus set of documents (see p. 167).

Participation may vary around several other dimensions and variables that are relevant to weblogging as well, such as the scale and visibility of a 'project', one's level and degree of activity, the kind of activity involved, and so on. These variables can be related in interesting ways. Writing in 2003, Clay Shirky discussed the 'head' and the 'long tail' of the 'power law distribution' among blogs and some of the consequences of how attention and power are distributed in the blogosphere. The point here is that a tiny proportion of the vast number of blogs that exist account for a large proportion of the inbound links. Relatively few blogs get relatively vast attention, and the huge majority of blogs get little attention at all so far as readership and inbound links are concerned. This has interesting but obvious implications for 'participation'. Shirky explains, for example, that the more a blogger's audience grows, the less she can read other people's blogs, reply to their comments, link to other blogs, and so on. Such a blogger ends up, in effect, becoming 'a broadcast outlet, distributing material without participating in conversations about it' (Shirky 2003: n.p.).

Shirky could have been talking about a blogger like Michelle Malkin, a US-based syndicated columnist (Michellemalkin.com). The comments function on her blog has been disabled, and the only other service available for each post is a trackback link. Clicking on the trackback icon for a particular post enables the reader to see who has linked to that post in a post of their own on a blog in some other place. Malkin's work as 'material put out there' enters into larger discourse by being taken up in other people's blogs. Her material becomes a catalyst for participation by others, including others who link to the posts made by people who have incorporated Malkin into their posts. Malkin herself, however, is not in these conversations. She facilitates them but is not there as participant. This is close to pure broadcast. Meanwhile, says Shirky, things are very different along the tail of the blogosphere:

> [T]he long tail of weblogs with few readers will become conversational. In a world where most bloggers get below average traffic, audience size can't be the only metric for success. LiveJournal had this figured out years ago, by assuming that people would be writing for their friends, rather than some impersonal audience. Publishing an essay and having three random people read it is a recipe for disappointment, but publishing an account of your Saturday night and having your three closest friends read it feels like a conversation, especially if they follow up with their own accounts.
>
> (shirky.com/writings/powerlaw_weblog.html)

Besides operating a weblog and making regular posts (which is the bottom line for 'blogging' in any event), there are numerous ways (i.e., 'moves' a participant can make) in which bloggers *participate*, and different levels of intensity and involvement at which this participation might occur. For present purposes we can distinguish between participation that is directed to particular or specified others, participation that is directed toward a larger community, and participation that is directed at both. Two examples may suffice.

First, we may look at the post and comments sequence for Encaustic's blog *Because; We are Ordinary People* for 5 March 2006. The post is taking about attending the UK Education Fair. It concludes with the (lightly edited) remark:

> It's pretty sad the universities I am more interested in (Durham, UCL, King's College, Leicester, LSE) weren't at the fair. Oh, and the woman at Nottingham's booth was a … *laaa*. **'Sorry. Due to the high competition for the very limited places in Nottingham's Law School, the law faculty doesn't consider a diploma as an entry alternative.'**. I hate Nottingham now.
>
> (users.livejournal.com/encaustic_/15581.html; emphasis in original)

The comments sequence that follows involves an interchange between Encaustic and Sun_skittle:

> **Sun_skittle:** Hi there, Was just blog-hopping and came across your LJ. Durham's a great choice, and they definitely recognise and are willing

to accept TP's law diploma, although I'm not too sure what sort of grades they expect. All the best for the exams!

Encaustic: Wow. Cool. Haha I see that you were once in TP also. What course were you in? Did you also do Law at Durham? =)

Sun_skittle: Was from TP law too, and currently doing law in durham. Heh, yes ... that's why I'm shamelessly promoting it.

Encaustic: OH MAN URE GONNA BE MY IDOL OR SUMTHIN. I very much wld like to go to Durham. What is the grade average for all ur subjects throughtout the 3 years? Cumulative GPA? haha. I'm sure Durham would take into consideration other factors like CCA participation, leadership positions and the likes rite? haha. sorry for hounding you with all these questions. But its like, 'OMG SOMEONE'S IN DURHAMMMM!!' haha

Sun_skittle: Whoa ... easy there. I can't recall offhand what my GPA was like (prob a B average?), but yeah, they do take your grades and activities into consideration amongst other things, although not as strictly as the Singapore unis do. I think there's a book at the British Council on what the various law depts look out for. It's pretty useful. But do keep your options open...:)

Encaustic: May I add you as a friend?

Sun_skittle: sure:)

This sequence shows a chance meeting on a blog that gets followed through a brief exchange of information to the point where the blogger gets permission to add the commenter as a 'friend'. This opens up possibilities for further contact and introduction to other blogging networks on the part of both participants. Equally, it might lead to nothing. The interaction is one-to-one, quite intense (at least on the part of Encaustic), related to specific matters, and unlikely to reach far beyond the two participants.

In marked contrast we might consider a short chain of links that we followed from a post made by Steven Johnson on 2 June 2004, under the heading 'Bloggers save the world'. Johnson said in his post (original hyperlinks underlined): 'My buddy Jeff Jarvis alerted me to the laudable Spirit of America site.' Clicking on the first hyperlink led to Jarvis' site and a post that Jarvis had made the previous day (1 June) containing information on the Spirit of America initiative, which was organizing donations of items to be sent to Iraq in the wake of the US-led invasion of that country. Scrolling through Jarvis' post one could read a list of tributes to people who had supported the initiative. At the end of the tributes there was a comment with a hyperlink: 'Surprise, surprise, surprise: <u>Dave Winer dissents</u>.' Clicking on the hyperlink led to Winer's posting for 1 June, on his *Scripting News* blog (scripting.com). This post concludes as follows (original hyperlinks are underlined in the following text):

> <u>Jeff Jarvis is promoting</u> a site called <u>Spirit of America</u>. I don't know much about it, and I don't sign up for political causes I don't know much about. I see other bloggers <u>singing</u> glowing praises for it, but sheez, how could they know? I don't think bloggerdom should be used like TV talk shows. I said I don't stand up for causes I don't understand. I guess that's a polite way of saying that I don't even *like* what they're doing. I think we need to get over ourselves in America, our time is just about over, unless we stop guzzling so much gas and start electing leaders with brains, morals and courage. I feel I have to say I like Jeff, I really do, he's come through for me twice at BloggerCon, and I appreciate that. But his politics are 180 degrees opposite mine, even on tactics. I think the best thing the US can do for the world is get our own house in order and stop trying to fix the world, something we're exceedingly bad at.

Jarvis' post, replete with hyperlinks opening out to diverse blogging spaces germane to the invasion of Iraq at that time, as well as to people supporting the Spirit of America initiative can be found at: buzzmachine.com/archives/ 2004_06_01.html. And for some of the fruit on higher branches of the blogging as participation tree, there are pickings to be had at Britt Blaser's blog: blaserco.com/blogs/2004/06/02.html. Point of view is important, and expressions of truly courageous point of view – even if polemical – can be priceless. While many of the comments on Winer's blog post that ensued were low-level knee jerks and *ad hominem* comments of a kind that are common in any 'popular opinion space', the fact remains that the opposing positions at the heart of the interchange present a context for serious and potentially fruitful dialogue that could hardly, if at all, be bettered by a formally published text.

Tools for participation
Strictly speaking, one can participate actively and on many levels in the world of weblogs without operating a blog of one's own – although depending on the policies and preferences of the provider of the blog one wants to comment on and/or of the blogger in question, it may be necessary to have registered a blog account with that provider in order to be able to post comments on someone else's blog. Beginning bloggers typically start

out from a free hosting service like Blogger (blogger.com) or LiveJournal (livejournal.com). These (in conjunction with meta-blog services; see earlier) provide the basic tools for participatory weblogging. The following account is based on Blogger.com as the standard.

The most straightforward medium for participation is the comments function, which is accessed by clicking on an icon or hyperlink at the end of each blog post (see Figure 5.3). As noted, whether or not one can comment may be a function of parameters that are set by the blogger or the blogger's host service. Where anonymous commenting is permitted, there are no hoops to jump through. Most bloggers are keen to receive comments – other than spam and other forms of abuse – and aim at opening the door as far as possible. From a commenter's point of view, as seen earlier, this mode of participation can be extended by commenting on the blogger's response to someone's comment. From the blogger's standpoint, they can respond to comments (if they choose to) in two main ways. They can add a comment themselves in response to a comment. Alternatively, they may pick up on a comment made to a post and make it the subject of a subsequent post.

A second reasonably straightforward means of participating is by means of making a link. Links are of two main kinds: to a blog and to a specific post on a blog. In the case of a blog, you find interesting and wish to be associated with – perhaps as a way of signalling to others that part of who you are is someone who reads blogs like this one – is by linking that blog to your own (e.g., adding it to your blog roll in your template sidebar, adding a blog to your 'friends list'). In the case of a particular post you find interesting and want to follow up in a post on your own blog, it is a matter of using the 'Links to this post' function (or the 'permalink' hyperlink in other kinds of blogs, as described in Chapter 3) immediately following the post to which you intend to link (see Figure 5.3). Clicking on this link opens a dialogue box where you can compose a post around the permanent URL for this blog post and then send it directly to your own blog as a complete post. In Blogger there is also an email function that allows you to email the original post directly to yourself or to some other person. In these ways a reader takes an initial step toward opening someone else's post up to a wider audience.

// posted by Colin @ 11:18 AM 1 comments links to this post ✉ ✎

Figure 5.3 A sample comments link following a blog post

Incorporating a link to someone else's blog post into a post of one's own creates, in effect, an annotated link. The annotation will involve expression of some point of view on the original post (see the Winer example on p. 161–162). From there, other people can 'click through' to the original post, and maybe link to that, as well as to your own post, branching the discussion or commentary outwards. This works in a further way as well. When B makes a link to a post by A, this is signalled by a 'trackback' function at the end of A's post. That way somebody else, C, reading A's post, can get to B's post by clicking on the trackback link (in Blogger, the 'Links to this post' serves this purpose as well, by listing all the blogs that link to that particular post). Where several links have been made to a post on different blogs, there is already a network of participation in place, which can be accessed via the trackback function. All such links are registered by aggregators like Blogdex or search engines like Technorati, which means that other people who are searching by keywords or tags in areas covered by the blogs in question have a better chance of arriving at a well-linked-to post and reading or engaging more actively with what is going on in that web of links.

The final elementary tool for participation we will cover here is syndication – of which the aforementioned Dave Winer was a key developer. The process is widely referred to as RSS, or really simple syndication, and involves a stretch of internet-friendly code that establishes a 'subscription feed' for a blog. The code allocates a 'syndication' address for each blog (the code originally ended in the *.xml extension, but different coding systems mean that these 'feed' URLs can also end in *.opml, *.rdf, and other extensions now). The syndication address is rarely the same as the actual internet address of a blog. For example, the URL for our *EverydayLiteracies* blog is everydayliteracies.blogspot.com, but the RSS feed URL is everydayliteracies.blogspot.com/atom.xml. Internet browsers can't 'read' syndication URLs in the way that they can read ordinary URLs. Online or harddrive-based subscription software and interfaces instead manage subscriptions and reading feeds.

Syndication might be thought of analogously to getting on an update mailing list. So, for example, when we wanted to be kept up to date with what Dave Winer was writing on his blog we went to Bloglines.com, and set up a 'feed'. This involved entering the syndication URL for Winer's blog (i.e., scripting.com/rss.xml) into the feed 'subscription' window and automating 'subscribing' to his blog. Thereafter, whenever we want to find anything new that has been blogged by Winer, or anyone else whose blog we have subscribed to, we just log on at Bloglines and check our 'feeds'.

Using Bloglines involves going to the site and logging on whenever one wants to catch up on new blog entries.

Alternatively, one can use a subscription service like Squeet.com and have information about updates to self-selected, syndicated blogs delivered to one's email inbox. Once again it is a matter simply of setting up an account and then entering the blogs you want feeds for into a dialogue box. Thereafter, whenever an update is available, you receive an email message and can read the updates in your email client. Any hyperlinks contained in the posts can be accessed directly from your email browser by clicking on them. Getting started on participation could hardly be easier.

Reflection and discussion

Go to http://www.bloglines.com or some other aggregator from wikipedia.org/wiki/List_of_news_aggregators and sign up. Experiment with subscribing to some of the blogs we've mentioned so far in this chapter, or use the search function accessed from inside Bloglines to find blogs of your own to subscribe to.

- Based on your subscription experience, to what extent and in what ways do you think subscribing to blogs means you are participating in something?

- Why do a blog's actual URL and its RSS subscription URL differ? What does this tell you about how the blogosphere, or the internet more generally, works?

Blogging participation in action: concrete examples

In this section we showcase three quite different examples of participation in the blogosphere. We begin with the 'LiveJournal Batgirl Meme' that took on a life of its own on 13 January 2006, then go back to the latter part of 2004 and the 'Case of Bloggers vs Dan Rather's Evidence,' before returning to the present (March 2006) and 'Blogging Project Runway'.

The LiveJournal Batgirl Meme
We can begin a few days after the event with a 16 January post on davidbau.com's *A Dabbler's Weblog* (davidbau.com/archives/2006/01/17/ draw_batgirl_day.html). This asks if readers noticed how the previous Friday 'everybody on LiveJournal dropped everything to draw Batgirl'. A LiveJournal blogger, Andi Watson, posted about how another blogger's post reminded him of some character designs he had created in the late

1990s for a 'cute Japanese Batgirl' (see andiwatson.livejournal.com/ 37925.html). He included an image in his post of some of the sketches he had come up with. This sparked a discussion among a couple of people on his Friends list, one of whom, Jamie Dee Gailey, responded with his own version of Batgirl (himynameisjamie.livejournal.com/342720.html).

From that point a significant portion of LiveJournal's webspace seems to have exploded into an impromptu high octane comic aficionado affinity space. Over the next 24 hours several hundred responses to the initial posts flooded in, each offering their own version of Batgirl. Some latercomers were still posting near the end of January. Contributions included carefully drawn images submitted by professional comics artists through to the quixotic renderings done by people clearly quite unused to drawing the human figure. The first respondent, Jamie Dee Gailey, generated a list of participants seemingly to serve as a record of the event (himynameisja-mie.livejournal.com/345568.html). The early links appear to be organized chronologically and act as a kind of history trail for how the short-lived meme began.

The Case of Bloggers vs Dan Rather's Evidence
Jason Gallo claims that:

> [n]ews-oriented blogs have created a *real-time virtual feedback loop* that disrupts the temporality of the traditional news cycle [and] are helping to usher in a new form of hybrid journalism that merges traditional newsroom practices with the decentralized intelligence of individuals and groups spread across the Internet.
>
> (2004: 1, original emphasis)

This real-time virtual feedback loop refers to the way in which the immediacy of blogs is linked to the relative ease of quoting from, linking to, commenting on, elaborating upon, critiquing or challenging any given post within the blogosphere.

Interconnectedness occurs not only among people with blogs who happen to know each other, but is assisted by the kinds of tools we have mentioned earlier: online indices or portals (e.g., Eatonweb.com); diffusion or popularity indices that track most-linked to blog posts on a given day (e.g., Blogdex.com, Popdex.com); email alert services that let subscribers know when a particular blog has been updated (e.g., Bloglet.com, Squeet.com); blog-oriented search engines that search for blogs and/or keywords within blog posts (e.g., Technorati.com, Daypop.com, Blogpulse.com); and syndication services.

This interconnectedness means that many discussions about and critiques of news reporting within the blogosphere are collaborative affairs, with each poster building on or adding to an analysis from their particular point of view and range of expertise. Collective nouns, like 'hive brain', have been lifted from science fiction to describe this distributed expertise and analysis effect because common-use nouns simply do not capture the remarkableness of this phenomenon. Kelly McBride's (2004) observation that '[w]e journalists are no longer the gatekeepers in the marketplace of ideas' rings true within the blogosphere. Ironically, given journalists' initial tendency to disparage the quality of blogposts and commentary, mainstream media journalists have increasingly found themselves reporting on blog posts as significant sources of valid opinion, analysis and critique.

An example of this occurred in the second half of 2004, when Dan Rather, anchor for the US television news show, *60 Minutes*, reported on a series of memos that threw doubt onto whether George W. Bush had completed his National Guard service during 1972 and 1973. Before Rather had signed off on the segment, bloggers were critiquing the validity of the memos (McBride 2004; Ooi 2004). Nineteen minutes into the broadcast, TankerKC (his posting name) made a post to the highly conservative Freerepublic.com – an online discussion board and news blog portal. TankerKC suggested that the style and format of the memos did not match those used when he was in the US military (Ooi 2004). Four hours later, Buckhead (his posting name) posted a comment to the same discussion board critiquing the font in which the memos were printed (Ooi 2004). Buckhead pointed out that each of the documents shown on CBS was printed in a proportionally spaced font (e.g., Palatino or Times New Roman). In the early 1970s, however, personal memos within the military were produced mostly by means of typewriters, which use monospace characters (e.g., Courier, Letter Gothic). Buckhead used his knowledge of the evolution of fonts to argue that the memos were forgeries. He turned out to be right.

Buckhead's critique spread rapidly through the blogosphere. Issues connected with the memos, the then-upcoming federal elections, and how the exposure of the fake memos effectively deflected attention from Bush's actual incomplete National Guard service, were taken up and discussed at length within blogs spanning the political spectrum. Buckhead's critique was subsequently reported in mainstream media, including *The Washington Post*, the *New York Times*, the *LA Times*, *The Australian*, the BBC, and CNN among others. Many of these venues also focused on how the issue was taken up and discussed within the blogosphere itself.

Blogging Project Runway

We think there is a major study to be made of the *Blogging Project Runway* phenomenon (bloggingprojectrunway.blogspot.com). This, however, remains for others to do. All the signs in March 2006 were that this blog constitutes a significant popular culture and participation phenomenon.

For the uninitiated, BravoTV's *Project Runway* is a 'reality' television show in the broad genre of shows like *American Idol* and *Survivor*. It runs as a serialized competition with a focus on fashion design. For each episode the participating designers are given a fashion design challenge and their resulting creations are modelled by their chosen model (who is also up for elimination should 'her' designer not make the next round) and judged by a panel comprising a supermodel (Heidi Klum), a highly regarded fashion magazine editor (Nina Garcia), a famous American designer (Michael Kors) and a guest judge who changes each week. For example, Episode 9 in the second series was called 'Flower Power' and designers were required to create a dress using only natural materials purchased in the New York Flower District and within a tight budget. Each week a model and a designer is eliminated until there is an overall winner. The stakes are high: a sizable cash prize, a luxury car (in the second series), a one-year apprenticeship at Banana Republic (a North American clothing line), and the opportunity to show a collection of designs at the internationally famous and trend-setting New York Fashion Week.

In early June 2005, a blogger named Laura K made a modest initial posting on a new blog called *Blogging Project Runway*, hosted by the free provider, Blogger.com (see bloggingprojectrunway.blogspot.com). Under the post title 'I Miss Project Runway', Laura entered:

> Okay, this might be a bit obsessive but I miss Project Runway [season 1] and I want to be totally prepared for next season [airing December 7]. I intend to blog away after every episode and I hope others will join me with fascinating comments. In fact . . . bring on the comments now if you'd like! I'd appreciate any help I can get. Please pass on any PR news or information – thanks.

> Also, I'd like to keep this Rated G for ALL audiences – I have five children who enjoy reading my blogs. Thanks for your consideration.

> *posted by Laura K at 9:59 PM* 0 comments

Assuming the comments count in the archives is correct, during the first month of the blog's operation only two comments were posted (by Barb and Bathany). Both endorsed Laura's dislike of a particular contestant in the past season's line-up of competing designers. During the second month most of Laura's posts received comments, mainly from Barb, who was the only person to make comments during August 2005. In September there was only one comment (Anonymous) and one comment had been removed by the blog administrator. During September and October 2005 there were more posts – with one of these posts receiving seven comments (some of them seemingly facetious). Barb was absent, but showed up again in November. She was house sitting and had access to Bravo TV again. Laura was responding to some of the comments, expressing delight – 'How great. Another fan' – when one reader described *Project Runway* as her life. There were six posts in November, and a total of six comments. Two of these were for a post that contained a photo of one of the final three contestants from the previous season, Wendy Pepper.

The comments increased dramatically in December 2005 when season two of *Project Runway* began. Laura K's posts were becoming more regular and complex. She began using a high proportion of photographs in her posts as well. Copying and pasting just the posts for December into Word resulted in a 34-page printout. Posts were made on 19 days that month, and around 140 comments were posted that month.

Two months later, at the end of February 2006, three additional contributors to the blog were listed along with Laura. The printout for February's posts alone ran to 138 pages and we counted 3600 comments in all. February was the month in which the competition was whittled down to the final three contestants who would show collections at New York Fashion Week before the final winner was announced. Reading the comments on the days when the episodes were running, or when some 'live' event associated with the show was happening on the blog (e.g., televised interviews with final candidates, or with other personnel from *Project Runway*), reveals very interesting commenting patterns – in some cases individuals are interacting frenetically with others, making comments in a manner akin to chatroom conversations (for example, see Jan the Dan Fan's comments under 'This Post is for the Party' on Wednesday, 22 February 2006).

What is to be said about 'participation' on this blog? This question constitutes a research goldmine, and patterns are likely to change between periods when each new season is running and the periods in between. A preliminary survey we have made of the blog posts and comments from June 2006 to the end of February 2006 has suggested some questions that may be worth asking. These include:

- Which participants abide over time? Who is still visible on the blog in, say, February or June 2006 who was there in June to December 2005 when the blog was just getting started? For example, 'asarkees' made comments in December 2005 and was still commenting in February 2006. Will 'asarkees' still be commenting later in 2006?

- In the case of individuals who make comments and who abide over time and make significant numbers of comments, to what extent does their participation reflect continuity or change? If there is change, what kind of change?
- What categories of participants can be identified? For example, those at home, people from the TV show, the designers, high profile bloggers, the main contributors, people who comment once and not again, people who comment on different kinds of issues, people who set up blogs of their own on the show (do they link to this one and participate visibly in it)?
- Can we identify patterns of interaction between participants? Who seems to be talking to who?
- Which participants seem to get noticed, or otherwise seem to bear significant power? Which ones do not?
- What categories of posts can be identified?
- What categories of comments can be identified – e.g, by theme, quality, uptake or other traces of significance?
- Do comments get taken up in posts? Which, if any? Whose? What about?
- What kinds of artefacts are generated via the posts? What might be done with them, by whom? How are they being taken up by participants (e.g., there are embedded videos, audiofiles, transcripts, etc.)?
- Does the blog go through 'identity' changes and, if so, do these changes seem to be associated with changes in participation?
- What might be said about Laura K (the blog founder) as participant? For example, to what extent and in what ways does the Laura K of June 2005 resemble the Laura K of February 2006 or (projecting ahead from the time of writing) in June 2006 or December 2006?
- To what extent can the participants be identified as *fans*: of the show, of particular designers, of fashion in general, of the blog? How is their participation related to their identity as fan?

The social universe of *Blogging Project Runway* participants and participation is rich, complex and interesting. In one space we have Barb, who was there at the start. Her photo that accompanies her comments reveals an open face with a happy friendly smile. She made one of the two comments to Laura's 'My Barbie' post of 14 December 2005, asking: 'Do you have a degree in Fashion design, Laura? If not, then WHY NOT? It's not too late. I know you sell your clothes now, but why not further the process? Sounds like it was your calling all along.'

In another space we have The Scarlett, who offers a comment on who qualifies as a socialite in response to Laura's post of 30 December, 'Is this a Socialite?' (The post referred to the episode where the designers were told they would be designing for a 'socialite', who turned out to be Nicky Hilton, a young North American woman famous for being famous). In late January The Scarlett makes some candy heart icons available to the blog that are imprinted with names of key figures in *Project Runway* (e.g., Tim Gunn, Santino, Andrae), or slogans signalling particular fandoms (e.g., 'Pick Nick', 'Dan Fan'), along with information on how to add these icons to one's profile or insert them in a blog post. By February The Scarlett is a full blog contributor making regular posts.

In other spaces we have some of the designers themselves and key personnel (e.g., Tim Gunn) associated with the show providing material in the form of emails to Laura (with permission to post the letters to the blog) and generating a virtual carnival of comments in response. In addition, various other people interested in the show and the blog contribute a range of additional materials. These include scanned magazine pages that showcase interviews with one of the season's designer hopefuls, video clips or stills grabbed from each episode, links to online interviews or profile pieces of designers, links to spoofs and remixes associated with key figures in the show, links to photographs of the final collections shown at Fashion Week prior to that particular espisode airing, accounts of real-life encounters with the designers or, even better, with Tim Gunn. (By day Gunn is a professor at Parsons College of Design in New York. He has acquired cult status in the design appreciation world thanks to *Project Runway*.) Manolo the Shoe Blogger (shoeblogs.com; 'Manolo Loves the Shoes') offered blogging advice to Laura, which she took and acknowledged in a post of 29 January 2006: '[Manolo] gave me the most excellent advice for BPR, which I will pass on. He advised me to post frequently and to aim to "amuse." I think of this every day. He also sent me some valuable encouragement when I really needed it.'

And so on.

From our perspective, *Blogging Project Runway* provides a very interesting case of blogging as participation. It is one kind of case and, at least in the US, is a high profile case. It affords insights into particular kinds of participation. So, at a different point on the continuum, do blogs like *Because; We are Ordinary People* (users.livejournal.com/encaustic_) and the tens of millions of other blogs that constitute the blogosphere. If we are to understand new literacies well there is no better place to begin than with weblogs, in all their diversity.

Medicasting: from linking to audio files, to audioblogging, to full-on ubiquitous podcasting and videocasting

With the exception of a brief reference to photoblogging in relation to journaling, our discussion of blogging thus far has emphasized conventional written posts (words plus links). While the majority of links made by bloggers are to other written texts, it is worth mentioning that links to other kinds of media files have been reasonably common for more than a decade now. Basic sound and video capacity has been standard on computers for more than 10 years, and the 'annotated links' format of mid-1990s blogs was not infrequently linked to sound and image files. Until recently, issues to do with bandwidth and file size limited the extent to which these media could be used effectively. But for purposes which justified the time it took to load a file and listen to it, or view it, the capacity to link to audio and video files had a place.

For example, the audio despatches made by Kevin Sites on his blog (kevinsites.net) during the days immediately preceding the US-led invasion of Iraq added a valuable dimension to his blog. Sites' audio casts (e.g., audblog.com/media/2498/11969.mp3, audblog.com/media/2498/12487.mp3, audblog.com/media/2498/12323.mp3) from the Northern Iraq border with Iran in Kurdish villages provided a strong sense of context that would not otherwise have been available, given constraints against making transcriptions in the field.

In the context of writing this book it has similarly been useful for us to make a blog link to an audio file. In 2005 we spoke at a conference in Norway where Lawrence Lessig was one of the other speakers. We had read his published work and were eagerly anticipating his presentation – although were not prepared for the bounty it was to bring – and had taken a recording iPod to the session. In his presentation Lessig gave a much more detailed and illustrated account of his argument about remix as writing than is available elsewhere to this time (March 2006). Lessig's presentation convinced us that remix practices could and should be identified as new literacies. For these reasons we count our recording of Lessig's presentation as among our most valuable academic resources and it has entered into this book as a full participant. At the same time, the fact that it serves as a key reference in this book – it is the work referenced as Lessig 2005 – means that it should be available for scrutiny by anyone who wants to check our use of primary source material. For that reason, we converted the recording to an mp3 format, uploaded it to a streaming server, and created a blog post containing a link to the audio file itself, at everydayliteracies.blogspot.com/ 2006/02/lessig-and-writing-in-remix-culture_20.html.

Around 2003, developments in blogging tools and media file formatting, and the expansion of broadband services and accessibility to high speed internet access created the possibility for full-on audioblogging. This is the idea of entire posts being presented as audio (or video) files, and not simply as embedded links within a post. From the outset, critics recognized potential abuses of the technological capacity to audioblog. In 'An Audioblogging Manifesto', Maciej Cegłowski (2003) advocated remembering some fundamental internet principles before jumping on 'the audioblogging bandwagon'. He argues that much of the force of the web comes from the power to choose that it bestows on users; 'You make your own trails, and your own links. You read what you like and skip the boring bits.' He suggests that audioblogging undermines this choice, turning listeners into a passive audience that cannot skip the boring bits or excerpt from a post effectively. It marginalizes those who can read a language better than they can hear it, and forces accomplished readers to take in information at the speed of speech when they could read it so much faster.

Developments that have occurred since the time Cegłowski published his audioblogging manifesto make it important to distinguish between the concept of a blogger who is *audioblogging* and a blogger who is *podcasting*. For what Cegłowski envisaged happening – namely, a situation in which bloggers would speak their blogs rather than write them – has not happened to any great extent. Rather, what we see happening is an explosion of podcasting and videocasting. While mediacasters *may* use blogs as their preferred interface for podcasting they can in fact use *any* web interface from which syndicated feeds can be made (or even no web interface at all, using instead just a webserver from which the mediacasts are accessed by a syndicated feed command and a mediacast aggregator like *iTunes* or *Firefox* to play each file).

It is important to understand the principle underlying podcasting and videocasting and how this differs from mainstream blogging. In lots of ways this parallels the difference between watching TV and recording a TV programme on a recorder for watching later when it is convenient. The thing about mainstream blogging is that it is an online experience. We log on, go to a blog, interact with it and with any other blogs we choose, update our own blog and then go do something else.

By contrast, podcasting and videocasting – whether done by bloggers or by other kinds of 'casters' – is designed to meet the principle of 'where I want it when I want it'. In other words, why sit at a computer to listen to a concert, watch a video presentation, listen to a conference paper, or whatever, when you can do it on the train to work, or driving home? Moreover, why go to your computer to manually check what is available, when you can have the information automatically fed directly to your computer or internet-enabled mobile device via RSS for you to check and transfer to a listening or viewing device of your convenience at a time of your convenience to be listened to or viewed at a time *and* a place of your convenience? When you have a 40 gigabyte audio or videodevice that interfaces with your computer, that can play through earphones, through audio speakers, or be tuned to a car's sound system, *and that can fit in your pocket*, it is possible to check your mediacast subscriptions at your convenience (or automate your mediacast aggregators to do this for you as well, every time you open the aggregator while logged on to the internet), download them to your device and listen to them or view them anywhere anytime.

When a blogger (or some other 'mediacaster') *podcasts*, they take advantage of the development of high-capacity audio players and high quality audio file types (like mp3 and ogg vorbis files), and the introduction of automated online syndication or subscription services for blogs to begin podcasting. While 'podcasting' is a spin on Apple's iPod music and media file players and 'broadcasting', it is not limited to iPod players as presentation vehicles. Podcasting involves recording a series of spoken language or other sound files in digital format (generally not a music file *per se*; although a podcast could include an entire live *concert*), and then uploading each file to the internet and making them freely available to listeners to download and play on their computer or portable audio file player. Early podcasts tended to comprise public radio shows (cf., npr.org), regular commentaries produced by regional newspapers (e.g., sfgate.com), series of esoteric commentaries by experts and non-experts alike, entire sets of conference presentations, music concert series and other similar events. More recently, podcasting has evolved to include journal-like recordings, such as:

- travelogues (e.g., amateurtraveler.com);
- conversations about anything and everything (e.g., The Dawn and Drew Show at dawnanddrew.com);
- spoken comedy shows (e.g., Keith and the Girl at keithandthegirl.com);
- reviews (e.g., Geek Comic Speak);
- videocasts – often referred to as 'vlogging' or 'vodcasting' – such as those found at stevegarfield.blogs.com/videoblog or ryanedit.blogspot.com (see also www.vlogdir.com).

According to *How Stuff Works* (computer.howstuffworks.com/podcasting1.htm):

> Podcasting was developed in 2004 by former MTV video jockey Adam Curry and software developer Dave Winer. Curry wrote a program, called iPodder, that enabled him to automatically download Internet radio broadcasts to his iPod [instead of having to listen to them as 'streamed' files]. Several developers improved upon his idea, and podcasting was officially born. Curry now hosts a show called *The Daily Source Code* [dailysourcecode.com], one of the most popular podcasts on the Internet.

The syndicated feed dimensions of podcasting are what sets it apart from simple audio file download practices or audiofile streaming. A single audiofile made available for download is not technically a podcast because it is not a syndicated and repeated event, although this distinction is beginning to fade in everyday use of the term 'podcasting'. Podcasting is not like streaming audio either, which requires users to 'tune to' or access a particular internet radio location using their internet browser software. The first successful syndication software (that could be embedded or enclosed within existing feed aggregators) was created by Dave Winer and called RadioUserland. It was designed initially to work with Userland blogs, affirming that blogs are excellent vehicles for podcasting. Each audio file can be posted in chronological order from the least recent to the most recent, and the syndication feed elements of blogs make it easy for users to subscribe to podcasts. Blogs comprising mostly podcasts were referred to originally as 'audioblogs' (along with other kinds of audioblogs already mentioned) before the term 'podcasting' caught on. Radio programmes and television shows have been quick to make use of podcasting as either an alternative listening format (e.g., The National Public Radio Station in the US regularly podcasts weekly shows via its blog), or as an addition to broadcast content (e.g., Tim Gunn's commentaries on each episode of Bravo TV's *Project Runway*).

Radio has taken quickly to the medium. US National Public Radio logged 4 million downloads of its 17 different weekly shows in its first two months of podcasting (paidcontent.org/pc/arch/cat_podcasting.shtml). All 17 appeared in *iTunes'* weekly 'Top 100' podcast rankings, and many of them within the top 10 podcast rankings each week at the time of the report in November 2005 (ibid.). Adam Curry was among the first to become an A-list podcaster (being referred to as the 'Podfather' in some circles). He is a key player in the podcasting portal and index *Podshow* (podshow.com), which organizes podcasts by category (e.g., business, comedy, technology, culture, music, and education). Duke University, North Carolina, hosted what was billed as the world's first podcast of an academic conference in September, 2005 (isis.duke.edu/events/podcasting/casts.html).

Subscribing to a podcast

Method 1: If you have *iTunes* installed on your computer (free from itunes.com), open the program and click on 'Advanced' in the menu bar. Under 'Advanced' click on 'Subscribe to Podcast.' Inside the dialogue box insert the URL for the podcast feed that you want (as provided by the website where the feed is coming through). For example, the podcast feed for Tim Gunn's podcasts that align with BravoTV's *Project Runway* television show is: http://www.bravo tv.com/Podcasts/Project_Runway_2/Episodic.xml. Each audiofile already posted will load automatically in iTunes, and subsequent files will be automatically downloaded as they become available. When each audiofile has downloaded you can listen to it directly in *iTunes*, or else transfer it to a portable device for on-the-go listening.

Method 2: Go to Squeet.com and create an account by following the online instructions. Key in the subscription URL for the podcast feed that you want, or else use the *Project Runway* podcast URL provided above. Click on the 'Add' button. When the file shows up under Feed Title, go across to the right end of the frame and click on the icon immediately to the right of the blue XML button. (If you hold the cursor over this icon you will see it says 'Email me this feed right now'.) Go to your email and look for the sender, DoNotReply @squeet.com. Open the email file (if you have used the *Project Runway* podcast URL this file will be Project Runway: Tim Gunn) and click on the link. This should open a media player and play the audio file for you.

Videocasting, or 'vodcasting' is a relatively new phenomenon and appears to have emerged as a result of low-cost video recording and editing devices and software now widely available. Vodcasting operates on the same principles as podcasting and is quite different to internet webcam streaming in that the latter tends to be locationally fixed (e.g., tied to a computer in a room somewhere) and to occur in real time. Videocasts, on the other hand, can be filmed anywhere it is possible to film action or an event, with the resulting file digitized and stored online for viewers to download at their convenience. Vodcasting is set for take-off as a communication medium following the release of Apple's portable iPod video player. *Wikipedia* identifies the low-budget, high-quality Canadian *Tiki Bar TV* series, first launched on 13 March 2005, as the first independently-produced fiction/ talk show style videocast series (en.wikipedia.org/wiki/Videocasting).

Steve Garfield is widely recognized as being the first do-it-yourselfer to post a videocast online – in November 2004 (see stevegarfield.blogs.com/ videopodcast/2004/11/videopodcast_20.html). His blog, Steve Garfield's Video Blog (stevegarfield.blogs.com), is a good place to start for anyone new to videocasting, and it is interesting to compare the blog as it was at the time of his first videocast and its look, feel and fare today. The dynamics of participation around mediacasting from a weblog are the same as with a conventional blog. Clicking on the permalink for a post in Garfield's blog and copying the URL into a post in one's own blog makes the contents of that post available to anyone visiting your blog. Readers can comment on the blog, and do regularly and, in many cases, enthusiastically. Garfield has a good rate of responses to comments. His blog offers an array of RSS options that make it easy to have his posts delivered direct to one's own computer, for example, by iTunes or Squeet, which then sets up various file sharing and remixing possibilities. Clicking on the Creative Commons Licence Icon on the blog informs participants that they are entitled to make 'derivative works' from Garfield's content. This invites users to take up forms of participation occupying the kind of remix spaces addressed in the previous chapter.

Reflection and discussion

- What is the difference between a blog that includes some audio files and an audioblog? Do you think this distinction is important? If so, why? If not, why not?

- Why have podcasting and vodcasting become so popular? What implications does this have for our conceptions of literacy?

Under these kinds of conditions it is easy indeed to see what is new about new literacies with, respect to the 'ethos stuff' and 'technical stuff' alike. How all this might interface with school-based learning is a question that arises immediately. We make a modest start to considering some dimensions of this question in Part 3.

Classroom Learning Meets New Literacies

CHAPTER 6

Planning Pedagogy for i-mode: Learning in the Age of 'the Mobile Net'

Introduction: the arrival of the mobile Net

During the past decade rapid developments have occurred in the scope, uses and convergence of mobile hand-held computing, communications and information devices and services. These have seen the emergence of what Howard Rheingold (2002) calls the coming of 'the mobile Net' or 'i-mode' (after the pioneering Japanese DoCoMo wireless internet service). The developments leading to the mobile or wireless internet include the convergence of mobile telephony, radio chips, the internet, and location awareness capacity (e.g., Global Positioning Systems).

In a manner reminiscent of Jeff Bezos's distinction between first- and second-phase automation, Rheingold argues that the mobile internet will not just involve doing familiar computing and communication things on the move but, rather, will see people inventing and doing all kinds of things that simply could not previously be done. Learning within formal contexts marks one important site in which such 'inventions' and 'doings' might occur. This chapter will examine early initiatives in school and higher education settings, and suggest some principles and possibilities for pedagogy in the context of the mobile internet.

We are now familiar with mobile phones and their text messaging, camera and video capacities. Texting and photographing with mobile phones are common practices (notably among young people) across diverse social and economic groups in countries worldwide. To date, however, with only a few exceptions (e.g., Japan, and some larger North American and European centres) full wireless internet connectivity has not emerged on anything like the scale of phone texting and photography. Nonetheless, 'always on', large-scale, full internet wireless connectivity is just around the corner. It is projected that most countries will experience the conjoining of mobile communications and the information processing power of networked computers by 2010. If it has not already happened, in the very near future the number of mobile (wireless) devices connected to the internet will surpass the number of internetworked personal computers. It is important to recognize that this trend is not confined to wealthier countries alone. Mizuko Ito (2005b: n.p.) refers to countries outside 'the high tech Euro-America-East Asian axis' using wireless network technologies to 'leap frog from a struggling landline infrastructure into the information age'. In short, i-mode is imminent globally.

Drawing on observations he made during 2000–2 in leading edge telephony cities like Tokyo and Helsinki, and on trends he was tracking in North America, Britain and Western Europe, Rheingold (2002: xv) predicted that 'the personal handheld device market is poised to take the kind of jump that the desktop PC made between 1980 and 1990'. This is the jump from merely being 'a useful toy adopted by a subculture to a disruptive technology [impacting on] every aspect of society' (ibid.). Today's mobile phones, says Rheingold, 'have become tiny multimedia Internet terminals'. Furthermore, the 'infrastructure for global, wireless, Internet-based communication is entering the final stages of development' (ibid.). We are looking at the looming large-scale convergence of 'portable, pervasive, location-sensitive intercommunication devices' that are useful to groups and individuals alike across many facets of their daily lives (ibid.).

Similarly, in a commissioned literature review on learning with mobile technologies, Laura Naismith and colleagues (n.d.: 36) identify current trends in mobile computing as being toward devices that are more and more 'embedded' in our everyday routines, 'ubiquitous and networked'. They anticipate the 'capabilities of mobile phones, PDAs [personal digital assistants], games consoles and cameras [merging] within the next five to ten years to provide a networked multimedia device that is always with you'. Among other consequences, the 'entire internet will become both personal and portable' (ibid.). What this might mean for formal learning is the subject of this chapter.

i-mode, wireless and mobility

We want to clarify as much as possible at the outset what our focus in this chapter is and is not. We are interested in *mobile access to the internet as an integral component in learning work*, pure and simple. We are not interested here in just any kind of mobility, and we are not interested in just any kind of wireless connectivity (e.g., infrared or Bluetooth machine-to-machine connections). It is important to make this point because to date the overwhelming majority of studies about what is referred to widely as 'm-learning' – learning with mobile digital electronic devices – within school education contexts and reported in the literature have not involved internet connectivity. The comprehensive review of learning with mobile technologies conducted by Naismith and her colleagues (n.d.) contains no cases of m-learning initiatives for K-12 education in which internet access – and, particularly the World Wide Web – is mentioned specifically, let alone foregrounded. (The only study in their sample in which the internet is explicitly mentioned involved youth who had left school.)

The academic literature abounds with examples of school students using global positioning system (GPS)-equipped PDAs to engage in games and activities using virtual reality simulations in woodland habitats or open spaces near to schools (e.g., Facer *et al.* 2004; Klopfer and Squire in press), using drill and skill and classroom response applications on PDAs, accessing foreign language activities on mobile phones, sending digital photos by phone to a class or school intranet (Mattila and Fordell 2005), etc. But to date there is little or nothing remotely reflecting Bryan Alexander's (2004: 31) observation of a growing interest in 'new learning spaces such as information commons, where wireless, mobile connectivity admits the full informatic range of the Internet into any niche or conversation'.

That this could be simply an infrastructural issue seems unlikely, given the expense and infrastructure involved in many of the m-learning initiatives documented in the literature. It is true that accessing the internet on a small PDA screen is not optimal, although there are any number of highly portable machines in the range between a PDA and a full-scale laptop and, of these, many are competitively priced alongside smartphones and connectivity plans. Moreover, laptops have hardly been seen as obstacles to mobility in other walks of life. They are highly portable. Rather, Jeremy Roschelle (2003: 265–6) seems to get closer to the heart of the matter in his account of 'unlocking the learning value of wireless mobile devices', where he presents three case studies of mobile technology use in learning. He points out that:

> The most common [mobile] Internet applications can be quite problematic in classrooms. Schools, for example, have been tempted to ban instant messaging because it enables cheating and disruptive behaviour (Pownell and Bailey 2001). Further, attention is a teacher's most precious commodity, and no teacher wants her students' attention focused on messaging with friends outside of class (Schwartz 2003).

Consistently with this, none of Roschelle's case study applications 'require connectivity beyond the local classroom, nor [does] any require a generic messaging capacity that would allow students to "pass notes"' (Roschelle 2003). Interestingly, had this 'ideal' been applied in earlier times it would have meant the removal of paper and pencil from classrooms.

Not surprisingly, when we come to describe current i-mode initiatives in school curriculum and pedagogy we are going to have to 'cheat' a little ourselves and draw on examples that are *like* i-mode but not really, and that are school-*like*, but not really (because they are derived from tertiary or non-formal settings).

Three windows on mobile internetworking, learning and everyday life

We will use three ideas to frame our discussion in this chapter. The first is Rheingold's claim (2002: xix) that by around 2012 a new kind of digital divide will separate those who know how to use the new media to band together to benefit themselves through cooperative-collaborative activity from those who don't.

The second is Naismith *et al.*'s claim (n.d.: 36) that formal learning 'will move more and more outside of the classroom and into the learner's environments, both real and virtual [and that learning] will involve making rich connections within these environments to both resources and to other people'. They advance this claim at the end of their review of literature that addresses learning with mobile technologies.

The third is Chris Bigum's (2002: 130) observation that for more than 20 years now attempts to integrate computing and communications technologies (CCTs) into classrooms have been characterized by schools and school systems trying to find 'educationally useful things to do' with whatever CCTs are in vogue at a given time.

We will briefly contextualize each of these 'windows' by reference to the wider arguments of their respective authors, beginning with Rheingold's (2002) account of 'smart mobs' making use of the mobile net to enhance their lives. Smart mobs are people who cooperate in ways never before possible because they carry devices that possess both communication and computing capacities. Even though the individuals who constitute a smart mob may not actually know each other, they are able to act together for shared purposes. The mobile devices that galvanize and mediate their efforts to act in concert are devices that 'connect them with other information devices in the environment as well as with other people's telephones' (ibid.: xii).

Rheingold argues that under conditions of the 'mobile net' new kinds of smart mob behaviours will become increasingly prevalent and dominant within everyday life. Early examples that have been documented by Rheingold and others (see Knobel and Lankshear 2004b, for examples) include studies of adolescent practices and 'ways' that are mediated by mobile phones (e.g., Kopomaa 2000; Mäenpää 2001; Plant 2001; Ito 2003, 2005b; Bryant *et al.* 2006); mobile or 'ubiquitous' game playing through physical and virtual spaces using mobile phones, PDAs, laptops and home computers (Björk *et al.* 2002; Flintham *et al.* 2003; Lankoski *et al.* 2004; Smith *et al.* 2005); mobile weblogging, podcasting, and 'skyping' or voice-over-internet services (Bradner and Metz 2005; Oliver 2005; see also Godwin-Jones 2005), etc.

Reflection and discussion

Spend some time exploring all the capabilities of your cellphone. Try these:

- Logging onto your service provider's website and sending your mobile phone a text message from there.

- Instant messaging or chatting via your mobile phone.

- Downloading and installing a new ringtone.

- Playing all the games that came already installed on your mobile phone.

- The voice recording function on your phone if it has one.

- Accessing the internet if you're able to (check your account details online to see if you have this enabled on your phone).

- Making a note-to-self on the note function (if you have it).

- Taking a phone camera picture, and using Bluetooth (a wireless data transfer system a little like infrared), email from your phone, or your phone cable to transfer your pictures to your computer.

- Changing your screen's theme.

- Changing your screen's wallpaper (try using a picture you've taken with your phonecam).

- Sorting out how SIM cards work and how it is possible to transfer them among different compatible phones.

- Getting the hang of predictive text keying.

- Seeing if your phone can double as an MP3 player, and adding some music files to it.

- The walkie-talkie function on your phone if it is enabled.

Do you think good use could be made of these various features in a school setting? If so, how and why? If not, how not and why not?

Many forms of smart mob behaviour are quite mundane or, what Ito (2005b) calls 'pedestrian'. Ito's observations revealed that Japanese teenagers and twentysomethings 'usually do not bother to set a time and place for their meetings. They exchange as many as 5 to 15 messages throughout the day that progressively narrow in on a time and place, two points eventually converging in a coordinated dance through the urban jungle' (Ito 2003: 2). In this way, they arrange to meet 'on the run', turn shopping expeditions into contexts for group communications, and generally stay in touch with the members of their personal community (often four or five very close friends). As Ito explains, for young people in Japan '[t]o not have a keitai [mobile phone] is to be walking blind, disconnected from just-in-time information on where and when you are in the social networks of time and place' (ibid.). In i-mode, time and place become fluid and flexible – negotiable on the fly: if you have a phone you can be late; much worse than being late is to forget your phone or allow the battery to die (ibid.).

While such behaviours may seem mundane, they nonetheless account for a lot of the 'stuff' of human life. They add up to how people *do* their lives. Being able to negotiate times and places on the run may be a key to reducing stress, making meetings more enjoyable, consolidating relationships, and so on, as well as contributing to more functional values like being more efficient with time and other resources. Rheingold also envisages diverse forms of cooperation on the run between people previously unacquainted with one another. An example might be where a friend or friendship network acquaintance brokers a ride by car for another person at short notice. A knows that B is driving to X that afternoon and that C needs to get there. A can vouch for C and reach B who is already on the road. Alternatively, a planned dinner at a restaurant is in jeopardy because of a reservation error. An alternative restaurant of similar kind and quality and in the vicinity is located via internet information accessed by phone or PDA (personal digital assistant, like a Blackberry or iPaq) and the venue is changed and the booking made on the run.

Less mundane examples of smart mob behaviour might be linked to professional life, citizenship and so on. For example, a college professor receives a message from a colleague at a conference where an international expert is going to be presenting a keynote address on X later that day. The professor knows of two other colleagues with courses that deal with X and text-messages the conference convenors to ask about the possibility of recording and podcasting the conference. This kind of example could be varied for contexts of participation in environmental groups, political lobbies, news reporting. Of course, it is obvious that there is more involved here than just the mobile net. Smart mob behaviour presupposes membership in networks. Without being socially networked there are strict limits to the potential attaching to being technologically networked. As we have seen, however, the tools of techno-networking are, precisely, tools of social networking *par excellence*.

The claim by Naismith and colleagues that learning will increasingly move out of classrooms and into virtual and physical spaces for learners to make rich connections to people and non-human resources is informed by an expansive conception of mobile learning advanced by Vavoula and Sharples (2002: 152). This view identifies three dimensions on which learning can be seen as mobile:

> [L]earning is mobile in terms of *space*, i.e. it happens at the workplace, at home, and at places of leisure; it is mobile between *different areas of life*, i.e. it may relate to work demands, self-improvement, or leisure; and it is mobile with respect to *time*, i.e. it happens at different times during the day, on working days or on weekends.
>
> (cited in Naismith *et al.* n.d.: 7, emphases ours)

Naismith *et al.*'s review of literature focuses mainly on uses of personal hand-held devices like mobile phones and PDAs within a dynamic range of learning activities. Their concept of activities highlights the *active* connotation of mobility. It is not a matter simply of using mobile devices to support learning activities that are currently supported by more static arrangements (Naismith *et al.* n.d.: 9). Examples include learners accessing simulations via PDAs, in some cases within habitats analogous to those the simulations are concerned with (such as woodlands), or using mobile devices to access databases for making observations in community settings. It is a natural progression from this 'context' of discussion to a 'wider than classroom' conception of formal learning.

Bigum's observation about the tendency for school uptake of new technologies to proceed on the basis of trying to find educationally useful work for the tools to do is made in the context of arguing for a 'knowledge production' approach to school-based learning. We will return to this theme later in the chapter. Meanwhile, it is worth noting some key claims in Bigum's account of why schools have tended to proceed as they do and what some of the consequences of this are. He identifies three important assumptions about new technologies in school-based learning, all of which he questions. One is the assumption that CCTs are good in and of themselves and, hence, the more that they can be deployed in classroom learning, the better education will be. A second is that new technologies are mainly about information. This is not surprising

> [since] schools have always acted largely as *consumers* of knowledge and information. From text books, to material available on the Internet, information flows into schools far outweigh the information that flows out. The relationships that schools have with the world outside is therefore largely framed by their consumption of information and knowledge.
> (Bigum 2002: 135)

The third is the assumption that the educational uses of new technologies in classroom learning are now well understood, and that integrating CCTs into learning is mainly a matter of 'mastering the intricacies of each new technology as it appears' (ibid.: 135). This sets in train a never-ending logic of looking for seemingly useful things to do with new waves of technology. The end result is massive amounts of 'digital busy work' (ibid.), a lot of 'old wine in new bottles' (cf., Lankshear and Bigum 1999), and a lot of whistles and bells 'whizzbangery' that generates such top heavy, quaint uses of new technologies as designing webpages to retell stories. There is no reason to expect the current moment of development in hand-held devices to fare any better in schools than have preceding waves of digital technologies if the underlying assumptions guiding their curricular and pedagogical take up remain intact.

Mobile digital technologies

The scope of mobile digital technologies discussed in relation to formal learning mediated by the internet varies considerably from project to project and author to author in accordance with their different orientations, emphases and purposes. In this section we will locate our own approach in relation to two alternatives.

One of these is the position adopted by Naismith *et al.* (n.d.), which we find interesting and useful at the conceptual level. They develop a classification of mobile technologies along two axes: 'Portable—Static' and 'Personal—Shared'. Most (although not all) of the technologies they identify as mobile (and all the ones their concrete cases deal with) fall into the quadrant formed by the 'Personal'—'Portable' intersection. They specifically identify PDAs, mobile phones, games consoles, tablet PCs and laptop computers. In the 'Portable'—'Shared' quadrant they identify kiosks (the 'portability' being a function of the learner's mobility through space). Classroom response systems are located in the 'Personal'—'Static' quadrant because while they are small and are often assigned to individual learners, their use is confined to the classroom, although users can move around within that space. These include things like wireless PDAs that students use to record responses to tasks or tests. Most tools falling in the 'Static'—'Shared' quadrant do not qualify as mobile technologies. In the event, with the exception of a drill and skill maths game using a Nintendo hand-held games system, the concrete cases actually discussed by Naismith *et al.* are confined to uses of PDAs and mobile phones.

The second position is a particularly high tech option being used in a project currently under development in Finland with primary schools in the wireless city of Oulu. The project portends the kind of device convergence anticipated by Naismith *et al.* and shows how far advanced this convergence has already gone so far as developing a complex *tool* for networked school-based learning is concerned. The 'MOOP' (an m-learning environment) project is being developed as a public–private sector collaboration between three schools in Oulu, the Education Department, and three companies (Nokia, Elisa and Viestimaa). We will discuss the project in the following section, but of immediate interest is the 'technology' component. This comprises a purpose-designed mobile phone networked to a project local area network, or LAN. The phone uses the

Symbian S60 operating system and with a specially designed interface. It comes with text, photographic, voice, video and GPS (i.e., global positioning system) capacities. It also has a 'walkie-talkie' type function for teachers to communicate directly with learners in the field without having to use the main calling function. Students in the field can log-on with a user name/password and make observations and gather information using any of the media functions. The GPS locating information is used to navigate physically to points designated for gathering information and programmed into the phone. Data collected as digitized speech, text, photo image or video can then be transmitted directly from the field to a server, from which the information can be transmitted between the various mobile terminals (phones), web browser and data base. Data collected in the field can be edited in the field prior to learners sending it to the server. Thereafter the data are available to them via computers in the school lab or via their own computers (via login) (Mattila and Fordell 2005: n.p.). In effect, then, the phone is a networked multimedia data collection device that accommodates in a single piece of hardware multiple more common everyday devices of the kinds we will talk about later. In terms of its 'Whizzbangery Quotient' (WQ), it is a matter of Point, Snap/Press/Click, Edit, Save, Send – from field to remote server to data base in a heartbeat. While the device being used in the MOOP project does not employ full internet capability but only a local area network, full internet capability could be employed to extend the accessible information base almost infinitely.

Our own position varies from the above in two important respects, namely, the range of devices in question and ownership. With respect to the range of devices we include such things as digital voice recorders, digital cameras and video recorders, thumbdrives, iPods and other mp3 players. These are devices that cannot directly link to the internet, but that can readily upload information to devices that *can* link to the internet.

Our reasons for including such devices are in part related to our position on 'ownership'. There are two sides to this. In the example of MOOP and the examples cited by Naismith and her colleagues, the equipment is the property of the school. It is set up by the school, maintained by the school and owned by the school. One implication of this is that if a school does not have the equipment, the students are not going to be able to use mobile networking for learning on the run, whereas if they are at liberty to use their own 'toys' and are willing to do so, such constraints need not apply. The extra devices we have mentioned are devices that are widely owned by young people. The other side to the matter of ownership is that while some young people might choose *not* to implicate their own personal digital devices in school-based learning, others might positively *welcome* the opportunity to integrate artefacts that can have deep personal meaning to them into practices beyond those they use them for in their own time and space. There is also an issue of trust in here. The default mode is that learners can't be permitted to use their own gadgets because they may become disruptive or, worse still, the students might use them in 'unapproved' ways. Our personal position on this is that it is time to extend some trust, and that given the will to do so, teachers, parents and students could easily enough arrive at some workable arrangements – at least until it were evident that extending this kind of trust is not warranted.

Our other reason (besides the matters of ownership) for extending the range of devices has to do with the way 'school gear' is set up. Whether they are high on WQ (Whizzbangery Quotient), like the MOOP 'phone', or not, educational hardware usually comes with built-in assumptions and agendas that can constrain creative problem solving, pre-empt 'making do' and, as a result, sap initiative. Working out how some collective personal gadgets could be mobilized to tackle a learning task involves precisely the kind of imagination, trial and error creativity that 'boffins' and other experimenters have engaged in to give us the wireless internet – indeed, *any* internet – in the first place.

For these reasons we prefer to take as wide a perspective as possible on what count as mobile technologies for the purposes of formal learning mediated by use of the mobile internet.

Current i-mode initiatives in curriculum and pedagogy

In this section we will briefly describe three fairly typical 'i-mode-like' initiatives that are either school-based or are of a kind that could be, and will comment upon them in light of our three framing statements.

The MOOP interactive m-learning project

The MOOP project involves primary school students using a GPS-equipped mobile phone in field settings to make observations relevant to a pre-set problem, analyse their surroundings in light of that problem, and communicate within groups in the process of resolving the problem (Mattila and Fordell 2005). The pedagogical principles identified as underpinning the project are inquiry learning, information gathering and knowledge building skills, creative problem solving, and interactive and cooperative learning. The knowledge building model employed begins from the question 'What is your topic?' (based on a problem framed by the teacher), and proceeds to the learner documenting what s/he knows about it (e.g., using mind maps), and what information s/he obtains from the text book. Once a plan for the topic has been made and approved by the teacher the learner considers the kind of observational information required, where it can be obtained locally, etc., and then goes to the field. Observations in the form of photos, speech, and text are collected using the phone, and are saved and refined on the phone itself, then sent to the network learning platform at the school. By means of group activity and individual work the learners resolve their problems and write the study up, observing an 'Update, Edit, Check, Publish' sequence. The final outcome is construed as 'constructed knowledge' rather than 'memorizing facts'.

A single practical example is provided: 'According to legend a Mr Taavetti Lukkarinen was hung from this tree. Explore to see whether this is likely.' The learners are required to construct a context that is anchored to the curriculum and to real life. 'The pupils have to philosophise to form the final answer by themselves' (ibid.). They find that the tree in question has only been there a short time and so it is unlikely that the legend is true.

While it is not entirely fair to comment on a project in the light of a single example, even if it is the *only* example provided, the obvious question to ask in this case is how and why resolving this kind of problem requires the elaborate technological set up devised for the project. To be sure, the learners are getting out into the field. But the example looks like a classic case of what Bigum refers to as 'digital busy work' and of having to find educational things for the technology to do. Moreover, the kind of collaboration described in the project is quite different from the kind of banding together for cooperative benefit that Rheingold attributes to smart mobs. The latter comes from 'real life' in a serious sense of the term. The example in the project is based on pure 'pretend'.

'Nomadic' web content in a museum

In a delightfully candid discussion, Sherry Hsi (2003) reports a study investigating participants' experiences with using a hand-held computer with a wireless connection to a website established to augment learning experiences in a hands-on museum (The Exploratorium in San Francisco). The hand-held computer served as a kind of electronic guidebook based on a concept of nomadic inquiry. This is the idea that as humans move between different physical spaces and settings they get access to different kinds of experiences, resources, and perspectives related to knowable phenomena. New contexts may generate new kinds of 'driving questions' or possible explanations and so on. In a hands-on museum the exhibits present a context for doing some learning work. But what users can make of this context will be a function of the set of interactions they can conceive of initiating with the exhibit. This set of interactions can potentially be enhanced by bringing a virtual environment into play with the physical environment. This amounts to a virtual environment that is complex and 'nomadic', representing different spaces (whether a game space or an information space; a question space or an explanation space). Web content for each of several exhibits was developed, and each hand-held wireless computer was equipped with a sensor that triggered the appropriate URL for that exhibit. Once the user went to the relevant webpage associated with that exhibit, they could move between a range of options (listen to information, view videos, access suggestions or questions related to how they might interact with the exhibit, and so on). The aim was to achieve a seamless integration of the physical and virtual that provided new kinds of interactions prompting new hypotheses, explanations, and knowledge of phenomena.

Interestingly, the results obtained from a study population of students and other volunteer 'explainers', science teachers, and regular museum members were mixed. Participants reported a sense of isolation (from other people, the social scene of interactivity around the exhibit, and from the exhibit itself). For example, 'It was more like you were interacting more with the handheld than the exhibit. That [the handheld] becomes almost the primary exhibit'; 'I didn't really notice other people'; 'I was actually surprised by how much I didn't realize I was in a museum ... which sort of takes away from the experience' (ibid.: 314). Participants also reported certain difficulties with reconciling and integrating the virtual and physical contexts. On the other hand, most said the web content encouraged them to try new ways of interacting with the exhibit and to engage with a range of new ways of thinking about these exhibits.

Here again, the version of internet mobility involved is the antithesis of smart mob collaboration. The individual user is isolated and cocooned within a menu-driven set of stimuli, not socially networked collaboration. Users are certainly physically 'in the field' and away from the classroom, but equally, they are to a large extent 'away' from the museum. Some of the kinds of limitations described will doubtless be resolved as content designers become more experienced in integrating the physical and the virtual. Nonetheless, it is difficult to escape the view that the developers were striving to pack as much 'educational' use as possible into a tool they thought should probably be useful. The alternative approach would be to begin from a set of grounded experiences of people in the museum and seeking out where (if anywhere) having access to a hand-held device might actually augment the museum experience. Such grounded information might lead to finding that the device might be a very good tool for doing (just) X or, perhaps, X and Y. Why not, one wonders, just have a wireless space where people can use on demand the abundant resources on the internet to see what exists in cyberspace that is relevant to the exhibit? That would be equally nomadic, just user-driven rather than hand-fed.

Mobile blogging the 399th Sàmí winter market

Bryan Alexander (2004) cites the mobile blogging (moblogging) of the 399th Sàmí winter market in the north of Sweden during February 2004 by a team of four students from Umeå University (blog.humlab.umu.se/ jokkmokk2004). The market, which is held on the first Thursday through Sunday in February in the Lapland town of Jokkmokk near the Arctic Circle, has been an annual event since 1605. The students drove to Jokkmokk, recorded concerts, interviewed participants, survived a network crash which prevented them streaming the closing concert live – although they obtained permission to audio blog it for a period after the festival – and posted material on the blog as audio files, video clips, photos, other graphics, and text: 'Students applied their academic learning about the Sàmí to the real world, interviewing participants, conducting follow-up digital research on the fly, and uploading and expanding on commentary online' (Alexander 2004: 31).

The outcome is a cultural artefact of depth and richness, that conveys far more about the event than any of the commercial or public relations sites manage. One of the blog posts relates receiving

> an email from one of our readers in Australia who is also planning a trip to Sweden. She got an email from someone she met at her son's swimming club recently. They are both interested in Sweden and this other woman sent our reader a link that she had received in a newsletter from Sweden. In this newsletter there was information about a website in Sydney which contained news about Sweden (and the Jokkmokk moblogging project). Our reader summarized the chain as follows: news from Brisbane about news from Sweden about news from Sydney about news in Sweden.

This is, at the very least, an extreme field trip. It is a trip, however, that was made with and for a much larger public than the participants alone. Rich as a resource that can be drawn on by people from diverse communities and with diverse interests anywhere in the world for all manner of purposes, the blog reflects collaboration that is close indeed to the heart of smart mobbery – including getting permission to stream the concert after the event when the network in Jokkmokk went down. Participants had all the right tools for the job and could adapt on the fly to a major glitch in their plans. The cultural experience rather than the tools were in the saddle. The result is a potentially valuable exercise in knowledge production.

Reflection and discussion

Visit the Smartmobs.com website and survey some recent developments in i-mode applications. Explore these in terms of both use and technical development.

To what extent do you think any of these applications have significant implications for literacy education? Which ones, and why? If none, why not?

Some principles and criteria for planning 'pedagogy for i-mode'

Having outlined and commented on some typical examples of current initiatives, we now turn to some general questions about how formal pedagogy and curriculum ought to take account of i-mode, and on what basis (which principles, what criteria, etc.) decisions about potential uses of the mobile net should be made. Clearly, curriculum and pedagogy must not be hostages to technological change at the level of artefacts. To a large extent this has been the history of CCTs in schools to date, with the result that all sorts of contrived practices have been created in order to find ways of accommodating new technologies to classroom 'ways'. As Bigum (2002, 2003a) observes, this has not worked. It has 'wasted' the potential of new technologies to provide bridges to new forms of social and cultural practice that school education could and should be interested in, like critical engagement with new literacies. It has simultaneously 'wasted' the potential that new technologies have for doing more efficiently the kinds of familiar 'knowledge things' that schools *should* be engaging learners in – such as forms of analysis and synthesis associated with evaluating and producing knowledge in expert-like ways.

To advance our argument, we will identify some educationally appropriate principles and criteria on which to base judgements and decisions concerning curriculum and pedagogy in relation to the mobile internet. These reflect the status of formal education as ethically informed practice – such that education does not become simply a reflex of the values and interests of the most powerful social groups – whilst simultaneously holding education accountable to a society's legitimate claims upon it. The entire history of educational thought is, of course, nothing less than the collective record of the search for such principles and criteria. So we won't pretend to resolve the matter here! On the other hand, several educational principles and related criteria derived from a sociocultural perspective and to which we are committed seem especially relevant to our concerns here. Four stand out in particular. These are:

- the principle of efficacious learning;
- the principle of integrated learning;
- the principle of productive appropriation and extension in learning;
- the principle of critical learning.

We will describe these briefly in turn.

The principle of efficacious learning

According to this principle, for learning to be efficacious it is necessary that what somebody learns *now* is connected in meaningful and motivating ways to mature or insider versions of *Discourses*. Discourses are understood as sets of related social practices composed of particular ways of using language, acting and interacting, believing, valuing, gesturing, using tools and other artefacts within certain (appropriate) contexts such that one enacts or recognizes a particular social identity or way of doing and being in the world (Gee *et al.* 1996: 4). This involves thinking of education and learning in terms not of schools and children (place-related and age-specific) but, instead, in terms of human lives as *trajectories* through diverse social practices and institutions (ibid.). To learn something is to progress toward a fuller understanding and fluency with doing and being in ways that are recognized as proficient relative to recognized ways of 'being in the world'. Participating in Discourses are things we get more or less right or more or less wrong. Mature or insider forms of Discourses are, so to speak, 'the real thing': the way a Discourse is 'done' by 'mature users' who 'get it right'. They are 'authentic' rather than 'pretend' versions of the social practices in question. In this sense, for learning at times to be efficacious, it must involve doing something that genuinely puts the learner on the right track toward becoming a competent participant in 'the real thing' – whatever the Discourse in question might be.

The principle of integrated learning

From a sociocultural perspective, learning is integrated to the extent that three conditions are met. These all relate to the key idea that learning is inseparable from Discourses.

The first condition is that integrated learning occurs *inside* a practice rather than at a distance (as where one learns something *about* a practice at remove from participation in the practice itself, with a view to applying the learning *in situ* at some subsequent time). This is not to say that worthwhile learning cannot be decontextualized and subsequently applied; only that to this extent the learning is not integrated in the sense intended here.

The second condition extends the first. Learning is integrated when the various 'bits' of social practices that go together to make up a practice as a whole – and where the various 'bits' of related social practices that go together to make up a Discourse as a whole – are learned in their *relationships* to one another, as a consequence of learning them *inside* the practice(s). In integrated learning we learn to put the various 'bits' (the speaking bits, tool and artefact-using bits, action/behaviour bits, valuing and believing and gesturing and dressing, etc., bits) 'whole' and 'live'. We learn them *organically* in their relationships to each other, not as 'chunks' to be articulated later.

The third condition is that our learning is *the more integrated* the *less* it clashes with who and what we are and do in the other discursive dimensions of our lives. The less the 'identity' we are called to be in *this* learning instance is in conflict with the identities we are called to be – and *are at home with* – in the rest of our lives, the more integrated the learning can be. Steve Thorne (2003) provides an interesting example of how strongly students can feel about issues associated with the use of new technologies in learning. He describes a French foreign language course in which part of the course grade was based on a component requiring students to email a keypal in France. One student (Grace) chose to opt out of this component (and receive a lower grade as a result) because she associated emailing with 'communication between power levels and generations' (Thorne 2003: 7). She said emailing was what you did with teachers or parents. With friends you use Instant Messaging. Grace considered email an inappropriate cultural tool for the kinds of exchanges occurring between the US learners and their French keypals. Trying to get Grace to learn conversational-friendship French by means of email could not be *integrated* in this sense. Grace was, in effect, being asked to 'mean against' some of her other social identities and values that were important to her. Other things being equal, the less conflict learners experience with their other social identities, the more effectively and willingly they learn.

The principle of productive appropriation and extension in learning

This principle is partly an extension of the integrated learning principle, and partly the time-honoured principle that learning should build on what learners already know and have experienced. With respect to the first aspect, this principle involves looking for ways to reduce or ameliorate conflict between social identities during learning. For example, if an educationally acceptable appropriation of Grace's cultural construction of age–peer/friendship communication (e.g., via IM) could be made within the French course, this would help integrate and strengthen learning by putting cultural, personal, technological, and epistemological aspects in sync.

With respect to the second aspect, if learners already know how to perform discursive roles and tasks that can legitimately be carried over into new discursive spaces, this can be used to advantage to enable learning and proficiency in a new area. For example, knowing how to archive downloaded music onto an mp3 player like an iPod for personal entertainment purposes can readily be transferred to archiving interview data that has been recorded digitally for research purposes, without compromising either practice. The kinds of clash between cultures of use evident in the example of Grace are not likely to arise in this case. Of course, this aspect of the present principle – building learning on, and integrating into present learning, relevant knowledge and competence the learner already has – is practically self-evident. It is certainly widely recognized by educators. At the same time, it is systematically ignored or subverted on a massive scale within classroom learning.

The principle of critical learning

In various places, Gee (1996, 2004; Gee *et al.* 1996) states very clearly a major dilemma with respect to effective learning construed socioculturally as processes of achieving fluent mastery of Discourses. This concerns the fact that becoming fluent in a Discourse is best achieved through processes of learning *inside* the Discourse. But the more effective this learning is, the less critically reflective the learner's perspective on the Discourse will be. The more effective learning inside a Discourse is, the more deeply 'indoctrinatory' it is likely to be. As Gee notes, Discourses cannot countenance criticism from within, since that would be to invite their own demise or transcendence.

This is problematic if we believe education should help prepare learners to understand the limitations and constitutive nature of each and every Discourse, and to be committed to and capable of playing active roles in trying to shape social practices in progressive and expansive ways on the basis of what they believe and value. From this standpoint, it is necessary to create spaces for developing and negotiating differing points of view on social practices, social identities, social institutions, and the like. This means creating spaces for experiencing different and competing Discourses and deciding how to handle this divergence.

Reflection and discussion

- Which, if any, of these principles do you think are sound from an educational perspective?

- In the case of those you think are sound, what are your reasons?

- In the case of those you think are unsound, what are your reasons?

- Do you prefer other principles? If so, which ones, and why do you think they are better?

Toward criteria for decision-making

These principles suggest a number of criteria for helping us decide on the extent to which and manner in which characteristically *contemporary* literacies – comprising technologies, artefacts, practices, and cultures of use – engaged by young people beyond the school might become integral components of school-based learning in ways that *strengthen* education. These include (but are not exhausted by) criteria such as their conduciveness to 'promoting approximations to expert practice', 'authentic/non-contrived uses', 'collaborative activity', 'recognition of distributed knowledge and expertise', 'efficacy for *in situ* use', 'capacity to mediate whole practices', and so on. If some of these criteria are not immediately apparent as derivations from our principles, the links become readily apparent when we acknowledge that Discourses are distributed networks of knowledge, expertise, competence. Without collaboration and expertise, there can be no Discourses, and without Discourses, there can be no learning.

This brings us to a crucial point in the argument we are trying to develop, which concerns the *purposes* of school-based learning and participation in school-based Discourses and the relationship between school-based learning and participation in the 'mature' Discourses to which the school Discourses are presumed to relate. Apart from when it is a senseless activity, learning is always 'a process of entry into and participation in a Discourse'

(Gee *et al.* 1996: 15). School learning certainly involves entry into school Discourses, but the further question is: 'To what end?'

If school learning is simply for initiation into school Discourses, that is one thing, and we are left without a significant problem here – since there would be no reason why school learning *should* have to take account of non-school practices. If, on the other hand, we believe that school-based Discourses of learning (school projects, school history, school science, physical education, etc.) should contract significant relationships to 'mature' Discourses beyond the school, we have an issue of major proportions. This is because schools 'separate learning from participation in mature Discourses' and, moreover, 'render the connection entirely mysterious' (ibid.: 15). Hence, our immediate questions about whether and how aspects of practices like blogging, instant messaging, text messaging, and generally being in 'i-mode' can, with integrity, be taken into account in school-based learning becomes a subset of a much larger and more fundamental question.

We take the view that school Discourses of learning can and should relate transparently and efficaciously to learners' lives as trajectories through diverse social practices in myriad social institutions and, to that extent, should seek progressive approximations to 'mature' or 'insider' versions of Discourses.

Knowledge-producing schools: a grassroots initiative on the side of education

In looking for clues as to how school-based learning might take educational account of the kinds of examples we have described in the core of this book we find some exciting possibilities inherent in a new initiative being developed in Australia (Bigum 2002, 2003b; Lankshear and Knobel 2003: Ch. 8). The initiative began from work by Chris Bigum with principals, teachers and students in a small number of schools in regional and remote parts of Queensland. The protagonists shared an interest in two related questions. One was how learning might become more about producing rather than consuming knowledge (and, to this extent, more connected to the everyday lives of school communities). The other was how to *deschool* classroom uses of new technologies – to move away from trying to find things for communication and computing technologies to do within the established routines and ways of classroom learning.

A key premise underlying the development of knowledge-producing schools (KPS) is that school uses of communication and computing technologies are based on a mindset that understands new technologies in terms of information (Bigum 2002; Schrage 2001). Bigum (2003b) notes that the many changes associated with communication and computing technologies (CCTs) that we have witnessed in such spheres as business, entertainment and commerce have been described as a result of 'the information revolution'. However,

> as Michael Schrage (2001) suggests, this is a dangerously myopic lens with which to view these changes. He argues, for instance that to 'say that the Internet is about "information" is a bit like saying that "cooking" is about oven temperatures; it's technically accurate but fundamentally untrue.' Schrage goes on to argue that 'the biggest impact these technologies have had, and will have, is on *relationships* between people and between organizations'. Seeing CCTs in terms of a *relationship* revolution is perhaps not as catchy some of the other descriptions in common use but it provides a way of thinking about CCTs in schools that opens up some useful possibilities.
>
> (Bigum 2003b: 5)

From this standpoint, schools can consider how communication and computing technologies might be used productively in terms of new relationships that could be developed and mediated using these technologies, rather than in terms of information delivery or of doing old things in new ways. The model of knowledge-producing schools builds on the idea that, as knowledge *producers* in a new and significant sense, schools can develop and consolidate new kinds of relationships within and outside the school.

The concept of knowledge producers/production in question here needs clarifying. There is a sense in which students have always been involved in producing knowledge within the classroom. But this is almost always an artificial, 'pretend', non-expert-like production of 'knowledge'. It is dominated by what Bigum calls a 'fridge door' mindset for student work – the idea that the teacher sets a task, students complete it, the teacher assesses it, and the student takes it home where it might be 'published' temporarily on the fridge door. There is no real problem, no real demand, no real need, no real knowledge *product*.

The knowledge-producing schools model actively tries to move beyond the fridge door approach. The schools in question have begun to develop new and interesting relationships with groups in their local communities, by engaging in processes that generate products or performances that are valued by the constituencies for which they have been produced. An important part of negotiating the production of such knowledge is that the product or performance is something that students see as being valued by the consumer or audience of their work. The students know their work is taken seriously, and that it has to be good or else it will not be acceptable to those who have commissioned it. The level of engagement and the quality of work and student learning to date have been routinely impressive. These are not teacher projects with peripheral student involvement. Rather, they are projects – in the sense in which developing and producing commercial movies or motor cars are described as projects – that are given to students as problems to solve or, as has frequently been the case, problems the students have raised with a view to solving them. The following examples are typical:

- The principal of one school was invited to talk about developments at the school to a state conference of primary school principals. She commissioned a group of Year 7 students to document the use of CCTs in the school on video and to produce a CD. The students planned the shoot, collected the footage using a digital camera, did the editing, voice-overs, supplied music and credits and burned a CD-ROM. The students then presented the product to an audience of over two hundred principals at the conference.

- Following a classroom incident, a group of Year 7 students designed and produced (using presentation software) a CD-ROM to offer advice to students about bullying. They scripted, filmed and edited six role plays, each with three alternative outcomes to illustrate the consequences of what they labelled 'weak', 'aggressive', and 'cool' responses to a bully. They launched the interactive CD-ROM at a public meeting at the school and have marketed the CD-ROM to other schools.

- Groups of Year 6 students worked in collaboration with the local cattle sale yards to produce a documentary of the history of the sale yards for a Beef Expo in 2003. They video-interviewed representatives of different sectors in the cattle industry, recorded *in situ* footage of activities, provided voice-overs and bridges between sequences, and edited the components to produce the documentary as a CD-ROM. The product CD-ROM was used at an international beef festival and by the local council to promote the region.

- A group of students interviewed local 'characters' and filmed them at tourist sites in an old mining town with high unemployment and that is trying to establish itself as a tourist location. The students shot the film, edited it, and burned the product to CD. The data will be available at various sites around the town on touch-screen computers so visitors can get a sense of what the town has to offer (cf. Bigum 2003b: 5–6).

It is important to briefly note four points here. First, these examples come from the primary or elementary school level. The knowledge-producing schools initiative involves learners from their first year at school onwards to Year 7. Obviously, engaging in knowledge production with such young learners would be extremely difficult if it rested primarily on *written* language. Accordingly, the schools from which our examples are drawn have established practices of 'writing with cameras' – recording digital visual images, still and video – alongside formal initiation into print literacy. They have invested very modestly in communication and computing technologies, with no more than two or three computers per class and a small central facility that supports image editing. In some classes, students routinely employed digital cameras to do their work.

Second, the strategy of writing with cameras quickly led to the development of a broad base of expertise by teachers and students in preparing audiovisual presentations, usually stored on CD-ROM or VHS tape. This is not, however, expertise devoted to using digital imaging equipment *per se*. Communication and computing technologies are not the *focus* or purpose of the work. They are media that play useful roles in supporting student work that has genuine value to outside groups and audiences. According to Bigum (ibid.), the fact that the communication and computing technologies provide learners with an additional mode of expression has been a pivotal factor in the success of most of the projects (and not all projects employ communication and computing technologies).

Third, the knowledge-producing schools approach is based on a view of education as a 'whole of community responsibility'. It contracts deep and committed relationships between the schools and their communities. These relationships go multiple ways. It is not simply a matter of community groups having the role of being the source of problems and demand for projects. On the contrary, the community provides an essential source of relevant expertise: the expertise that is needed for the student work to approximate to proficient performance in 'mature' Discourses. The beef industry does not want a 'pretend documentary'. It has to be good or it will be rejected. There is no space for patronizing here. In fact, the entrée to digital visual media work in one of the schools came via a student teacher with a sibling who was employed in digital video production and who provided free expertise. As Bigum puts it:

> Not only has community become a source of problems on which to work but also students access specialist communities for support in working on some of their projects. As Moore and Young (2001: 459) recently suggest, there are now strong grounds for 'reorienting debates

about standards and knowledge in the curriculum from attempts to specify learning outcomes and extend testing to the role of specialist communities, networks and codes of practice'.

(2003b: 7)

Finally, there is a sense in which many of the components of these examples, taken individually, are not new. Nor is there anything especially remarkable about the projects. The novelty of knowledge-producing schools is that 'all of these elements are drawn together under a new logic: that of schools as producers of knowledge as sites where serious knowledge production and research can occur' (ibid.). The invitation here is 'instead of thinking of a school as a place where 300 young people attend to be provided with an education, try to think about a school as a research site populated with 300 ... researchers' (ibid.: 10).

Reflection and discussion

- To what extent do you think a KPS approach, or something like it, could work in your professional context?

- What ideas do you have for how such an approach could be improved or made to work under conditions with which you are familiar?

- If you wanted to take a KPS approach to learning, where would you begin? What kind of project might be possible in your context? What expert resources would be needed and how could you access them?

Some vignettes of non-contrived possibility: mobile, cooperative, contemporary, expert knowledge production

This account of the KPS initiative provides a springboard from which the following kinds of fictional vignettes are but a short and plausible jump.

Vignette 1

Soloranzo High School has assembled a research team of students drawn from History, English, and Social Science subjects across grade levels 8 to 12. The team is working in collaboration with three History professors at a local university. The project, commissioned by the municipal council, is to develop an oral history of long-established migrant groups in the city. It involves conducting life history interviews with elderly residents, focusing on their experiences of settling in their adopted country.

Ben (8th grade) and Monica (11th grade) meet at McDonald's to go over their interview questions. Their information about the couple that they are to interview has given rise to doubts about two of their proposed questions. Unsure what to do, they call their university research partner on Monica's mobile phone and ask her advice. They talk for five minutes and revise the interview schedule accordingly. The university professor tells them she will be in her office for the next two hours and asks them to call her back when they reach that part of the interview. When they arrive at the house, Monica text-messages the teacher coordinating the project to confirm that they have arrived and everything is ready for the interview.

Ben takes the digital voice recorder from his pocket and gets it ready for recording. The recorder has a built-in camera that Ben will use throughout the semi-structured interview, having obtained the necessary formal consent from the couple. On this occasion Monica will play the main interviewing role, although both will prompt and probe when appropriate as the professor has coached them to do. They call the professor at the arranged point in the interview. She talks with the couple by means of the loudspeaker function built into the mobile phone, recording the conversation at her end, while Ben continues recording the conversation *in situ*. When the professor has finished, Monica and Ben conclude the interview, thank the couple, negotiate a follow-up if needed, and leave.

They have one hour before their next interview, so they go to a nearby public library they know has wireless internet access. Ben uploads the digital audio and visual file from the voice recorder to the small highly portable notebook on loan to them from the university, and Monica uses iMovie software to combine the photos and audio file into a single file and saves it in a Quicktime viewing format which can be read across different digital devices and platforms. Monica saves the original audio and image files to a small external hard-drive that she has plugged into one of the computer's USB ports. Later, another project member will collate and archive these 'raw' files on a back-up CD-ROM. When the Quicktime file is finished, Monica opens an FTP client that enables her to transfer the original 'raw' files and the unedited Quicktime file to a space on one of the university's network servers that has been dedicated to the oral history project. Ben simultaneously logs on to the internet using a PDA borrowed from the school set and adds a short post to the project's team blog that includes a direct hyperlink to the new Quicktime file and includes some details about the interviewees, interviewers, time and date of the interview itself in his post. He also lists the artefacts displayed and discussed by the couple during the interview and records the professor's participation during the interview. When they have finished, they text-message their teacher again and set off for the next interview.

Vignette 2

Karl (Year 10) oversees Soloranzo High School's reputation system for the school's various formal projects and maintains a registry of community expertise that has been made available to project teams. He and a group of peers researched a range of well-known formal rating systems (eBay, Amazon.com, Plastic.com) and developed a five-point rating scale and space for brief feedback statements by clients. At the completion of each project Karl and his teammates email the clients, providing a brief explanation of the rating and feedback system, a reference number, and politely inviting them to log their evaluation on the automated form on the school's project website. (Karl's team developed this form in collaboration with some undergraduate university students enrolled in a computer engineering degree. Those involved worked long hours to create a web-based version of the feedback interface that could be read using multiple web browsers, as well as a mobile version that could be used on mobile phones and PDAs.) The clients enter their project reference number into the form (feedback cannot be left without this number), select a rating from a drop-down menu, and provide up to 50 words of descriptive feedback in the text window. This feedback is automatically posted to the project reputation webpage, which is public, and Karl then adds hyperlinks to online websites and other materials associated with each 'rated' project.

These ratings provide a formal public record of the school's level of performance as assessed by clients, as well as evaluative data on individual projects that contribute to team members' assessment portfolios. This public record of reputation is an integral part of the process by which the community develops a new perception of the nature and role of contemporary school education. Karl's school recognizes that to function effectively as a knowledge-producing school, it (and other KPSs) needs to be 'at least partially remade in the minds of the local community', and that 'project by project it [is] possible to build up a repertoire of [publicly recognized] research skills and products in consultation with local needs and interests' (Bigum 2002: 139).

Karl also maintains a registry of community expertise that has been made available to the school in the course of its project work. This registry is public and serves multiple purposes. In part, it is a record of resources that might be available to the school and/or other (non-profit) community groups for appropriate future activities. It is also a mechanism for community networking. In addition, and very importantly, it provides a public statement of the community service/collaborative–cooperative dispositions of those who have demonstrated their recognition that education is a whole of community responsibility. Of course, the record of projects on the school website also identifies those community groups and organizations that have supported the reconstitution of education as 'mature' knowledge production by commissioning projects.

Vignette 3

At Soloranzo High the research teams have each been assigned server space for project blogs and websites. Sarah (Year 10) is 'responsible' for overseeing and maintaining the oral history project blog. This blog works in tandem with the project's archival server space provided by the local university (for which Sarah is also responsible in terms of troubleshooting file transfer processes and blog hyperlinks to archived data, liaising with the university, etc.). The blog is used to document the team's research process as it unfolds. As we have seen, student interviewers in the field can use the blog to update their teammates in real time (e.g., by PDA from a wireless hotspot).

Sarah has general oversight of the blog, although all team members are registered and can post to it. Sarah follows up on comments posted to the blog by readers, organizes the structure of the blog, edits spelling, maintains a list of hyperlinks related to the project and displayed in the blog sidebar, troubleshoots broken links of HTML commands in posts made by team members on the run, and posts a regularly updated timeline of tasks to be completed and generally performs the kinds of tasks undertaken by webmasters. The blog serves as an audit trail for the project and as a repository of the team's thinking over time. For example, team members blog ideas about patterns they are starting to see in the data. They also blog issues and suggestions for how the final oral history website should be organized (as a museum-like archive or as a cross-referenced wiki network?; how should each Quicktime file be edited to produce a polished final file?; should they include already-existing online hosting spaces like Youtube.com – a digital video file hosting space – in their final product?). They post links to online resources relevant to an aspect of the study (e.g., examples of other oral history projects online, links to papers on oral history research methods), and list brief summaries, citations, and location details of relevant offline resources (books in local libraries, newspaper articles, artefacts in local museums), etc. The blog also accommodates ideas, information and suggestions (e.g., things to follow up on, other people to interview, artefact information) relevant to the study that are suggested by members of the public at large using the comments function built into the blog.

The server-based data archive is a password-protected database containing all digital archival material generated in the project. It can be accessed by all team members for their various research purposes from any location that has internet access and the necessary file transfer software installed. These purposes include uploading new data, keeping tabs on what has already been collected (and not), preparing data for analysis and printing out data to be analysed, storing multimedia files that can be edited for final presentation purposes, and so on. It is not only the main digital database for the project, but also a potential future source of secondary data for subsequent projects, subject to ethical research considerations and approval overseen by the relevant formal research ethics body. Sarah oversees the team's use of their server space, ensuring that files are stored in a logical manner, that folder and file names are suitably descriptive and accurate, and so on, all in collaboration with her counterpart in the university and her History teacher (who is the staff member assigned to this project).

Reflection and discussion

Try to think of as many possible objections as you can that might be raised by teachers, education administrators, parents, community members, and education policy-makers to the approach to learning outlined in the vignettes.

- What seem to you to be the most plausible or convincing objections?

- If you were committed to the kind of approach outlined, how would you respond to these concerns?

- If you do not think the approach is educationally appropriate or viable, what are your reasons? What would you do instead?

Conclusion

These vignettes may be fictional – which is almost inevitable given the poverty of school engagement to date with the mobile net – but they are by no means far-fetched. At the same time, they show how a range of characteristically contemporary technologies and social practices and cultures of use engaged outside of school can be incorporated into learning on terms that satisfy the kinds of principles and criteria we have identified. The fact that the students are working with experts to acquire bona fide research skills integral to mature practices of research that could serve them well in life after school meets the criterion of efficacious learning. This learning, moreover, is integrated. The team is learning by doing *in situ* and members are acquiring the various components of the process in conjunction with each other. For example, they are learning data management techniques in the process of learning to collect data, and are learning the complementary roles of research tools and which tools are best to use on particular occasions and for particular purposes. The learning builds on what the young people already do and know, and it offers non-domesticating spaces for these to be drawn on in different but non-alienating contexts and ways. With respect to the critical dimension of learning, the project envisaged in the vignettes offers wide scope for serious reflection on discursive difference. The data analysis phase will call for developing and negotiating points of view. The necessary reflection and negotiation will focus partly on matters of cultural difference and, perhaps, tension. It will also provide focused opportunities for reflection and discussion about particular aspects of doing oral history (e.g., sensitivity to issues to do with privacy, dignity, intrusion, validity and verification, and of who benefits).

Finally, the fictional experiences described in the vignette cohere well with the three perspectives that frame this chapter: we can educate now to minimize future social divides; we can educate in ways that transcend well-recognized constraints associated with classroom enclosures; and we can fit learning tools to educational ideals rather than sacrificing these ideals at the altar of technology. These perspectives provide a frame for planning pedagogy that is not merely *appropriate* for our times but, rather, that significantly defines captures an educational *obligation* to our next generation.

CHAPTER 7

Memes, L/literacy and Classroom Learning

Introduction

In Chapter 4 we briefly mentioned the idea of internet memes (pronounced 'meems') as a dimension of cultural production and transmission within the context of describing examples of photoshopped remixes. In this chapter we will look at some examples of what are recognized by internet insiders as online memes and consider some possible links to thinking about classroom learning under contemporary conditions.

To introduce this discussion it is important to distinguish the level at which we will be talking about memes in this chapter from the way they are talked about in the emerging formal discourse of Memetics. There are some broad surface similarities between how 'heavy duty' memeticists conceive memes and how people involved in using the internet to 'hatch memes' conceive memes. But we think that these similarities do not run very deep. It seems to us very unlikely that many, if any, so-called internet memes of the kinds we talk about here will have even remotely the kind of shelf life that serious memeticists assign to memes. By the same token, participants in popular practices of online 'meming' would not typically be interested in buying into the deep issues that engage serious students and theorists of memes, such as whether memes are actually associated with physical neural manifestations in human brains. Nonetheless, there are some very interesting and worthwhile points to be discussed around online memes, and these points resonate structurally – even if on a rather superficial level – with 'hard core' conceptions of memes. It is these points that are of interest to us here.

The concept of memes

As noted in Chapter 4, memes are contagious patterns of cultural information that are passed from mind to mind and directly shape and propagate key actions and mindsets of a social group. Current interest in memes and the contemporary conceptual and theoretical development of memetics dates to ideas advanced by the geneticist Richard Dawkins in 1976. In his ground-breaking book, *The Selfish Gene*, Dawkins proposed a substantial evolutionary model of cultural development and change grounded in the replication of ideas, knowledge, and other cultural information through imitation and transfer. His definition of memes posited actual biological changes in brain neurons when brains become infected with memes. This position is controversial among those who study memes and has helped contribute to 'mutations' in the ways memes themselves are conceived within the field.

Dawkins (1999) has retrospectively recalled that his purpose in invoking a term like 'meme' to refer to good ideas, 'tunes, catch-phrases, clothes fashions, ways of making pots or of building arches' (1976: 192), was to argue for the importance of small units of information like genes and memes in biological and cultural evolution (1999: xvi). In the *Selfish Gene* Dawkins argued that the 'real unit of natural selection [whether speaking biologically or culturally] was any kind of replicator, any unit of which copies are made, with occasional errors, and with some influence or power over their own probability of replication' (ibid.).

Issues with 'memes'

For Dawkins, memes are not metaphors for the transmission of ideas, but are 'living structures' that reside within the brain; that is, they comprise a physical structure in each person's neural network (1976). Even Dawkins himself, however, seems taken aback by the vigorous debates that emerged subsequent to the publication of *The Selfish Gene* and which focused on theorizing the definition of a meme more thoroughly than Dawkins had done. These debates have tended to fall into three camps, characterized by biological, psychological, and 'sociological' definitions of memes respectively.

Biological definitions tend to follow either an evolutionary gene model of memes (e.g., Dawkins 1976), or argue for an epidemiological conception of memes. The latter uses disease metaphors to explain what memes are and how they work, and treats memes as pathogens in analyses of meme dynamics (e.g., Goodenough and Dawkins 1994, cited in Wilkins 1998: 2). Biological conceptions of memes tend to focus on the effects memes have on behaviour (Aunger 2002; Brodie 1995).

Psychological and cognitive conceptions of memes tend to pay closer attention to decision-making processes *prior* to action (Aunger 2002: 37). From this perspective, the brain becomes a selective information processor – unable to process all the information received from moment to moment, and continuously engaged in selecting those units of information deemed worth attention. Interest in selective attention and information processing focuses on the ways memes affect decision-making. Memes are defined from this perspective in terms of being ideas spread by 'vehicles' that are physical manifestations of the meme (Dennett 1995, cited in Brodie 1996: 30).

Sociological definitions of memes downplay any physical neural quality of memes and instead pay attention to the effects of social organization on meme success. For example, from this perspective, memes are 'those units of transmitted information that are subject to selection biases at a given level of hierarchical organization of a culture' (Wilkins 1998: 2). That is, social structures like family, religions, schools and their defining values, mindsets, ways of doing, etc., directly impact which memes are most likely to be successfully contagious.

A tendency across all three perspectives to give too much autonomy to memes has long been criticized within the memetics literature (cf., Brodie 1996; Wilkins 1998). A more metaphorical use of the concept, 'meme', that draws on elements of all three theoretical orientations towards memes and takes into account human predilections for patterns, decision-making processes, and social structures, contexts and practices may prove more useful within the field of education. This enables the examination of modes and means of cultural production and transmission that do not confine analysis to discrete units of information, but take into account the ways in which memes themselves are caught up in realizing and propagating social relations. Memes are therefore usefully defined as contagious patterns of cultural information that are passed from mind to mind by means of selection, infection and replication. An idea or information pattern is not a meme until someone replicates it by passing it on to someone else, and, as previously noted, the probability of a meme being contagious within a group is directly tied to the values, beliefs and practices of that group (cf. Grant 1990).

This latter position is closest to the one we will take up in this chapter. Before turning to the prosaic everyday world of online memes, however, there are two further points to be made.

Memes and electronic networks

The first has to do with the significance of the internet for current interest in memes. Numerous researchers interested in memetics – the study of memes – have argued that electronic networks along with personal predilections and interests provide ideal conditions for propagating and dispersing memes (e.g., Blackmore 1999; Adar *et al.* 2004). One useful way of conceptualizing the ways in which memes are shared and transmitted within and across groups of people and activities is to appropriate Gee's concept of 'affinity spaces'. Affinity spaces are those online and/or offline interactive spaces comprising people held together either loosely or tightly by means of shared activities, interests, and goals (Gee 2004). Although meming – the practice of generating and/or passing on memes – has always been a part of human practice (Blackmore 1999), we think meming that makes use of relatively well-defined affinity spaces and electronic networks can usefully be identified as an example of a 'new' literacy practice that deserves attention in relation to literacy education (Lankshear and Knobel 2003).

Characteristics of memes

The second point concerns characteristics of memes. Dawkins (1976) identified three characteristics of successful memes: fidelity, fecundity, and longevity.

Fidelity

Fidelity refers to qualities of the meme that enable relatively straightforward 'copying' of the meme (e.g., an email containing a contagious idea) that keep it relatively 'intact' as it passes from mind to mind. Units of information that make sense or are meaningful to a person and can be successfully imitated or reproduced will more easily become memes than units of information that are not easily copied or understood. As Susan Blackmore explains, memes may well be successful because they are *memorable*, rather than because they are important or useful (1999: 57). Dawkins provides a useful example of how memory, fidelity and ease of copying may work to promote one meme over another. A little before Dawkins coined the term 'meme', an alternative synonym, 'culturgen,' was proposed (Dawkins 1999: xiv). Dawkins suggests that 'culturgen' never really caught on because it was polysyllabic rather than monosyllabic; did not lend itself easily to developing sub-category words (e.g., unlike meme, which has been hived off into 'memeplex', 'memeticist', 'metameme', 'meme pool', etc.); and was not similar in sound or spelling to a similar or related concept in the way that 'meme' and 'gene' can be connected. 'Meme' began to catch on and automatically generate much more attention than 'culturgen'. Soon it became the dominant concept for explaining the transmission of ideas from mind to mind.

Susceptibility is an important part of meme fidelity as well. Susceptibility refers to the 'timing' or 'location' of a meme with respect to people's openness to it, the meme's relevance to current events, its relation to previous well-established memes, and the interests and values of the affinity space in which the meme is unleashed. Ideal conditions of susceptibility will let the 'hooks' and 'selection attractors' built into the design and function of the meme itself take hold more easily and in ways that maximize the possibilities for the meme to 'catch on' and be transmitted rapidly from person to person without being hindered or slowed by early warning filters or other forms of cultural immunity (cf., Bennahum, in Lankshear and Knobel 2003).

Fecundity

Fecundity refers to the rate at which an idea or pattern is copied and spread. In other words, the more quickly a meme spreads, the more likely it is that it will capture robust and sustained attention, and will be replicated and distributed (Brodie 1996: 38). This is partly why students of memes have seized on the significance of electronic networks for transmitting memes.

Richard Brodie has recently added a further dimension to Dawkins' concept of fecundity, arguing that memes tend to infect minds more quickly when the meme is transmitted by 'trustworthy others' (ibid.: 152). To this, Susan Blackmore, a prominent memeticist, adds the argument that the 'effective transmission of memes depends critically on human preferences, attention, emotions and desires' (1999: 58).

Longevity

The longer a meme survives, the more it can be copied and passed on to new minds, ensuring its ongoing transmission. Longevity assumes that optimal conditions for a meme's replication and innovation are in place. A classic example of a long-lived meme that has made its way into cyberspace is what has come to be known as the 'Nigerian letter scam'. The email versions of this letter can vary in terms of contextual details, but the gist of the email remains constant: a relative of or ex-government official for a deposed dictator of an African country needs to launder an enormous amount of misappropriated funds through a mediating bank account and offers the reader a generous proportion of the total sum for providing a temporary holding account for the money. Victims provide bank account numbers and soon find their accounts are emptied and the 'relative' or 'dignitary' is nowhere to be found (Glasner 2002; Wired 2002). Some reports claim that the Nigerian letter scam actually generates higher median losses per victim per year in the US than does identity theft, even though the identity theft meme is given much more airplay in media venues (see di Justo and Stein 2002).

Internet memes

Among internet insiders 'meme' is a popular term for describing the rapid uptake and spread of a particular idea presented as a written text, image, language 'move', or some other unit of cultural 'stuff'. This use of the term begs the question of longevity – since in terms of serious meme time the internet has not been around long enough for any kind of evolutionary longevity to have been established – and blurs the distinction between a meme *per se* and a new vehicle for an old meme, as the Nigerian letter scam meme attests. In this case, the meme itself is as old as recorded time – how to get rich quick. What is new is the vehicle; dressing the old meme up in contemporary garb which, in this case, ranges from using email to trading on money laundering as a high profile everyday focus.

Notwithstanding such slippages, which doubtless incline some serious students of memes to frown on populist appropriations of a concept that should be taken altogether more seriously, it is interesting and informative from the standpoint of interest in learning to consider some examples of relatively long-standing and successful memes carried on the internet, as well as some lesser 'flashes in the pan', like the LiveJournal Batgirl meme described in Chapter 5. Purists might question whether this is a meme in any recognizable sense of 'meme' because it was all over in a weekend. On the other hand, what is interesting to us is the fact that one or two early 'movers' saw the potential in the original posting of the Batgirl designs for a 'mass event'. They brought into existence the possibility for a short-lived meme (albeit one that will live on for some time in LiveJournal lore and, perhaps, more widely on the internet) by recognizing a good potential.

As we will discuss in more detail later in this chapter, they drew on a kind of meta knowledge to see how fuelling this spark might create a blaze. Here was an example of a popular Discourse (Bat-everything) in combination with an online environment and easy access to graphics software and uploading facilities. Conditions were in place for a 'swarm', and in no time at all the long tail of the web was in full evidence. Members of online communities were in a position to participate, and they participated frenetically. After a while, of course, the meme ran its course and posting pictures of batgirl on one's Livejournal no longer had any 'cool' cachet. In a weekend the 'meme' potential was exhausted. It had insufficient existential significance – a key ingredient in survival value – to induce further effort (unlike the 'get rich quick' meme of the Nigerian letter scam emails). So it became part of internet history, over almost as quickly as it began. But while it was there, it drew deeply on the quintessence of popular internet culture where, after all, 10 nanoseconds might be quite a long time, and five minutes – as the saying goes – can seem like more or less for ever.

A study of some internet memes

During 2005 we made a small study of internet memes in the stripped back sense of 'memes' employed in this chapter for the five-year period spanning 2001 to 2005.

Data collection

To generate a 'meme pool' we used some different types of well-known online search engines on the assumption that successful online memes would have the kind of presence that registers with such search engines. The search engines used to generate this 'meme pool' were selected on the ground that they would obtain maximum coverage of likely meme conduits (e.g., website archives, blogs, broadcast media sites). In the first instance we used Google.com, to search websites in general, and Technorati.com, to search weblogs in particular. These wide-ranging searches were then supplemented with targeted searches. We trawled Wikipedia.com because it has excellent coverage of popular culture phenomena (Scholz 2004), using its search functions and following up references in articles or forums (e.g., following links mentioned in the *Wikipedia* entry on memes, searching for information on a meme mentioned in a *New York Times* article). We also trawled popular image and animation archives and forums like Something awful.com, Milkandcookies.org and Fark.org for mention of popular internet phenomena.

To finalize the data set we used four criteria:

1   Modified versions of Dawkins' characteristics of successful memes (*fidelity, fecundity* and *susceptibility*, and *longevity*).
2   Transmission is via *online* media.
3   The memes can be deemed '*successful*' in respect of being sufficiently strong and salient to capture online and offline broadcast media attention in the form of full-blown reports through to side-bar mentions in newspapers, television news reports or talk shows, widely read trade publications or general-audience magazines. With respect to this criterion, we used three databases to verify broadcast media reports of memes generated by the first phase of searching the internet: Proquest (ABI/Inform), LexisNexis, and WilsonWeb. All three survey broadcast media items, require paid subscription and, to this extent, are considered reliable indices to and archives of mainstream media reports and articles.
4   Even if the memes themselves draw on ideas or concepts that can be identified as established memes (e.g., 'get rich quick', spoofing an icon, caricaturing, etc.), they take forms that are sufficiently *distinctive* for their manifestations to be seen as memes that began their lives online.

The meme pool is summarized in Table 7.1. Limiting the cases to the period 2001–2005 ensured a robust set of online memes that post-dated the widespread take-up of online internet practices by the general public (at least within developed countries), and reflected the more widespread possibilities of access to the internet that can be dated from roughly 2000 onwards (cf., demographic reports published by Nielsen-Netratings.com).

All 19 memes received mentions in regional and/or national newspapers and magazines. The Star Wars Kid was mentioned in *Time Magazine*, *Wired Magazine*, BBC reports, Toronto's *Globe and Mail* newspaper and the *New York Times*. The Numa Numa Dance video meme was the focus of several *New York Times* articles, as well as being mentioned on CNN (a major US news broadcast network) and also playing on the *Today Show* and *Countdown* television shows in the US. Each meme in the final data

Table 7.1 The meme pool

Oolong the Rabbit (2001)

Nike Sweatshop Shoes (2001)

All Your Base Are Belong To Us (2001)

Bert is Evil (2001)

Tourist of Death (2001)

Bonsai Kitten (2002)

Ellen Feiss (2002)

Star Wars Kid (2002)

Black People Love Us (2002)

Every time you masturbate ... God kills a kitten (2002)

'Girl A'/Nevada-tan (2003)

Badger, Badger, Badger (2003)

Read My Lips, Bush–Blair Love Song (2003)

The Tron Guy (2003)

Lost Frog/Hopkin Green Frog (2004)

JibJab's This Land is My Land (2004)

Numa Numa Dance (2004)

Dog Poop Girl (2005)

Flying Spaghetti Monster/Flying Spaghetti Monsterism (2005)

Note: Memes are ordered from earliest to most recent.

pool has generated a range of homage or spoof websites or other artefacts (including themed merchandise).

Data analysis

We were interested in exploring these memes in terms of features that may provide useful 'windows' on literacy education specifically and classroom learning more generally. To this end our analysis of the memes as data was informed by three considerations.

1   What light can these memes shed on the 'fidelity', 'fecundity' and 'longevity' of online memes, in senses of these terms that are adapted to and appropriate for contexts and instances of popular cultural online practices?

Table 7.2 Prompt questions for analysing online memes

Referential or ideational system	The focus is on the meaning of a meme: • What idea or information is being conveyed by this meme? How do we know? • How is this idea or information being conveyed? • What does this meme mean or signify (within this space, for certain people, at this particular point in time)? How do we know?
Contextual or interpersonal system	The focus is on social relations: • Where does this meme 'stand' with respect to the relationship it implies or invokes between people readily infected by this meme? What tells us this? • What does this meme tell us about the kinds of contexts within which this meme proves to be contagious and replicable? • What does this meme seem to assume about knowledge and truth within this particular context?
Ideological or worldview system	The focus is on values, beliefs and worldviews: • What deeper or larger themes, ideas, positions are conveyed by this meme? • What do these themes, ideas and positions tell us about different social groups? • What do these memes tell us about the world, or a particular version of the world?
Social practices and affinities	• What is going on here and who is involved? How do we know? • Who would recognize this meme as part of or relevant to their affinity space and what tells us this? Who would not recognize this meme and what might be some of the consequences of this? • What kinds of affinity spaces might most readily embrace this meme, and what suggests this? What do people 'learn' as a result of engaging with this meme? • What ways of doing, knowing and using resources (i.e., social practices) seem to be part and parcel of this meme?

2 Ideas derived from approaches to discourse analysis that we had found useful in other contexts: especially, the concepts of 'referential or ideational system', 'contextual or interpersonal system', and 'ideological or worldview system' (e.g., Fairclough 1989; Kress and van Leeuwen 1996).

3 The idea of literacies as social practices that are often played out in affinity spaces.

Our analysis drew on prompt questions summarized in Table 7.2.

Outcomes: in relation to characteristics of successful memes

Our analysis suggested that 'fidelity' might be better understood in terms of 'replicability' where online memes are concerned. As we will see a little later, many of the online memes in our pool were not passed on entirely 'intact' in the sense that the meme 'vehicle' often was changed, modified, mixed with other referential and expressive resources, and regularly given idiosyncratic spins by participants. In other words, while the meme or contagious idea itself remained relatively intact, the 'look' of the meme wasn't always held constant. These 'mutations' seemed in most cases to help the meme's fecundity in terms of hooking people into contributing their own version of the meme. A concept like 'replicability' includes remixing as an important part of the overall meme mix, where remixing includes modifying, bricolaging, splicing, reordering, superimposing, etc. original and other images, sounds, films, music, talk, and so on.

Reflection and Discussion

Compare the following two sets of memes:

- Nike sweatshop email exchange: geocities.com/infotaxi/nike.html
- JibJab's 'This Land': jibjab.com (filed under 'classics')
- Badger, Badger, Badger: weebls-stuff.com/toons/badgers
- Tron Guy; tronguy.net

- All Your Base: planettribes.com/allyourbase/index.shtml
- Hopkin Green Frog: lostfrog.org
- Bert is Evil: bertisevil.tv
- Star Wars Kid: www.jedimaster.net

> On the basis of your comparison, why do you think some online memes might remain relatively intact, while others spark a veritable avalanche of remixes?
>
> What do you think it is about the memes listed here that seems to lend them readily to replication, other than the fact that they are digital?

With respect to the life of memes, as distinct from longevity in a strict sense, the search and selection process used to generate the data set showed how easy it was to find ample online archives of original meme texts, images, and video clips and other footage, etc. as well as detailed accounts of the origins and spread of different memes and their various permutations. In terms of distribution, the blogosphere in particular seems an ideal vehicle for transmitting memes, with weblogs replacing email and discussion forums as a chief way of spreading memes (especially for memes emerging from 2002 onwards). This resonates with the ongoing work of Eytan Adar and his colleagues at the Hewlett Packard Dynamics Lab which focuses on tracing what they call 'information epidemics' spread via weblogs, which they see as potent fields for spreading contagious ideas (Adar et al. 2004: 1). Analysis of the contextual or social 'systems' of the memes in this study also suggested three distinct patterns of characteristics that seem likely to contribute particularly to each meme's fecundity. These are some element of humour, a rich kind of intertextuality, and the use of anomalous juxtaposition. We take these points up under a new sub-heading.

Outcomes: in relation to discursive features and sociality

The online memes we studied were often rich and diverse in humour, including the quirky and offbeat, potty humour, the bizarrely funny, parodies, and the acerbically ironic. Intertextuality was a regular feature, most notably in the form of wry cross-references to different everyday and popular culture events, icons or phenomena. The use of anomalous juxtaposition usually involved images. We will look at these features in turn.

Humour

Humour is a key feature of almost all our memes (recognizing that humour is notoriously subjective). Perhaps the most famous and enduring among our memes is the All Your Base Are Belong To Us meme (c. 2001; see Figure 7.1). The syntactic and semantic hiccups within the English sub-titles created for a US audience of gamers and used in the opening animated sequence of the Japanese video game, *Zero Wing*, seemed to resonate immediately with what a *Times Magazine* article about this meme identified as 'geek kitsch' humour (Taylor 2001). In short, this sequence establishes the context for the game and is set in an intergalactic, war-torn future. It involves the sudden appearance of Cats, an evil-doer, inside a space craft. Cats announces that he is the victor in this particular war, but the Captain responds valiantly by calling for the ZIG fighters to be launched, and emphasizes that all of earth's fate is in their hands. And then the game begins, with the player in role as a ZIG fighter and working to help the Captain defeat Cats.

```
In A.D. 2101
War was beginning.
Captain: What happen?
Mechanic: Somebody set up us the bomb.
Operator: We get signal.
Captain: What !
Operator: Main screen turn on.
Captain: It' s You !!
Cats: How are you gentlemen !!
Cats: All your base are belong to us.
Cats: You are on the way to destruction.
Captain: What you say !!
Cats: You have no chance to survive make your time.
Cats: HA HA HA HA. . . .
Captain: Take off every 'zig' !!
Captain: You know what you doing.
Captain: Move 'zig' .
Captain: For great justice.
```

Figure 7.1 Dialogue for English language version of the opening context-setting sequence for the computer game, *Zero Wing*
Source: planettribes.com/allyourbase/story.shtml.

The seriousness of the dialogue about a threatened global takeover coupled with language translation glitches struck a chord and the clip quickly caught on among video game-players and software programmers first, and later within wider audiences (especially when a voice track and sound effects were added to the clip). The original clip sparked a remixing epidemic, with active meme participants generating a range of new, very funny, photoshopped takes on the 'All Your Base' catchphrase, including a reworking of the iconic Hollywood sign, as well as remixed billboards, road signs, high-profile advertisements, official documents, food products and toys, and so on to announce to everyone that, 'All Your Base Are Belong To Us' (see planettribes.com /allyourbase/index.shtml). These remixes are in many ways funnier than the original clip due to the creative uses of key phrases and the celebration of the quirkiness that they embody. The catchphrase, 'All your base are belong to us', now regularly appears in news or political reports in the broadcast media or the blogosphere, and is used to describe clumsy, heavy-handed take-over bids for positions of power and the like. The longevity of this meme seems assured, and recent remixes of this meme include the Danish production: 'All Your Iraq Are Belong to Us' (mb3.dk/ayiabtu).

A second example, the Ellen Feiss meme (c. 2002), began as a television advertisement by Apple for its campaign to entice PC users to 'switch' to Apple. When the advertisement aired on television, 15-year-old Fleiss appeared to be quite 'out of it' (she later claimed filming had occurred close to midnight and that she had taken a strong dose of anti-allergy medication for her hayfever just before filming began). Her awkward eyebrow lift, uncoordinated hand movements, and her use of sound effects to describe her computer crashing coupled with lengthy pauses in her monologue, caused much hilarity around the world. Apple cancelled the advertisement as soon as it was realized why it had become so popular, but not before it had been digitized and archived on multiple websites. Ellen quickly reached iconic status among young, male programmers, Apple Mac users, and male college students (see: ellenfeiss.net). Her story was reported in books and newspapers. Her response was to go to ground, and she has turned down numerous invitations to appear on major talkshows within the US. Nevertheless, more than three years after the meme began a tee shirt series celebrating Ellen Feiss is still available for purchase. Numerous tribute and remix sites remain active (see, for example, ellenfeiss.gloriousnoise.com; jeffwilhem.com/files/ellen1.mov), and pictures of contestants in the Ellen look-a-like contest held in Europe are still archived online (see: feiss.mac-freak.org/index.html).

In addition to quirky and situational kinds of humour, five of the memes examined in this study put humour to use in biting social commentary. The Nike Sweat Shop Shoes meme is a good example of this. During 2000, Jonah Peretti had a series of email exchanges with the Nike company concerning Nike's iD campaign that allows customers to customize their shoes (Peretti 2001). Peretti's request to have 'sweatshop' embroidered on his new shoes had been denied and came at a time when Nike was under fire for exploiting workers in under-developed countries. Despite persistent questions on Peretti's part, the company hid behind company policy statements and did not provide a logical rationale for the cancelled order. In

January 2001 Peretti gathered these exchanges together in a single email and sent it off to a few friends (see an excerpt from the exchange in Figure 7.2).

From: "Personalize, NIKE iD"
To: "'Jonah H. Peretti' "
Subject: RE: Your NIKE iD order o16468000

Your NIKE iD order was cancelled for one or more of the following reasons.
1) Your Personal iD contains another party's trademark or other intellectual property.
2) Your Personal iD contains the name of an athlete or team we do not have the legal right to use.
3) Your Personal iD was left blank. Did you not want any personalization?
4) Your Personal iD contains profanity or inappropriate slang, and besides, your mother would slap us.

If you wish to reorder your NIKE iD product with a new personalization please visit us again at www.nike.com

Thank you,
NIKE iD

From: "Jonah H. Peretti"
To: "Personalize, NIKE iD"
Subject: RE: Your NIKE iD order o16468000

Greetings,
My order was canceled but my personal NIKE iD does not violate any of the criteria outlined in your message. The Personal iD on my custom ZOOM XC USA running shoes was the word "sweatshop." Sweatshop is not: 1) another's party's trademark, 2) the name of an athlete, 3) blank, or 4) profanity. I choose the iD because I wanted to remember the toil and labor of the children that made my shoes. Could you please ship them to me immediately.

Thanks and Happy New Year,
Jonah Peretti

```
From: "Personalize, NIKE iD"
To: "Jonah H. Peretti' "
Subject: RE: Your NIKE iD order o16468000

Dear NIKE iD Customer,

Your NIKE iD order was cancelled because the iD you have chosen
contains, as stated in the previous e-mail correspondence,
"inappropriate slang". If you wish to reorder your NIKE iD product
with a new personalization please visit us again at www.nike.com

Thank you,
NIKE iD
```

Figure 7.2   An excerpt from the 'Nike Sweatshop Shoe' meme
Source: snopes.com/business/consumer/nike.asp; accessed 7 March, 2005.

The satiric humour and social commentary contained in the set of email correspondence caught popular attention and soon reached thousands of people via email networks. This in turn sparked mainstream broadcast attention, and Peretti's meme was the subject of a range of news and magazine reports, including *Time* magazine, and Peretti himself was interviewed on the *Today Show*, a popular news events talk show in the US.

Other examples of humour in the meme pool include the oft-linked-to website known as Black People Love Us! (blackpeopleloveus.com). This meme, which also was created by Jonah Peretti, in collaboration with his sister, is a wry – 'scathing' might be a better word – commentary on white American liberal paternalism towards black Americans. The faux 'personal' website comprises a series of 'testimonials' from a middle-class white couple's black friends that emphasize much of the condescension that can occur in naïve liberal positions on social and cultural difference (e.g., references to 'being articulate', white people demonstrating 'solidarity' by speaking Black English and claiming a preference for rap music).

Another well-known social commentary meme that makes effective use of sardonic humour is the Bush–Blair Love Song meme described in Chapter 3 (see p.68).

Reflection and discussion

Access these three social critique memes:

- Read My Lips' Bush-Blair Love Song: atmo.se/zino.aspx?
  articleID=399

- Nike sweatshop email exchange: geocities.com/infotaxi/nike.html

- Black People Love Us! blackpeopleloveus.com

Discuss who you think might *not* find these memes particularly funny and why they might not.

Does this tell us anything about the contagiousness of successful online memes? If so, what?

See if you can locate any further examples of successful online memes of the social-political critique variety. What makes them 'successful'?

Rich intertextuality

Cross-references to a host of popular culture events, artefacts and practices also characterize many of the successful memes in this study. Perhaps the most widely known intertextual meme is the Star Wars Kid (c. 2003). This meme began when schoolmates of a 15-year-old, heavily-built Canadian schoolboy, Ghyslain, found a video recording he had made of himself. The tape showed him miming somewhat awkwardly a light sabre fight inspired by *Star Wars* movies using a broomstick-like golf ball retriever. His friends uploaded the footage to Kazaa – a now-defunct person-to-person file sharing service – where it was found by millions of viewers, many of whom added music, special effects and highly recognizable Star Wars sounds (e.g., the light sabre 'swoosh-hum') to create the now-famous Star Wars Kid meme (e.g., screamingpickle.com/members/StarWarsKid).

Subsequent remixes of this video clip include Ghyslain cast as Gandalf in *Lord of the Rings*, as William Wallace in the movie *Braveheart*, and as Neo from the *Matrix* movies, among others. One version mixes a very early email-distributed meme, the Dancing Baby (or Baby Cha-Cha; c. 1996), and Gyhslain in a faux trailer for a Hollywood buddy movie, while another mixes the clip with Tetris, an enormously popular, early video game. These cross-references to popular movies, an earlier meme, and games clearly tap into an affinity space that recognizes and appreciates this intertextuality, while at the same time they serve to blur the line between an ordinary life and the extraordinary lives of characters in movie and game universes. The popularity of the Star Wars Kid remixes even produced an online petition to Lucasfilm to include Ghyslain himself as a character in *Episode III* of the *Star Wars* prequel series (petitiononline.com/Ghyslain/petition.html). The Star Wars Kid meme has in turn become a popular culture touchstone and regularly appears as a reference in animated cartoon series and video games.

The Lost Frog meme described in Chapter 4 likewise alludes to a range of popular culture phenomena as it remixes and mutates the text of a lost pet announcement (c. 2004). The remixed images include typical 'missing persons' announcement vehicles (e.g., broadcast media news reports, milk cartons), crowd scenes seemingly devoted to spreading the news about the lost frog (e.g., 'lost frog' banners at a street march and at a crowded soccer match), and a host of other 'remember Hopkin' scenarios (e.g., lost frog scratch-it lottery tickets, Hopkin's ID on someone's instant message buddy list, Hopkin as a 'not found' internet file image). As with the Star Wars Kid meme, references to popular culture artefacts and practices abound, and include reworked book covers, music album covers, video games, eBay auctions, fan conventions, and so on. Other images spoof advertising campaigns (e.g., an Absolut Vodka spread becomes 'Absolut Hopkin'; a 'Got Milk?' advertisement becomes 'Got Frog?'). Many of the lost frog images refer to other memes as well. For example, an aeroplane pulling a lost frog announcement banner also appeared earlier in an All Your Base Are Belong To Us remixed image, as did photoshopped highway signs. This rich layering of cross-references appears to help the fecundity of a meme by encouraging subsequent photoshoppers to make their own engaging cross-cultural popular references that add layers of meaning for 'those in the know' to an already humorous contribution.

Reflection and discussion

Access Lostfrog.org.

- As you click through each image, try and identify as many *intertextual* references as you can, using internet searches as necessary (e.g., the eBay auction for Hopkin Green Frog on a slice of toast is, among other things, a direct cross-reference to the Virgin Mary grilled cheese sandwich that was auctioned off on eBay in 2004 for $28,000 USD).

- Compare your final list with someone else's and discuss the impact that the cross-references to a range of popular culture and everyday icons, artefacts and events on your list have on your interaction with and response to this meme.

Anomalous juxtaposition

In addition to humour and intertextual references, more than half the memes we selected include what could be called anomalous juxtaposition among their 'hooks' for maximizing the susceptibility of the idea being passed from mind to mind (cf., Oolong the Pancake Bunny, Bert is Evil, Bonsai Kitten, Tourist of Death, Nevada-tan, Numa Numa Dance, God Kills a Kitten, All Your Base, Lost Frog, and Star Wars Kid). The juxtapositions are of different kinds.

One kind involves incongruous couplings of images. The Tourist of Death figure is set against backdrops from a range of tragic events, beginning with the attack on New York City's Twin Towers. The meme began from a picture of a real person at the top of the World Trade Center. Someone then photoshopped the image, added an aeroplane, and posted the picture with a bogus story about the camera being found at the disaster site. After that other people took the same smiling, posing tourist and inserted him into all manner of disaster scenes: the *Titanic*, hurricanes, ferry accidents, and so. This juxtaposes a conventional smiling tourist pose usually found in travel photos of famous landmarks with disastrous events and implies that death and mayhem are to be found wherever this particular, seemingly innocuous tourist goes. More recent mutations of the Tourist of Death show him in all sorts of incongruous roles (as a sports reporter, as a video game character, as a political adviser, etc.).

Another kind of juxtaposition involves the deliberately provocative or bleakly satiric. In this vein the faux Bonsai Kitten website (c. 2002) presents 'illustrated' step-by-step instructions for altering the shape of pet cats by feeding kittens muscle relaxant drugs and stuffing them into bottles and jars for a few months so that the cats take on a rectilinear shape. The photos were photoshopped and fake, but realistic enough to cause international furore over what appeared to be an intensely cruel practice. The realism is certainly aided and abetted by the very serious promotional text found on the hoax website. In this case, a ludicrous set of images juxtaposes with deadpan and carefully formulated instructions, satirizing home decorating trends that shape and constrain living things to suit an imposed aesthetic.

The Bert is Evil meme provides a good example of anomalous juxtaposition (c. 2001). This meme was spawned by an actual event. It began with a photograph of the muppet, Bert, a character from the popular and long-running children's television show, *Sesame Street*, being photoshopped into a picture of Osama bin Laden and uploaded as a joke to an online photoshopper forum. The image was subsequently downloaded and used in Bangladesh on street march banners by supporters of Osama bin Laden.

The creators of the banners seemingly either did not notice Bert in the picture they downloaded or did not know who Bert was. The banner image caught wide broadcast media attention and rapidly prompted different people to create remixed images that added 'evidence' to the claim that Bert was indeed evil, rather than a harmless children's television character (see: bertisevil.tv). These photoshopped and animated images portray the muppet as being involved with the Klu Klux Klan, as implicated in President Kennedy's assassination, connected with the Charles Manson murders, and the like. The overall tenor of these remixed images tends to be one of 'moral bankruptcy'. There is an 'almost paparazzi' feel to most of the images, that are staged to look as though they were taken by hidden cameras or in off-guard moments. The juxtaposition of horrible, tragic or seedy scenarios with an innocuous puppet from a children's television show generates a kind of gallows humour, presenting documentary evidence that clearly cannot be true. The fecundity of this meme may also owe something to real-life stories concerning the public airing of hidden seedy or immoral lives of some movie and television stars including, particularly, stars of children's television.

A disturbing example of anomalous juxaposition concerns the Nevada-tan meme (c. 2004). This meme, too, was sparked by a real-life event. In 2003, an 11-year-old Japanese schoolgirl murdered a classmate by slashing her throat with a box cutter before returning to class, covered in her classmate's blood. The murderer subsequently became known as 'Nevada-tan', because images of her wearing a hooded sweatshirt emblazoned with the word, 'Nevada', were released online and in the broadcast media. Nevada-tan's age and her website – which was full of shock animations (e.g., The Red Room), and other gruesome internet culture references and artefacts – sparked national debates in Japan concerning the age limit for criminal culpability and the social effects of internet use. Nevada-tan has become a popular culture icon among certain groups; her 'character' features quite regularly as a manga or anime character in fanfiction texts, has generated homage websites, appears as a character in cosplay (i.e., in-person character role plays often built around anime storylines), and is mentioned in a number of Japanese pop songs. The juxtaposition of a young, ordinary-looking schoolgirl with a gruesome murder she did not even try to hide seemingly creates attention 'hooks' that turn Nevada-tan's case and persona into a meme within certain affinity spaces inhabited by people who are interested in shocking or gory news events and/or in Japanese culture and popular culture texts like manga and anime.

An outlier

While it is arguable that the fecundity of online memes may owe much to the use of humour, intertextuality, and anomalous juxtaposition – in varying combinations – one meme in the set draws on none of these features. The Dog Poop Girl meme (South Korea, 2005) is an outlier in this regard. It began with a photograph of a young woman and her dog on a train in South Korea. The dog had fouled the train carriage and its owner refused to clean up the mess, even after being asked a number of times to do so. A disgruntled fellow passenger took a phonecam image of the offender and her dog and posted it to a popular website. It was quickly picked up by the internet community and widely circulated online, both in its original form, and in slightly remixed poster versions. It took only a few days for the woman to be identified from this photo, and her personal information was published online as a way of punishing her for her failure to be a responsible citizen. The meme in effect became something of a witch hunt, and saw the woman hounded online and offline until she posted a very contrite apology for her actions to an internet forum. This meme attracted broadcast media attention around the world due mostly to its vigilante nature and the breaching of the woman's right to personal privacy.

Elements of a typology of memes

Drawing on findings for the questions used to analyse the memes in our data set we can map the beginnings of a typology of memes (Figure 7.3, see p.232). We will focus here on what we see as some aspects of the relationships between memes and identity.

Most of the memes in our pool seem to appeal to and draw on the creative energies of people who enjoy playful, absurdist ideas carrying little 'serious' content and/or who enjoy humorous ideas carrying serious content which may be considered to be social critique and commentary (with the Dog Poop Girl and Nevada-tan memes remaining the outliers here).

Playful and absurdist ideas include dignifying the banal and everyday with epically-scaled albeit imagined responses to real, fictional, or fantastical events, or with casting minor and trivial events and/or very ordinary/simple/humble people with global significance. The Lost Frog and Star Wars kid memes are examples of these. Equally, a penchant for the absurd underscores the popularity of quirky or anomalous images and video sequences like Oolong the Pancake Bunny and Gary Brolsma's Numa Numa Dance.

Wry and satiric humour is prevalent in those memes within our pool that are designed to serve purposes of social critique and commentary. For example, depicting a coy but intimate relationship between Bush and Blair satirizes the political-military alliances between the two countries and portrays them as, ultimately, self-serving. Blair's falsetto vocal spins bitingly off prevalent gender relations of power and servitude. All of the social critique memes in the pool exhibit playfully serious qualities.

Whether the memes are more 'absurdist' or more of the serious critique and commentary type, the forms of playfulness in most cases tap into shared popular cultural experiences and practices of various kinds. To 'get' the memes depends to a greater or lesser extent upon having particular forms of insider savviness. The memes we have interrogated can be seen as associated with – and, indeed, as helping to define – different kinds of affinity spaces. These include gamer spaces, photoshopper spaces, manga/anime spaces, left-leaning political spaces, 'good' community member spaces, Asian popular culture fan spaces, among others. These memes relate to and define particular affinity spaces through semiotic nods and winks to those 'in the know'. Most of the memes we analysed travel across multiple affinity spaces, as well. Nevertheless, 'outsiders' to these spaces will be hard-pressed to see the humour or point in many of these memes, and to know how to 'read' or 'take' them: whether seriously or playfully, or, as self-deprecating, or wryly/sardonically/wistfully, or in a 'if you didn't laugh you'd cry' kind of way, and so on (witness the hue and cry over the Bonsai Kitten hoax meme). This affirms Blackmore's (1999: 58) claim that the 'effective transmission of memes depends critically on human preferences, attention, emotions and desire'.

Reflection and discussion

Examine the memes listed in Figure 7.3.

- Which of these appeals to you most? Why?

- What this might 'say' about your own interests, worldviews, point of view?

- Do the same for the meme that least appeals to you.

- Compare your responses with those of one or more other peers or colleagues.

- What, if anything, do the comparisons tell you about 'meaning making'?

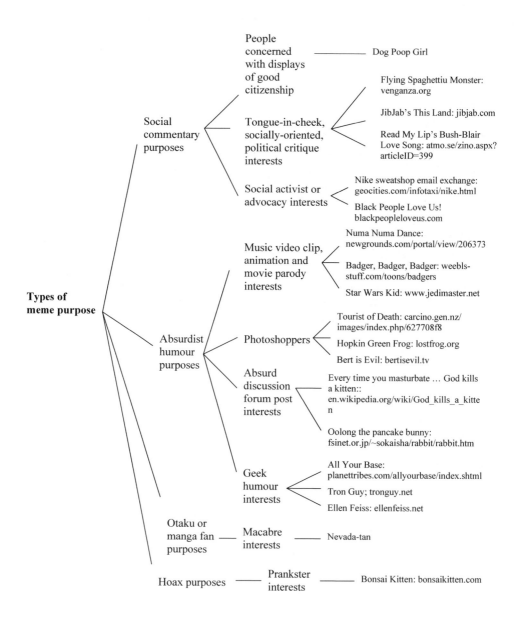

Figure 7.3 Meme typology

Memes, literacy education and classroom learning

How might memes and meming, as a kind of 'new' literacy, invite us to think about literacy education and, more generally, about classroom learning? What kinds of 'windows' or perspectives on literacy education and learning might be afforded to the kinds of people who 'hang around' or participate in memes, who 'get' memes, and who inhabit the kinds of online places that confer forms of insider awareness that memes recruit and spin off? We think this is an important question to ask. In fact, it is just one particular instance of a generic question that can be applied to any new literacy. For example, how might fanfiction or blogging or manga practices (as kinds of new literacies) invite us to think about literacy education and, more generally, about classroom learning? We conclude this chapter by briefly addressing four thoughts about literacy education and classroom learning that are highlighted for us by our discussion of memes.

The importance of a L/literacy perspective

Memes highlight the profoundly social dimension of language and literacy. In a nutshell, memes require networked human hosts in order to get established, to grow, and to survive. This social dimension of memes and meming emphasizes the importance for literacy education of focusing on practices that are larger than reading and writing. To make this point we will (shamelessly) remix one of our favourite academic memes – Gee's D/discourse meme (Gee 1996, 2004) – as L/literacies (with a big L and a little l).

Literacy, with a 'big L' refers to making meaning in ways that are tied directly to life and to *being* in the world (cf., Freire 1972; Street 1984). That is, whenever we use language, we are making some sort of significant or socially recognizable 'move' that is inextricably tied to someone bringing into being or realizing some element or aspect of their world. This means that *l*iteracy, with a 'small l', describes the actual processes of reading, writing, viewing, listening, manipulating images and sound, etc., making connections between different ideas, and using words and symbols that are part of these larger, more embodied Literacy practices. In short, this distinction explicitly recognizes that L/literacy is always about reading and writing *something*, and that this something is always part of a larger pattern of being in the world (Gee *et al.* 1996). And, because there are multiple ways of being in the world, then we can say that there are multiple L/literacies.

At the level of *l*iteracy we can see how producing a photoshopped image for, say, the Bert is Evil meme involves generating a text comprising a carefully designed montage of photographic and hand-drawn images together with written words or embedded sound effects. The multimedia dimensions of this text production involve understanding what software application to use to cut and crop and blend disparate images into a new 'whole'; what image manipulation tools to use and for what effects (e.g., using the 'blur' tool to soften the edges of imported or cut-and-pasted images so that they look more 'naturally' a part of the overall scene); how to generate and fix in place layers of images; how to add a sound track or printed stretches of text; how to save the resulting file in an internet-friendly form and how to upload the file to an archive or forum, and so on. In short, contributing a multimodal 'meme text' that has the maximum appearance of veracity, regardless of the actual absurdity of the content for this contribution, requires a range of finely-honed technical skills and competencies.

More important, however, are the 'big L' Literacy practices associated with meming that are invested in meaning making, social significance-making, and identity-making in one's life worlds. The texts and montages produced and read as part of being infected with and propagating a meme online are never free-standing. Rather, they are implicated in and generated out of networks of shared interests, experiences, habits, worldviews and the like that pick up on and use texts, events, phenomena, icons, cultural artefacts etc. in *particular* – and, often in socially idiosyncratic – ways. For example, posting a picture of a rabbit with pancakes on its head only makes sense in an online forum that celebrates quirky conversation responses. The Pancake Rabbit meme began when an image of a rabbit balancing what was referred to as a 'pancake' on its head, along with the caption, 'I have no idea what you're talking about ... so here's a bunny with a pancake on its head', was posted to a discussion forum (see kimsal.com/rabbit_pancake.jpg).

Hence, analysing the 'ideational system' of a given meme needs to be carefully nuanced in order to fully appreciate that successful online memes are often heavily ironic and tongue-in-cheek, and reference multiple texts, events, cultural practices and values. Looking for the meme to make 'sense' in its own right would be to overlook much that is important, especially with respect to absurdist memes. Similarly, analysing the contextual system of successful online memes also needs to be nuanced and pay close attention to the often collaborative, cumulative and distributed nature of these memes.

A 'big L' conception of new *Literacies* recognizes that everyday life is often amplified through participation of and interaction with people one may never meet and, moreover, that in online environments this interaction and participation may occur in ways not previously possible. The Lost Frog meme isn't simply about generating humorous images concerning the search for or the whereabouts of a child's lost frog. It plays out as a distributed collaboration that crosses national borders and languages (e.g., not all the lost frog images make use of English), and brings together people who probably do not know each other but who nonetheless value each other's contribution. The 'big L' dimensions of the Lost Frog meme include recognizing that amateurish or clumsy photoshopping will not produce a meme vehicle that is as memorable or as contagious as something that is slick and well-crafted in terms of design and technical proficiency alike. At the same time, however, it also encompasses knowing that a particularly humorous or conceptually clever version of the meme will win out every time over mere quality of technical execution. It also includes recognizing clever intertextuality in the form of cross-references to other memes or cultural practices, beliefs and phenomena (e.g., conspiracy theories, alien abduction theories, the significance of computer or web browser error messages, the social roles of remembrance ribbons and 'missing persons' announcement vehicles, etc.).

Some of the other 'Big L' Literacy practices discernible in the meme pool used in our study include the practices of video game playing, celebrating Japanese popular culture, being a fan (which can include writing fanfiction, setting up homage websites, linking to a meme archive via one's weblog, etc.), being privy to a plethora of online affinity space 'insider jokes', being familiar and up-to-date with Hollywood movies, or with fan practices such as lipsynching to pop songs or cosplay.

At the dawn of the mass internet, Ursula Franklin cautioned against taking an 'artefactual approach' to examining new technologies. She argued for focusing instead on technology use as part of a 'system of social practice' (Franklin 1990). Franklin's advice applies to studying new L/literacies, as well. When we examine memes as *Literacy* practices we see they involve much more than simply passing on and/or adding to written or visual texts or information *per se* (i.e., *l*iteracy). Rather, they are tied directly to ways of interacting with others, to meaning making, and to ways of being, knowing, learning and doing.

In short, the importance of teachers having a 'big L' Literacy mindset on memes cannot be over-stated. This, in turn, suggests the importance of seeing time spent in affinity spaces as a bone fide dimension of learning. More than this, it is *indispensable* – for teachers and learners alike. Some of the integral features of affinity spaces that enable learning are the very stuff of how literacies – and, particularly, *new* literacies – are constituted and experienced by people engaging in them. Gee (2004: 9, 73) describes affinity spaces as

> specially designed spaces (physical and virtual) constructed to resource people [who are] tied together ... by a shared interest or endeavor. ... [For example, the] many many websites and publications devoted to [the video game, *Rise of Nations*] create a social space in which people can, to any degree they wish, small or large, affiliate with others to share knowledge and gain knowledge that is distributed and dispersed across many different people, places, Internet sites and modalities (magazines, chat rooms, guides, recordings).

Among various other features concerning learning in particular, affinity spaces instantiate participation, collaboration, distribution and dispersion of expertise, and relatedness. Our focus on new literacies is interested in social practice as a whole, of which learning and sharing knowledge and expertise are a part. Our point is that the 'logic' of new literacies embodies general features and qualities highlighted by Gee's account of 'affinity spaces'. These features and qualities emphasize the relational and social aspects of any literacy practice and draws attention to various social and resource configurations within which and through which people participate and learn.

Reflection and discussion

Think about some of the digitally mediated affinity spaces you yourself 'inhabit' fairly regularly.

- What role do these spaces play in your everyday life?

- How did you first encounter these spaces and how did you learn to become a proficient participant in these spaces?

- What place might your own affinity space understandings and practices have within school contexts?

Memes and learning in relation to civic and ethical considerations

Meming is a fruitful practice for educators to consider when thinking about new forms of social participation and civic action in the wake of widespread access to the internet and involvement in increasingly dispersed social networks. Brodie (1996) has argued for more attention to be paid to the memes with which we are infected, and with which we infect others, as well as to the material effects of these infections. Not all the memes gathered for this study are benign and contribute to expansive ways of being in the world. The Dog Poop Girl meme, for example, rightly roused criticisms of the vigilante way in which the woman was identified and then publicly hounded until she apologized. The power of this meme to mobilize public censure of this woman was clearly significant in its reach and has opened a Pandora's box of issues concerning to what extent memes should be used to right relatively minor social wrongs and by what authority. In South Korea, academics and journalists alike have been openly discussing the importance of understanding the dangers of witch-hunt types of approaches to public castigation of a person. Indeed, participating in this meme by passing the woman's picture and personal details along to others is not an innocent, playful or morally clear-cut act, and provides teachers with a controversial event that promotes important discussions about the moral and civic dimensions of participating in certain memes.

The Star Wars Kid meme likewise provides fruitful ground for teachers and students to examine what happens when reluctant meme stars are 'adopted' by members of cybercommunities who spend considerable time and energy identifying who they are in meatspace, where they live, and who may unwittingly focus widespread broadcast media attention on them after broadcasting their names online. Ghyslain did not find anything funny about the Star Wars Kid meme. He and his parents regarded it as cruel and invasive. Ironically, perhaps, a group of cybercitizens who banded together and raised money to buy him an iPod were offended when he refused to have anything to do with them and their iPod and brought charges against some meme participants for invasion of privacy and related harm. Regardless of intent, the material effects of memes are not always beneficial to meme 'stars'. Nor do these 'stars' necessarily welcome the attention directed at them (cf. Ellen Fleiss and her television advertisement for Apple; the father of Terry, who lost his frog; Gary Brolsma of Numa Numa Dance fame). Examining memes like these can add new meaning to participating in memes, including the capacity and disposition to consider how far one's participation will reach.

Researchers like Adar and colleagues remind us that the most socially powerful and *influential* people online are not necessarily high profile persons and groups but, rather, those who *cause* idea epidemics (Adar, in conversation with Asaravala 2004; Adar *et al.* 2004). Interrogating memes is one way of considering the ideas, hooks and catches that infect us, how they may impact on our decision-making, actions, and our relations with others, and how we might respond to our understanding of these matters. *Counter-meming* is a well-established online practice. It involves purposefully generating memes that aim to neutralize or defeat potentially harmful ideas. (Compare, for example, the work of Adbusters.com. See also the strategies outlined at memecentral.com/antidote.htm, allyourbrand.org/why.htm, and dkosopedia.com/index.php/Meme).

To take a specific example, Mike Godwin (1994) documents how he began a meme to counter what he called a 'Nazi-meme' that he saw operating in different online discussion boards to which he belonged. He describes this Nazi-meme as a practice that was widespread at the time whereby discussants drew direct analogies between what another person had posted to the board and Nazism. Godwin felt compelled to counteract these glib and offensive analogies. He developed 'Godwin's Law of Nazi Analogies' and released this meme into discussion groups wherever he saw a gratuitous Nazi reference. His original 'law' stated that: 'As an online discussion grows longer, the probability of a comparison involving Nazis or Hitler approaches one' (Godwin 1994: 1). The meme quickly caught on and became a kind of 'marker' for judging the worth of a discussion thread. The original statement of Godwin's Law underwent a number of mutations at the word level, but the idea itself remained intact.

> As *Cuckoo's Egg* author Cliff Stoll once said to me: 'Godwin's Law? Isn't that the law that states that once a discussion reaches a comparison to Nazis or Hitler, its usefulness is over?' By my (admittedly low) standards, the [counter-meme] experiment was a success.
>
> (Godwin 1994: 1)

Godwin suggests that this kind of 'memetic engineering' makes an important contribution to the health of our social and mental lives and proposes that once we identify a harmful meme we may have a social and moral responsibility to confront it by releasing a positive counter-meme into the idea stream. Among the memes in the pool we collected, several rank as successful counter-memes (Black People Love Us!, The Flying Spaghetti Monster, This Land Is My Land, and the Bush–Blair Love Song). These memes are generative resources and, among other things, can be used to promote discussion and to encourage the development of informed points of view – by way of supplementary research and reading – on a range of social issues.

Reflection and discussion

- What are some of the ethical dimensions that need to be considered in any call to create a counter-meme?

- To what extent do you agree or disagree with Godwin's claim that we may well have a moral and social responsibility to launch positive counter-memes into the meme stream? Why, or why not?

Adopting an expansive view of meta-knowledge

Over the past 20 to 30 years, numerous researchers and writers have enriched our concepts and understanding of literacy education and learning more generally by identifying the role of meta-level knowledge within successful performance. Within literacy education, for example, writers working in areas like genre theory, critical literacy, discourse studies, comprehension theory, higher-order reading skills and the like have had much to say about meta-level understandings and skills. More generally, researchers and theorists working in fields like cognitive science and meta-cognition, and particulary those adopting Vygotskian approaches to social cognition, have provided further perspectives on the role and significance of meta-level knowledge and understandings for competent practice (for an introduction, see Gee, *et al.* 1996: Chs 3 and 7).

The approach to new literacies that we have taken throughout this book draws attention to something we think is very important so far as 'meta matters' are concerned. It is this: to date, most of the work that has been done has focused on 'metas' from conventional epistemological and ontological standpoints, as crunched through traditional disciplinary and, recently, cross/interdisciplinary approaches. Hence, we get an emphasis on such relationships as those between linguistic concepts like 'genre' and 'schemas', and epistemological ideals like 'propriety', 'correctness', 'rationality' and the like. Within wider vistas of learning we get an emphasis on relationships between mastery of concepts in physics or mathematics and effective reasoning and problem solving within these disciplinary practices themselves and within areas of life in which they are applied (see ibid. 1996: Chs 3 and 7). As we intimated briefly at the end of Chapter 3, conventional literacies and book space are closely linked with this whole enlightenment heritage. Yet, the current explosion of new literacies, and the progressive push toward realizing the second mindset seems to be opening up further dimensions of 'metas' that may need to be taken much more seriously in relation to learning and to literacy education than they have to date.

While we do not have space to go into it here (for a discussion see Lankshear and Knobel 2002, 2003: Ch. 5), the growing significance of what has been referred to in various ways as the attention economy or attention economics (e.g., Goldhaber 1997; Lanham 1994) converges with our concept of the second mindset and new literacies to indicate the growing significance of such meta-level matters as an appreciation of 'cool', of 'being there first and early', and of knowing 'how stuff best gets done' within a given space. The latter is especially interesting and a dimension of meta-knowledge that is regularly overlooked by education researchers interested in examining learning and practice. Knowing how to conduct oneself within a given network space includes knowing how to practise a generosity of spirit that spans giving advice to newbies through to giving stuff away free (e.g., posting open access images online, giving away items within a game, paying the costs of hosting a public fan website, providing unstinting feedback on fan writing or art). This generosity of spirit also needs to come with meta-knowledge about how to avoid being scammed. This is much like real-life of course, although it assume a particular form online, and involves a raft of meta-understandings about what to look for in a range of interactions. These include:

- Being savvy about when it is all right to divulge personal contact details online and when it is not.
- Being able to scrutinize the veracity of texts obtained via networks or online spaces that have very little to do with conventional 'information' or 'truth' criteria and everything to do with discursive understandings of how online practices work. For example: knowing how to read the source code of an email message claiming to be an urgent communiqué from a bank or online payment service wanting you to verify your account details and checking whether the click-through URLs contained in the message and hidden in the code match your bank's actual URL or are scam links; or understanding that the Bonsai Kitten website was a hoax because there were no methods available for purchasing bonsai kitten making kits and no contact details for the company; knowing how to access documentation on known scams within various multi-player online games.
- Knowing about specific scams like the Nigerian email scam and how they work.
- Knowing what to look for in computer virus warnings sent by email (e.g., who it's from, the veracity of the operational logic of the virus

claimed in the email, correct spelling and grammar), and how to double-check the veracity of the warning by conducting a search for the named virus (e.g., 'Good times', 'sulfnbak.exe') along with the keyword, 'hoax' (if the warning is a hoax, it will be documented online).

Particularly important meta-knowledge relevant to living online also includes:

- Knowing which blogs will lend you cachet if you link to particular posts and readers of these influential blogs then use the trackback feature of the blog post to arrive at your blog (i.e., you're much less likely to attract secondary attention if the influential blog doesn't have a 'trackback' feature for posts).
- Knowing how to use blog search engines to see who is linking to your blog and shoring up social networks and alliances – and your own influence – by linking to them in return, or posting a comment on their blog.
- Knowing that the quirky, humorous, and downright bizarre is far more likely to draw attention online than almost anything else, aside from large-scale disasters or political intrigue (e.g., posting instructions for how to make your own to-scale, knitted model of the human digestive tract is far more likely to attract attention online than an interminable account of what you watched on telly last night). Advertising companies are tapping directly into this feature of life online and are letting quirkiness and snappy ideas take precedence over traditional product branding techniques as witnessed by satellite broadcaster BSkyB's advertising video comprising a live re-enactment of the opening sequence to the popular cartoon animation, *The Simpsons* (youtube.com/watch?v= 49IDp76kjPw). The company deliberately chose to release the video online and not just on television with the result that during its first week online alone it was accessed by millions of viewers.
- Knowing that exploration and risk-taking online are rewarded and encouraged in ways that seldom happen in schools (e.g., exploring a new adventure space within a video game requires the gamer to get inside and move or click around and see what happens, knowing that the game can be restarted anytime and death is only fleeting); in schools, high stakes testing works the opposite way by insisting students have too few chances to 'get it right'.

If we take the example of 'cool' as well, it is evident that many affinity spaces on the internet attract people who are deeply into 'cool' and 'being cool'. Being and having cool are good for getting attention. This is not simply a matter of trendy fads in new areas. For us, Gee's D/discourse meme is one of the 'coolest' things to have gone around language and literacy related areas of studies since Ludwig Wittgenstein's 'forms of life' and 'private language' memes. As an attention grabber, it is second to none in the field. It works. And it works not merely as a 'hook' but, far more importantly, as a powerful intellectual resource that is overflowing with 'metas'. But there are 'internet cools' as well, and these are very important for successful performance of new literacies and for participation in new literacy practices, as well as for doing identity and esteem work.

Various internet-mediated affinity spaces attract people who are seeking and/or peddling 'cool'. Sites like Boingboing.net and Slashdot.com are associated with trend-spotting, undoubtedly 'cool people', and with reporting on the 'next big thing'. Such spaces always have a high 'cool quotient' and are seen as worth participating in – either as a contributor and/or as a reader and comment-maker – by anyone wanting to appear 'plugged in' to cutting edge cultural or subcultural evolution. Online, contributing directly to spreading a new, mutating meme is considered cool, and generating an entirely new meme is even cooler. Being among the first to spot a potential online mutating meme is perhaps coolest of all.

This bespeaks meta-level understandings and knowledge of a quite different order from those with which educational theory and research have been concerned to date. And if our arguments here are reading the trends of the current conjuncture at all accurately, it seems to us that these new metas are likely only to grow in significance during the decades ahead. They cannot be intuited out of a vacuum any more than conventional kinds of meta-awareness can. They presuppose experiences and practice of kinds that allow us to spot them and for them to stand out for us so that they can be spotted. To put it another way, you can't buy a ticket to Rio if you don't know it's there; likewise, you can't see new metas if you don't know to look for them.

The challenge of 'digital epistemologies'

Finally, our discussion of memes provides a window on what we have elsewhere (Lankshear *et al.* 2000; Lankshear and Knobel 2003: Ch. 7) identified as the challenge of 'digital epistemologies' for literacy and learning as conventionally understood and practised. The key idea here is that a large and seemingly increasing proportion of what people do and seek within practices mediated by new digital technologies – particularly, computing and communications technologies – has nothing directly to do with truth and with established rules, procedures and standards for knowing. This is most emphatically *not* to say that these matters are no longer important. Rather, it is to draw attention to the fact that today's learners are increasingly recruited to other values and priorities.

For example, the phenomenon of online memes challenges the growing dominance of 'digital literacy' conceptions of what it means to be a competent user of new technologies and networks. Increasingly, digital literacy is being defined by policy groups and others in terms of technical or operational competence with computers and the internet (cf., accounts in Lankshear and Knobel 2006), and/or as the ability to evaluate information by examining sources, weighing up author credibility, gauging the quality of writing and argument building in an online text, judging the 'truth value' of a text found online, and so on (e.g., Gilster 1997). Many of the successful memes included in this study would be discounted or ignored by digital literacy advocates because they do not carry 'useful' information or otherwise conform to the epistemological priorities of digital literacy. This seems to us to constitute a massive blind spot. Digital literacy mindsets do not pay sufficient attention to the importance of social relations in developing, refining, remixing and sharing ideas in fecund and replicable ways, or to the important role that memes play in developing culture and creativity (cf., Lessig 2004).

Applying conventional information evaluation criteria and digital literacy competency checklists (see, for example, certiport.com) to website-based memes like *Black People Love Us!* (blackpeopleloveus.com) will make little sense because the website itself is a deliberate parody of personal webpages and is not intended to be 'true' in any conventional way. The 'testimonials' made by Black people about the White couple who 'created' this page (and in reality, who are not a couple at all but, rather, brother and sister) may or may not be 'true' or 'authentic'. This, however, is completely beside the point. Peretti and his sister nonetheless use this website to try and infect us with what they see as a very significant message.

From a technical standpoint, the website is painfully cheesy in its design, and doubtless intentionally so. What matters most about this meme is the challenge it poses to 'liberal' attitudes that are patronizing in effect and that tend to reduce racial issues to superficial differences concerning, for example, skin colour and language use, rather than focusing actively on ameliorating structural, economic, historical, ideological and other inequities experienced by people of colour in their everyday lives. Similarly, while many of the remixed images in the All Your Base meme are technically sophisticated and polished, not all of them can be considered the work of proficient photoshoppers. Technical competence is clearly *not* a major criterion for successfully inserting an image in a meme stream. What does appear to be important is that the final image is clearly, recognizably and cleverly linked in some way to the idea being carried by the meme itself. This is more about being smart than being truthful, correct, or proficient in conventional terms. That does *not* make it right. It does, however, make it significant so far as thinking about literacy and learning under contemporary and foreseeable conditions is concerned.

CHAPTER 8

So What?

Introduction

Our aim in this book has been to develop a viable concept of new literacies – of what it is about particular social practices of encoding meaning that make it appropriate to think of them as *new* – and to discuss some prominent examples of new literacies thus understood. In so doing we have tried as far as possible to address these new literacies *in their own terms*, rather than in terms of their implications for formal learning in classrooms – and without any thought whatsoever of transporting them holus bolus into the curriculum. Certainly, we have tried to avoid any suggestion that new literacies should take over the literacy curriculum or displace established literacies. On the contrary, on those occasions in this book (eg., pp. 22–23, pp. 53–60) and in other places (e.g., Lankshear and Snyder 2000; Lankshear and Knobel 2003: Chs 3, 4; Goodson *et al.* 2002: Chs 3, 4) where we have considered what happens when new technologies get incorporated into school-based literacy education and learning more generally, our response has often been: 'Please don't do that. It is better to keep new technologies *out* of learning if the price of their "integration" would be to impose outsider ways on insider sensibilities.'

At the heart of this book is the idea that the concept of *new* literacies is attached to a mindset that differs in very significant ways from historically familiar and conventional ways of looking at the world. We have asked 'What is "new"?' with a view to raising questions about how *the new* might best be brought into a fruitful relationship with *the already established*. If, as educationists, teachers, teacher educators, administrators, policy developers, parents, learners or media commentators, we want to engage effectively in processes that will bring 'the new' and 'the already established' into productive conversation, we must first know where we stand in relation to new literacies.

Rather than advancing judgements about the place of new literacies within formal learning, we have tried instead to pose *questions* we think are worth reflecting on. These have been questions designed to encourage thinking about issues associated with new literacies generally and in relation to education, as well as questions about where we would locate ourselves in relation to the two mindsets and in relation to new literacies, and on what grounds we locate ourselves there. We have also posed questions pertaining to options that might be contemplated so far as taking up new technologies within formal learning settings are concerned.

In addressing our aim we have tried to present accounts of various new literacies in ways that will evoke interest and curiosity on the part of readers who are unfamiliar with them, such that they will be encouraged to 'take a look and see'. Indeed, we have tried to stimulate an interest in taking a look to see how these literacies might be experienced by those who are really *into* them, who are *insiders* of these new kinds of social practices. Unless and until we can do this as educators we have no effective base from which to even begin trying to envisage and develop pedagogical approaches that integrate new technologies into processes of taking learners from where they are to places we believe it will be good for them educationally to go. In this context, Jennifer Stone (2006: 5) observes that a burgeoning body of research into popular websites and other online spaces is contributing to deeper understandings of 'young people's out-of-school literate lives'. At the same time, she argues that this work harbours some important limitations. Apart from mainly focusing only on individual sites associated with some particular affinity space or other, they also 'tend not to deal in depth with how these sites support school-based literacies' (ibid.). Stone cites Hull and Schultz's (2001) belief that it is important to begin applying insights derived from study of such literacies to educational contexts.

This is consistent with the approach we have endorsed here of looking as far as possible at new literacy practices on their own terms, and then considering the extent to which and ways in which insights might be applied to classroom literacy education. The question is how to apply insights in ways that do not compromise the integrity of either the 'popular' cultural practices in question or our educational purposes.

Stone (2006) provides helpful examples of how applications of insights from research into non-school literacies might usefully inform classroom practice. For example, spending time in the kinds of online sites Stone has researched makes it clear that 'critical media literacy' approaches based on familiar forms of advertising will be inadequate for developing critical orientations toward the 'new' kinds of hooks and catches being developed around affinities as a means for recruiting consumer allegiances. If literacy education is to encourage approaches to critical evaluation of how certain kinds of websites that have strong appeal to adolescents work *ideologically* to recruit young people's consumer investments and allegiances, it will not be sufficient simply to assume familiar 'ideal types' of advertisements. This kind of application of research insights to classroom practice is not direct or straightforward. It calls for careful and sophisticated interpretation on the part of the researcher herself, as Stone's work shows. This is demanding work. It is not a matter of peeling off some straightforward application.

This raises a further complication. It is one thing for a careful and sensitive researcher to study a new literacy space, pursue some degree of insider participant understanding of what is going on, and then engage in the complex kind of interpretation that can inform an educationally constructive initiative. It may be another thing altogether for a teacher or curriculum developer to 'take' an insight from someone else's research report and translate it into a curriculum or pedagogy application. This is especially so if the reader has limited personal experience with the kinds of phenomena being researched. There are serious limits to what 'outsiders' can understand of 'insider' experiences and of the artefacts and other discursive trappings that constitute these experiences from written reports alone – no matter how well conceived and presented the informing research may be.

As we will argue below, we think that the best way for those involved in education to pursue respectful and potentially fruitful 'intersections' across different literacies spaces is by actively pursuing personal experience of the phenomena being reported in the research. This is experience of social *practices*, not merely of artefacts like texts and tools, or of specific technical operations like posting comments or navigating around a site. In Stone's paper, popular websites in adolescents' out-of-school lives point to social practices. The websites are merely portals. They lead to what is significant. Experiencing what is significant in the kinds of ways that may lead to educationally fruitful applications of *insights* – which, after all, are *sights* from the *in*side – calls for commitment to getting a feel for the practices and what constitutes them.

By way of following this argument further and concluding our account of new literacies in relation to everyday practices and classroom learning we will briefly address two points. The first relates to our idea in Chapter 3 that the current literacy conjuncture can be understood usefully in terms of a *dialectic* between established literacies and new literacies, on the one hand, and between an established mindset and an emerging mindset on the other. The tensions between established and emergent literacies and mindsets have to 'work themselves into' a productive *synthesis* that will itself, in due course, be challenged by a new round of change and development. The second point is to draw some tentative implications from the overall discussion.

A 'dialectical' approach to thinking about new and established literacies

In his book *Everything Bad Is Good for You*, Steven Johnson (2005) argues that active participation in contemporary popular culture is making young people in the US (and, by implication, in other relevantly similar societies) *smarter* on average. He describes a culture industry that recruits young people to engage with genuinely complex media that demand serious thinking and problem solving, reflection and comparison, recall, and hypothesizing at almost every point of engagement. He describes the complementarity of contemporary media whereby, for example, viewers of popular television programmes post their reflections online and stimulate discussion and debate and provide points of view and recounts that other viewers (fans) can interact with – thereby contributing to enhancing the critical, aesthetic and pleasurable experiences of all. For example:

> Devoted fans coauthor massive open documents – episode plot summaries, frequently asked questions, guides to series trivia – that exist online as evolving works of popular scholarship, forever being tinkered with by the faithful. Without these new channels, the subtleties of the new culture would be lost to all but the most ardent fans. But the public, collaborative nature of these sites means that dozens or hundreds of fans can team up to capture all the nuances of a show, and leave behind a record for the less motivated fans to browse through at their convenience. And so the threshold of complexity rises again. *The*

Simpsons creators can bury a dozen subtle film references in each episode and rest assured that their labors will be reliably documented online within a few days.

(Johnson 2005: 169–70)

The same thing applies in games (Gee 2003; Johnson 2005: 17–62) and, as we have seen, imaginative projections of it occur in fanfiction.

Building example upon example, Johnson mounts a convincing case for the claim that, far from spiraling downward into mind-numbing stupor, today's popular culture is actually more cognitively challenging – *much* more cognitively challenging – than in previous generations. He is not, of course, saying that this is all there should be to culture, and that this popular culture is sufficient in its own right so far as being educated is concerned. Far from it. Rather, he seeks to redress a balance. His case is, in part, a case against ignorance and blanket judgements that impute intellectual and moral poverty to popular culture. He is arguing that popular culture has changed dramatically in the period that coincides with the emergence and development of digital technologies. He is arguing in part that this change has been in the direction of greater complexity and cognitive challenge, especially in areas like television and games. He is arguing also that we should take a close and empirically grounded look at what is actually happening in popular culture rather than allowing any prejudices we may have to run familiar storylines about the moral and intellectual bankruptcy of popular culture. He shows that if we look we can find abundant evidence for the claim that popular culture contains much that is 'cognitively nourishing'.

At the same time, however, he homes in on a point that is fruitful and indicative for thinking about new literacies in relation to established literacies and, moreover, for thinking about education in terms of a conversation between these various literacies. Johnson compares books with networked texts in relation to the varying demands they make upon us and the varying opportunities and possibilities they respectively afford (see Johnson 2005: 185–7).

He begins by observing that far from spelling the death of alphabetic writing and its replacement by the image, the growth of the internet has resulted in people reading written text 'as much as ever' and writing more text than ever before (ibid.: 185). At the same time, however, he accepts the oft made observation that in the US 'a specific, historically crucial kind of reading has grown less common' (ibid.). This is the practice of sitting down with a lengthy book for a lengthy stretch of time 'and following its argument or narrative without a great deal of distraction' (ibid.).

With networked texts, says Johnson, we operate 'in shorter bursts' than with books, across a wider breadth of information, and in much more participatory ways. Networked texts are 'more connective' and more 'abbreviated' than are books. Moreover, '[c]omplicated, sequential works of persuasion, where each premise builds on the previous one, and where an idea can take an entire chapter to develop, are not well suited to life on the computer screen' (ibid.: 185).

Johnson says that for all the importance of email in his life and for all the intellectual nourishment he derives from his blog (Stevenberlinjohnson. com), there is no way he would dream of trying to convey the argument presented in his book using email or a blog. He sees networked texts as rating high on some intellectual riches and not so high on others. In the 'riffs, annotations and conversations' that thrive within online spaces we can, and do, encounter much that is intellectually dazzling. But the intelligence that dazzles here is different, says Johnson, from 'the intelligence that is delivered by reading [and, of course, by *writing*] a sustained argument for two hundred pages' (ibid.: 186). The book is the natural medium for transmitting 'a fully fledged worldview', and a parallel argument applies to fiction (the novel) with respect to re-creating 'the mental landscape of another consciousness', and to projecting ourselves into 'the first-person experiences of other human beings' (ibid.: 187).

While it might be argued that spending extended time on a substantial blog is likely to afford insights into the blogger's full-fledged worldview, we nonetheless accept Johnson's main point: there is a rich and powerful *literacy* that consists in a particular kind of reading associated with an established form of text (namely, *books*). Moreover, and of crucial importance, this literacy remains a very potent resource for attaining social, economic and cultural rewards. It continues to be central to academic and professional participation and success. For example, it is integral to research and scholarship, both scientific and literary or 'humanist'. It is also integral to engaging in many aspects and areas of professional life that depend upon the capacity to understand and evaluate different points of view and ways of doing things, and to develop alternatives as and where appropriate. Just as lawyers must be able to absorb, understand, analyse and synthesize large amounts of information to make their cases, so must business executives, management consultants, journalists, clerics, script writers, narrators and administrators, among many others.

This kind of literacy is often closely associated with becoming competent in *disciplinary* thinking, and knowing how to mount a sustained argument as a result of understanding concepts, elements of theory, the nature and significance of evidence, and the like that 'systems' of knowledge based on academic disciplines confer. The reading and writing that Johnson is talking about are associated with the development of a certain kind of mind, and with a certain kind of orientation toward understanding and approaching the world. Johnson's own book exemplifies this very point. Early on in his argument he notes that the changes going on in popular culture reflect a dynamic interaction between three important forces: the economics of the culture industry; appetites of the human brain; and changes in technological platforms (2005: 10). Johnson says that to understand these forces and how they interact it will be necessary to 'draw upon disciplines that don't usually interact with one another: economics, narrative theory, social network analysis, neuroscience' (ibid.: 11).

In other words, following Johnson's argument over two hundred pages is not a matter simply of following an extended sequence of *words* that carry ideas and interlocking components of argument. Rather, we are following Johnson's account of how these forces interact, which is informed by his analysis and interpretation of data, arguments, viewpoints, and so on that arise within and across these various disciplines. Johnson's book involves the development of an argument that is informed by work done by Johnson himself and by other people that is in turn based on academic forms of disciplined inquiry. In other kinds of books that involve the development of sustained arguments, narratives and points of view, authors may not be drawing on content, intellectual and interpretive tools, and ways of thinking that are more or less directly related to the academic disciplines *per se*. Nonetheless, they will be drawing on *some* kind or other of systemic (and systematic) ways of understanding and interacting with the world. These might be religious, commercial, vocational-occupational, aesthetic, grounded in popular everyday social and cultural routines. (For a relevant discussion of this point, refer to Gee *et al.* 1996: Ch. 7). That is, whenever we follow the argument or the narrative in a substantial book, we are (also) simultaneously following, reflecting upon, and evaluating content that emerges from *some* kind of 'system' of thinking, feeling, believing, interpreting, and judging.

Formal education has traditionally been conceived as a process of initiating learners into a particular range of such 'systems'; namely, those subjects and disciplines that define the school curriculum. The traditional ideal of educating learners has been one of trying to get them to approach their world *systematically* using models of inquiry that are based more or less directly on academic disciplines. Religions offer alternative 'systems', as do the worlds of work and popular culture. But historically, the role of education has been to make available to learners the opportunity to master a range of systematic ways of understanding and engaging with the world that they cannot be presumed to encounter elsewhere.

Johnson's work, along with that of numerous scholars doing popular culture research, attests to the capacity and disposition of young people (and, of course, not so young people) to master such *systems*. We know beyond a shadow of doubt that human beings are hardwired to manage systems. We see evidence of them doing so whenever we read accounts of young people's gaming practices, fanfiction production, active (i.e., not merely 'spectatorial') television viewing, and remixing.

At the same time, formal school-based learning is not doing well in terms of getting learners on the inside of either the academic discipline systems or the more vocationally-oriented 'ones' that jointly dominate the curriculum (cf., Gee *et al.* 1996: 159–65). Despite widespread claims of falling standards over the past two decades, we do not think this is a recent phenomenon. School-based curriculum has over-emphasized content and under-emphasized tools of thinking and analysis for generations – educational rhetoric notwithstanding. (For all the current espousals of 'constructivist learning approaches', how often do we find tenets of constructivism enacted in classrooms with anything like the depth, consistency, and sheer efficacy we routinely find when good gameware intersects with gamer energies and participation in online gaming affinity spaces?)

Moreover, current education policy seems to be pushing elementary education in particular *away* from anything approximating the kind of systemic/holistic mastery that young people get free in so many out-of-school Discourses. Policy is focusing inward to an alarming extent on piecemeal 'basic' literacy and numeracy 'skills'. One need only to compare Johnson's account (2005: 1–8, 196–9) of his informal numeracy learning around dice and card baseball games with the kinds of experiences youngsters have interacting with the kinds of curriculum packages and remedial learning 'resources' developed in conjunction with policies like *No Child Left Behind* and the various versions of *The Literacy/Numeracy Hour* to appreciate what is at stake here. As a 10-year-old, Johnson spent hours and hours playing a tables-based pencil and paper baseball simulation game called American Professional Baseball Association. Basically, the game required the player to choose baseballers to create a team, decide on a strategy, roll some dice and then consult a thick sheaf of printed 'look-up' tables to determine the outcome of the 'play' (ibid.: 2). Despite sounding relatively straightforward, the game was truly complex and required the player to take numerous variables into account. For example, Johnson quotes the full entry for 'Pitching' on the main 'Bases Empty' chart:

The hitting numbers under which lines appear may be altered according to the grade of the pitcher against whom the team is batting.

Always observe the grade of the pitcher and look for possible changes of those numbers which are underlined. 'No Change' always refers back to the D, or left, column and always means a base hit. Against Grade D pitchers there is never any change – the left hand column only is used. When a pitcher is withdrawn from a game make a note of the grade of the pitcher who relieves him. If his grade is different, a different column must be referred to when the underlined numbers come up. Certain players may have the numbers 7, 8 and/or 11 in the second column of their cards. When any of these numbers is found in the second column of a player card, it is not subject to normal grade changes. Always use the left (Grade D) column in these cases, no matter what the pitcher's grade is. Occasionally, pitchers may have A & C or A & B ratings. Always consider these pitchers as Grade A pitchers unless the A column happens to be a base hit. Then use the C or B column, as the case may be, for the final play result.

(Johnson 2005: 3–4)

Johnson goes on,

Got that? They might as well be the tax form instructions you'd happily pay an accountant to decipher. Reading these words now, I have to slow myself down just to follow the syntax, but my ten-year-old self had so thoroughly internalized this arcana that I played hundreds of APBA games without having to consult the fine print.

(ibid.: 4)

Of course, the quality of experience Johnson encountered with his appetite for games is widespread today, among young males and females alike, in countries like our own.

Yet, at a time when formal learning should be contending with popular cultural engagement for winning the learning allegiances of young people at the level of mastering systems of thinking and acting – which is what games and similarly complex popular cultural pursuits comprise – it is being pushed (where it is not running) in the opposite direction.

The problem is acute in teacher education where programme allocations are increasingly devoted to equipping teachers with 'classroom management skills' and 'strategies' for dealing with children who 'experience learning difficulties' or who are not 'ready to learn' (*sic*). These 'skills' and 'strategies' are often little more than cobblings of clichés and formulae (packages, kits, professional development 'opportunities', etc. For a critique, see Larson 2001). While all this is going on, increasingly less attention is given to ensuring that tomorrow's 'education professionals' come out of their preparation with 'substantial educational worldviews' based on coherent *systemic* ways of thinking about, interpreting, responding to, and evaluating their world, that they can draw on to make sense of formal learning under challenging contemporary conditions. The 'sense' that gets made all too often of contemporary challenges is at the banal level of 'ADHD', 'the difference between boys' and girls' brains' (or 'maturation rates'), 'no books in the home', and children 'not being ready to learn'. This is fatuous, and insulting to young people.

Reflection and discussion

Spend some time playing the free, massively multiplayer online game, *Kingdom of Loathing* (kingdomofloathing.com). Pay careful attention to how the game 'scaffolds' your participation as a 'newbie' by means of very explicit and increasingly more difficult tasks.

- What were the key things you paid attention to as you began playing this game?

- Why does the game itself come with such little 'how to play' documentation? What might this tell educators?

- What can educators learn about learning from playing digital games like this one?

- How does this game compare with games you played as a child? To what extent does *Kingdom of Loathing* bear out Johnson's claims about popular culture today?

Some tentative implications

So far as teacher education is concerned, redressing this trend is not a matter of simply finding more timetable slots for (decontextualized) classroom-like lectures on theory and content. The issue runs much deeper than that. The issue, in a word, is dialectical in the sense outlined in Chapter 3. While it would certainly be good for tomorrow's teachers to get greater exposure to educationally relevant theory than many are currently getting, and the opportunity to wrestle with arguments, and to apply ideas and explanations they encounter in texts to what they experience in practice, the fact is that this emphasis has often produced modest results in the past. On the other hand, if the invitation to wrestle with concepts, theories and arguments is integrated into an involvement in some *conceptually and methodologically sound* teacher research that pays due attention to framing questions and problems and developing valid designs for investigating them – a form of science, if you will – there is a good chance that teacher education students will be able to win through to an understanding of research as a systematic process that builds coherent explorations and arguments out of theory, concepts, data, analysis, design and argumentation: a high end version of 'problem solving'.

Alternatively, pursuing mastery of systemic kinds of approaches to understanding and interacting with aspects of the world in ways that might contribute to developing robust and substantial educational worldviews might be pursued through practicum experiences that work to support classroom teachers already in service who are trying to develop some version of a 'Knowledge-Producing Schools' pedagogy (deakin.edu.au/education/lit/kps), as described in Chapter 6. This would provide opportunities to explore what is involved in pursuing learning outcomes that meet real-world standards of proficiency and expertise, in the company of experts who can help learners and teachers keep theory and concepts, ideas and arguments, data and analysis closely related to generating viable and serviceable use values. The KPS approach is dialectical. It brings elements of the conventional and new that are often in tension within established educational set-ups and routines into a productive and risky 'conversation'. It works with these tensions to resolve and transcend them in ways that are fruitful for learning. The result is a different pedagogy that is neither wholly 'conventional' nor wholly 'new': yet it bears visible traces of both tendencies.

Another approach might involve some sustained participation in a fanfiction affinity space (or something similar) and bringing that experience into conversation with more formal immersion in an academic-scholarly version of literary criticism. This latter possibility suggests an interesting paradox. Engaging with a new literacy steeped in the ethos of the second mindset and the logic of Web 2.0 – emphasizing participation and collaboration, and mobilizing collective intelligence – may provide a conducive context for coming to understand and realize capacities and priorities typically associated with established and conventional literacy of the kind Johnson associates with reading a sustained argument in a book. The point here is that all too often we attempt to 'teach' these literacies without the kinds of participation, collaboration, and mobilization of collective intelligence that are absolutely integral to getting on the inside of 'systems'. Whether we are talking about a 'system' at the level of a language, or of systems at the level of Discourses, all such learning is saturated in the kinds of procedures and interactions that characterize the kinds of new literacies described in this book.

There is a further and *thoroughly dialectical* point to be entertained here. Just as we partly achieve a sense of identity of who we are by understanding ourselves in contradistinction to others – that is, in relation to who we are *not* – so we are likely to develop sharper awareness of what we consider *education* to be by contemplating it in relation to what we think education is *not* – in this case, certain popular cultural practices. Other people who are *like* us in relevant ways, but who are different from us in specific respects, provide vital points of reference for the kinds of differentiation integral to identity formation. Similarly, as Gee (1996, 1997) notes, we cannot critique a Discourse from within; we need to have access to some other Discourse from which to critique one that we are in. Without that external perspective we cannot attain the kind of meta-level awareness essential to critique. In like manner, popular cultural practices like fanfiction are 'relevantly like' formal educational learning yet, at the same time, 'relevantly different' from them. Engagement with an 'Other' to education may help us firm up our educational thinking and practice – an educational worldview – in unexpected yet fruitful and effective ways.

Consider, for example, literary criticism as a kind of knowledge we might want high school teachers to command. One route to 'grasping' literary criticism in ways that could usefully inform classroom approaches to teaching and learning might be to participate wholeheartedly in online fanfiction spaces and activities – producing one's own fics and reviewing other people's – and to reflect on the learning processes involved here in relation to one's formal academic study of literary criticism. Fanfiction writing and reviewing is *not* what high school English should be about – or, at least, not *all* that it should be about. Yet it is 'kind of' what bits of it are like. Where, then, do the differences lie, and what might a 'bona fide *educational* connection to fanfiction' look like?

A genuine strength of fanfiction practices consists in the ways participants support each other and provide fanfic 'guides' and tips for writing better fics. It is precisely through such participation, collaboration and mobilization of collective intelligence that expertise is developed in new literacies domains. Indeed, as previously noted, it is how people get to become 'insiders' to mature forms of *any* Discourse (Gee, Hull and Lankshear 1996: Ch 1). Yet such qualities and practices of collaboration, support and sharing designed to mutually produce 'insiders' are often conspicuous by their absence in formal learning. Various forms of collaboration are frowned upon, especially in the upper grades. Individuals are required to 'earn their own grades' and produce 'their own' work. Failure to observe well known norms of possessive individualism are regarded as 'cheating'.

Furthermore, the sorts of collaboration involved in fanfic spaces contrast markedly with familiar (yet strange) classroom narrative writing practices that ask students to each contribute one new sentence to a developing story in a sequence of turns, such that the resulting 'story' has little, if any, narrative structure or character development. They also go far beyond such common classroom practices as exploring character development by means of compare-and-contrast circles in Venn diagrams, which typically put the focus on physical characteristics, rather than on values, motivations, relations with other characters and the like. These latter are often emphasized in fanfic and, of course, in mature forms of fiction writing. Equally, the kinds of peer tutoring and paired learning found in many classrooms are pale imitations of what participants in online affinity spaces commonly experience online. Online participation may extend for hours at a time over weeks and months. By contrast with shallow, stop-start 'bits' of 'collaboration' encountered in formal settings, young people get to experience serious participation and collaboration in and through the kinds of online engagements people like Gee (2003), Johnson (2004), Jenkins (2004), Black (2005a and b, 2006), Lam (2000), Thomas (2006), Lessig (2004), Leander and Lovvorn (2006), Thomas (226), Unsworth and colleagues (2005), among others, have described so clearly and usefully.

In other words, building substantial online lives within affinity spaces and groups linked to areas of personal interest may prove to be a powerful way of coming to understand the tenets of participation and collaboration from the inside, and of gaining a standpoint from which to make effective transfers and appropriations to formal learning settings. That is, if we want to steep ourselves in pedagogical experiences that genuinely engage participants, support co-learners, make just in time and just in place information and understanding available in ways that enable effective learning, why not spend some sustained time and energy in spaces where this goes on? Why not spend time 'there' soaking up what is done and reflecting on the extent to which the ways it is done could be integrated beneficially into our own work as teachers and teacher educators? We know this is typically *not* done effectively in lectures, and we are starting to see that it is often equally poorly done within online learning management systems environments – replete as they frequently are with obligatory postings, passive content downloads, and requirements that the same old types of assignments developed during the pen and paper era get produced and submitted electronically.

Some other potential fruits of participation in online spaces

Educators who spend serious time hanging out and practising new literacies in online spaces devoted to interests they are passionate about are likely to understand how and why so much classroom appropriation of new technologies is ineffective, wasteful, and wrongheaded. For a start, they are likely to see that effective use of the internet calls for sustained continuous periods online with minimal constraints. They will come to understand the extent to which the purported risks associated with online environments are overstated and overplayed by 'concerned' groups within and outside education arenas. More importantly, they will become better equipped in knowing how to help learners keep themselves safe online. They are likely to get a good sense of how to integrate time spent online in formal settings into genuinely *educational* engagement. As part of this they are also likely to understand the extent to which potentially powerful educational appropriations of the internet are compromised and marginalised by a cult of fear operating in conjunction with conservative interpretations of 'duty of care.'

Reflection and discussion

Spend some time online searching for broadcast media accounts of young people's online practices (the search terms 'teenagers at risk online' is a good place to start). Compare claims across the items that you find, and then search for statistical and other kinds of empirical evidence that supports these claims.

- What do your findings suggest?

- How does this 'fit' with key arguments raised in the preceding chapters of this book?

- What is your own position on young people and their online practices, and what are your reasons for this position?

From a different angle, how might formal curriculum requirements be interpreted in ways that are consistent with uses of new technologies that pay due respect to insiders' sensibilities and passions *and also* pursue bona fide educational purposes? This question is much easier to address conceptually and in practice if one has some grounded understanding of insider sensibilities and investments and, at the very least, is aware that such things exist and are keenly felt. Hence, if there is a curriculum requirement to demonstrate competent production of a particular kind of text type and/or genre, might this be consistent with a learner presenting a 'walk through,' or an 'online guide,' or a photoshopped meme, or an annotated blog post, or a fanfic work (or review). In some cases the answer may be 'yes' and on others 'no.' But without some grounded experience of these new literacies there is no basis for making a reasonable decision or, even, for conceiving the question in the first instance. Need the item be produced in class time and space in order to count for meeting the curriculum requirement, or can learners bring it from home? Does it matter if they produce or refine this product in class while multitasking on their blog and in chat with friends? How much can it be produced collaboratively, and with whom? And how do we decide?

Alternatively, what might it be like for students who are learning in some area of science, history, French culture, or whatever to assume responsibility as groups for contributing and monitoring entries to knowledge items in *Wikipedia*? What constitutes an effective entry? How does one check sources? How does one anticipate audience? How does one respond to criticism in the form of other people editing one's entries? How does one wrestle with possible tensions between *Wikipedia's* policy of neutral entries and recognition that knowledge is inevitably inflected by theory, values stances and point of view? Educators who participate actively in online spaces are likely to have informed perspectives on such questions and to know how to draw on these perspectives to inform and enliven classroom teaching and learning activities. They are especially likely to be able to identify points at which classroom learning can build on learner sensibilities and how to create options for building on them.

Last writes

In the final analysis we do not advocate turning schools into 'playgrounds' for new literacies at the level of popular cultural engagement. Educational practice is distinct from and different to popular culture. The day we give that distinction away is the day we give formal education away. At the same time the two are far from mutually exclusive. Moreover, school literacy space is not and must not be exclusively the terrain of conventional literacies. That would be irresponsible. On the other hand, subjecting students in class time to constrained, stop-start, wrongheaded experiences of using new technologies within literacy education specifically and learning more generally is (unwittingly) to mis-educate.

Fortunately, the 'educational' and the 'popular cultural', and the 'conventional' and the new' can be brought into productive conversations and complementary relationships. This can happen when educators understand the differences and the overlaps, and can see where learner interests and capacities can be built upon for educational purposes. There is nothing new in this. Dewey (1916/1997, 1938/1997) expressed much the same idea a long time ago. Moreover, there is no single or easy path to resolving these dialectics of our times. One hopeful path, however, at least *begins* from opening ourselves to the worlds of new literacies and pursuing an open-minded, yet critically reflective, exploration of them – in conjunction with asking ourselves, regularly, what counts as an education that is appropriate for our times, and on what grounds do we hold this view.

References

Adar, E., Zhang, L., Adamic, L. and Lukose, R. (2004) Implicit structure and dynamics of blogspace, draft research report for the HP Information Dynamics Lab. hpl.hp.com/research/idl/papers/blogs/index.html (accessed 4 March 2004).

Adbusters (2002) www.adbusters.org (accessed 21 March 2002).

Aigrain, P. (2003) The individual and the collective in open information communities, debatpublic.net/Members/paigrain/texts/icoic.html (accessed 16 February 2006).

Alexander, B. (2004) Going nomadic: mobile learning in higher education, *Educause Review*, September/October: 29–35.

Allen, K. and Ingulsrud, J. (2003) Manga literacy: popular culture and the reading habits of Japanese college students, *Journal of Adolescent and Adult Literacy*, 46 (8): 674–83.

Amano, M. (2004) *Manga Design*. Köln: Taschen.

Amazon.com (2002) About Amazon.com. www.amazon.com/exec/obidos/subst/misc/company-info.html/ref=gw_bt_aa/102-1153992-2446513 (accessed 25 July 2002).

Anderson, C. A. (1966) Literacy and schooling on the development threshold: some historical cases, in C. A. Anderson and M. J. Bowman (eds) *Education and Economic Development*, pp. 347–62. Chicago: Aldine Publishing Co.

Asaravala, A. (2004) Warning: Blogs can be infectious. *Wired*. March. wired.com/news/print/0,1294,62537,00.html (accessed 7 March 2005).

Aunger, R. (2002) *The Electric Meme: A New Theory of How We Think*. New York: Free Press.

Barton, D. (1991) The social nature of writing, in D. Barton and R. Ivanič (eds) *Writing in the Community*. London: Sage.

Barton, D. and Hamilton, M. (1998) *Local Literacies: Reading and Writing in One Community*. London: Routledge.

Bigum, C. (2002) Design sensibilities, schools, and the new computing and communications technologies, in I. Snyder (ed.) *Silicon Literacies*, pp. 130–40. London: Falmer-Routledge.

Bigum, C. (2003a) The knowledge producing school: moving away from the work of finding educational problems for which computers are solutions. deakin.edu.au/education/lit/kps/pubs/comp_in_nz.rtf (accessed 16 February 2006)

Bigum, C. (2003b) Knowledge producing schools. Geelong: Deakin University. Mimeo.

Bigum, C. (2004) Rethinking schools and community: the knowledge producing school, in S. Marshall, W. Taylor and X. Yu (eds) *Using Community Informatics to Transform Regions*. London: Idea Group Publishing.

Björk, S., Holopainen, J., Ljungstrand, P. and Åkesson, K. (2002) Designing ubiquitous computing games: a report from a workshop exploring ubiquitous computing entertainment, *Personal and Ubiquitous Computing* 6: 443–58.

Black, R. W. (2005a) Access and affiliation: the literacy and composition practices of English language learners in an online fanfiction community, *Journal of Adolescent & Adult Literacy*, 49(2): 118–28.

Black, R. W. (2005b) Digital resources: English language learners reading and reviewing online fanfiction, paper presented at National Reading Conference, Miami, FL, 30 November.

Black, R. W. (2006) Not just the OMG standard: reader feedback and language, literacy, and culture in online fanfiction, paper presented at the Annual Meeting of The American Educational Research Association, San Francisco, 10 April.

Blackmore, S. (1999) *The Meme Machine*. Oxford: Oxford University Press.

Blood, R. (2002a) Introduction, in Editors of Perseus Publishing (eds) *We've Got Blog: How Weblogs Are Changing Culture*, pp. ix–xiii. Cambridge, MA: Perseus Publishing.

Blood, R. (2002b) Weblogs: a history and perspective, in Editors of Perseus Publishing (eds) *We've Got Blog: How Weblogs Are Changing Culture*, pp. 7–16. Cambridge, MA: Perseus Publishing.

Börjesson, M. (2005) Scenario planning resources. well.com/~mb/scenario (accessed 4 April 2006).

Bradner, S. and Metz, C. (2005) The continuing road toward Internet media, *Internet Computing, IEEE*, 9(4): 19–21.

Brodie, R. (1996) *Virus of the Mind: The New Science of the Meme*. Seattle: Integral Press.

Bryant, J., Saunders-Jackson, A., and Smallwood, A. (2006) IMing, text messaging, and adolescent social networks, *Journal of Computer-Mediated Communication*, 11(2): article 10. jcmc.indiana.edu/vol11/issue2/Bryant.html (accessed 16 February 2006).

Caldwell, R. (no date) Glossary for course on Anticipating the Future. ag.arizona.edu/futures/home/glossary.html (accessed 16 February 2006).

Castells, M. (1996) *The Rise of the Network Society*. Oxford: Blackwell.

Castells, M. (2000) *The Rise of the Network Society*. 2nd edition. Oxford: Blackwell.

Ceglowski, M. (2003) An audioblogging manifesto. idlewords.com/audio-manifesto.txt (accessed 12 March 2006).

Chandler-Olcott, K. and Mahar, D. (2003a) Adolescents' anime-inspired fanfictions: an exploration of multiliteracies, *Journal of Adolescent and Adult Literacy*, 46(7): 556–66.

Chandler-Olcott, K. and Mahar, D. (2003b) 'Tech-savviness' meets multiliteracies: exploring adolescent girls' technology-mediated literacy practices, *Reading Research Quarterly*, 38(3): 356–8.

Chatelain, J. (2003) Learning from the review culture of fan fiction. jodi.ecs.soton.ac.uk/Articles/v03/i03/Chatelain/fanfic.html (accessed 22 April 2006).

Christie, F. (1987) Genres as choice, in I. Reid (ed.) *The Place of Genre in Learning: Current Debates*. Typereader Publications No.1. Geelong: Deakin University, Centre for Studies in Literacy Education pp. 22–34.

Coates, T. (2003) posting to Plasticbag.org. 11 June 2003. On permalinks and paradigms. At plasticbag.org/archives/2003/06/on_permalinks_and_paradigms.shtml (accessed 16 February 2006).

Cope, B., Kalantzis, M. and Lankshear, C. (2005) A contemporary project: an interview, *E-Learning*, 2(2): 192–207. wwwords.co.uk/elea/content/pdfs/2/issue2_2.asp#7 (accessed 3 April 2006).

Cowan, J. *et al.* (1998) Destino Colombia: a scenario process for the new millennium, *Deeper News*, 9(1): 7–31.

Davies, J. (2006) Affinities and beyond: developing new ways of seeing in online spaces. *E-Learning*, 3(2): 217–234.

Davies, J. and Merchant, G. (2007) Inside out: academic blogging and new literacies, an autoethnography, in M. Knobel and C. Lankshear (eds) *A New Literacies Sampler*. New York: Peter Lang (in process).

Dawkins, R. (1976) *The Selfish Gene*. Oxford: Oxford University Press.

Dawkins, R. (1999) Foreword, in S. Blackmore, *The Meme Machine*, pp. vii–xvii. Oxford: Oxford University Press.

Dennett, D. (1995) *Darwin's Dangerous Idea*. New York: Simon and Schuster.

Dewey, J. (1916/1997) *Democracy and Education*. New York: The Free Press (first published in 1916 by Macmillan).

Dewey, J. (1938/1997) *Experience and Education*. New York: Touchstone (first published in 1938 by Kappa Delta Pi).

Dibbell, J. (2002) Portrait of the blogger as a young man, in Editors of Perseus Publishing (eds) *We've Got Blog: How Weblogs Are Changing Culture*, pp. 69–77. Cambridge, MA: Perseus Publishing.

di Justo, P. and Stein, T. (2002) The cost of online fraud in the U.S., *Wired*, 12: 44.

Doctorow, C. (2004) <boingboing.net/2004/11/06/all_your_basestyle_t.html> Saturday, 6 November (accessed 10 October 2005).

Facer, K., Joiner, R., Reid, J., Hull, R. and Kirk, D. (2004) Savannah: mobile gaming and learning? *Journal of Computer Assisted Learning*, 20(5): 399–409.

Fairclough, N. (1989) *Language and Power*. London: Longman.

Flintham, M., Benford, S., Anastasi, R., Hemmings, T., Crabtree, A., Greenhalgh, C., Tandavanitj, N., Adams, M. and Row-Farr, J. (2003) People at leisure: social mixed reality: Where on-line meets on the streets: experiences with mobile mixed reality games, *Proceedings of the SIGCHI Conference on Human Factors in Computing Systems*, pp. 569–76. New York: ACM Press.

Franklin, U. (1990) *The Real World of Technology*. Toronto: House of Anansi.

Freire, P. (1972) *Pedagogy of the Oppressed*. Harmondsworth: Penguin.

Freire, P. (1973) *Cultural Action for Freedom*. Harmondsworth: Penguin.

Freire, P. and Macedo, D. (1987) *Literacy: Reading the Word and the World*. South Hadley, MA: Bergin and Garvey.

Gallo, J. (2004) Weblog journalism: between infiltration and integration. *Into the Blogosphere*. blog.lib.umn.edu/blogosphere/weblog_journalism.html (accessed 22 October 2004).

Garrett, J. (c.2005) Eats, blogs and leaves. Blogger Help: Advice. help.blogger.com/bin/answer.py?answer=1058&topic=47 (accessed 24 January 2006).

Gee, J. P. (1990) *Social Linguistics and Literacies: Ideology in Discourses*. London: Falmer.

Gee, J. P. (1991) What is literacy? in C. Mitchell and K. Weiler (eds) *Rewriting Literacy: Culture and the Discourse of the Other*, pp. 159–212. New York: Bergin and Garvey.

Gee, J. P. (1996) *Social Linguistics and Literacies: Ideology in Discourses*. 2nd edn. London: Falmer.

Gee, J. P. (1997) Foreword: a discourse approach to language and literacy, in C. Lankshear, *Changing Literacies*, pp. xiii–xix. Buckingham: Open University Press.

Gee, J. P. (2000) Teenagers in new times: a new literacy studies perspective, *Journal of Adolescent and Adult Literacy*, 43(5): 412–23.

Gee, J. P. (2003) *What Video Games Have to Teach Us About Learning and Literacy*. New York: Palgrave.

Gee, J. P. (2004) *Situated Language and Learning: A Critique of Traditional Schooling*. London: Routledge.

Gee, J. P., Hull, G. and Lankshear, C. (1996) *The New Work Order: Behind the Language of the New Capitalism*. Sydney: Allen and Unwin.

Gevers, N. (2001) Future remix: an interview with Ian McDonald. *Infinity Plus.* infinityplus.co.uk/nonfiction/intimed.htm (accessed 22 April 2006).

Gillmor, D. (2004) *We the Media.* Sebastopol, CA: O'Reilly Media Inc.

Gilster, P. (1997) *Digital Literacy.* New York: John Wiley and Sons Inc.

Glasner, J. (2002) Nigeria hoax spawns copycats. wired.com/news/business/ 0,1367,53115,00.html *Wired.* June (accessed 7 March 2005).

Godwin, M. (1994) Meme, counter-meme. *Wired.* Issue 2.10. wired.com/wired/ archive/2.10/godwin.if_pr.html (accessed 24 November 2005).

Godwin-Jones, R. (2003) Blogs and wikis: environments for online collaboration, *Language Learning and Technology,* 7(2): 12–16.

Godwin-Jones, R. (2005) Emerging technologies: messaging, gaming, peer-to-peer sharing: language learning strategies and tools for the millennial generation, *Language, Learning & Technology,* 9(1): 17–23.

Goldhaber, M. (1997) The attention economy and the net, *First Monday.* firstmonday.dk/ issues/ issue2_4/goldhaber (accessed 24 April 2006).

Goodenough, O. and Dawkins, R. (1994) The 'St Jude' mind virus, *Nature,* 371: 24.

Goodson, I., Knobel, M., Lankshear, C. and Mangan, M. (2002) *Cyber Spaces/ Social Spaces: Culture Clash in Computerized Classrooms.* New York: Palgrave Press.

Graff, H. (1979) *The Literacy Myth: Literacy and Social Structure in the Nineteenth Century City.* New York: Academic Press.

Grant, G. (1990) Memetic lexicon. pespmc1.vub.ac.be/MEMLEX.html (accessed 5 March 2005).

Green, B. (1988) Subject-specific literacy and school learning: a focus on writing, *Australian Journal of Education,* 30(2): 156–69.

Green, B. (1997) Literacy, information and the learning society, Keynote address to the Joint Conference of the Australian Association for the Teaching of English, the Australian Literacy Educators' Association, and the Australian School Library Association. Darwin: Darwin High School, Northern Territory, Australia, 8–11 July.

Green, B. and Bigum, C. (1993) Aliens in the classroom, *Australian Journal of Education,* 37(2): 119–41.

Hale, L. (2005) An historical perspective on Mary Sue, *The Fanfic Symposium,* trickster.org/symposium/symp174.htm (accessed 8 October 2005).

Hatcher, J. (2005) Of otakus and fansubs: a critical look at anime online in light of current issues in copyright law, *SCRIPT-ed.* 2(4).

Hawkins, E. (2004) *The Complete Guide to Remixing: Produce Professional Dance-Floor Hits on Your Home Computer.* Boston: Berklee Press.

Heath, S. (1983) *Ways With Words: Language, Life and Work in Community and Classrooms.* Cambridge: Cambridge University Press.

Heylighen, F. (1998) What makes a meme successful? Selection criteria for cultural evolution, *Proceedings of the 16th International Congress on Cybernetics,* pp. 423–418. Namur: Association Internat. de Cybernetique.

Hicks, D. (2001) *Reading Lives: Working-Class Children and Literacy Learning.* New York: Teachers College Press.

Hirsch, E. D. Jr. (1987) *Cultural Literacy: What Every American Needs to Know.* Boston, MA: Houghton Mifflin.

Hirst, P. (1974) *Knowledge and the Curriculum.* London: Routledge and Kegan Paul.

Hoggart, R. (1957) *The Uses of Literacy: Aspects of Working Class Life.* London: Chatto.

Hsi, S. (2003) A study of user experiences mediated by nomadic web content in a museum, *Journal of Computer Assisted Learning*, 19(4): 308–19.

Hull, G. and Schultz, K. (eds) (2001) *School's Out! Bridging Out-of-School Literacies with Classroom Practice.* New York: Teachers College Press.

Ito, M. (2003) A new set of social rules for a newly wireless society, *Japan Media Review*, 13 March, 1–4. www.ojr.org/japan/wireless/1043770650.php (accessed 14 March 2003).

Ito, M. (2005a) Personal, portable, pedestrian: lessons from Japanese mobile phone use, *Japan Focus* (30 October 2005), accessed 16 February 2006 at www.japanfocus.org/article.asp?id=434

Ito, M. (2005b) Otaku media literacy. http://www.itofisher.com/mito/publications/otaku_media_lit.html (accessed 22 June 2006).

Ito, M. (2006) Japanese media mixes and amateur cultural exchange, in D. Buckingham and R. Willett (eds) *Digital Generations: Children, Young People, and the New Media* (in press).

Jenkins, H. (1988) Star Trek rerun, reread, rewritten: fan writing as textual poaching, *Critical Studies in Mass Communications*, 5(2): 85–107.

Jenkins, H. (1992) *Textual Poachers: Television, Fans, and Participatory Culture.* New York: Routledge.

Jenkins, H. (2004) Why Heather can write. *Technology Review.* 6 February. technologyreview.com/articles/04/02/wo_jenkins020604.asp (accessed 27 December 2005).

Johnnycakesdepp (2004) Eternity in bliss. fanfiction.net/s/2033837/1 (accessed 6 March 2006).

Johnson, S. (2005) *Everything Bad is Good For You: How Today's Popular Culture Is Actually Making Us Smarter.* New York: Riverhead.

Kalantzis, M. and Cope, B. (1997) *Multiliteracies: Rethinking What We Mean by Literacy and What We Teach as Literacy in the Context of Global Cultural Diversity and New Communications Technologies*, occasional paper no. 21. Haymarket, NSW: Centre for Workplace Communication and Culture.

Klopfer, E. and Squire, K. (in press) Environmental detectives: the development of an augmented reality platform for environmental simulations, *Educational Technology Research & Development* (in press).

Knobel, M. (1999) *Everyday Literacies: Students, Discourses and Social Practice.* New York: Peter Lang.

Knobel, M. and Lankshear, C. (2004a) Form and effect in weblogging, *International Journal of Learning*, 11: 1289–97.

Knobel, M. and Lankshear, C. (2004b) Planning pedagogy for i-mode: from flogging to blogging via wi-fi. Published jointly in *English in Australia*, 139 (February) and *Literacy Learning in the Middle Years*, 12(1): 78–102. (Special issue of the International Federation for the Teaching of English).

Knobel, M. and Lankshear, C. (2006) Weblog worlds and constructions of effective and powerful writing: cross with care, and only where signs permit, in J. Rowsell and K. Pahl (eds) *Travel Notes from the New Literacy Studies: Instances of Practice*. Clevedon: Multilingual Matters.

Koman, R. (2002) Lessig on the future of the public domain. oreillynet.com/pub/a/network/2002/04/02/lessig.html (accessed 22 April 2006).

Koman, R. (2005) Remixing culture: an interview with Lawrence Lessig. oreillynet.com/pub/a/policy/2005/02/24/lessig.html (accessed 22 April 2006).

Kopomaa, T. (2000) *The City in Your Pocket: Birth of the Mobile Information Society*. Helsinki: Gaudeamus.

Kress, G. (2003) *Literacy in the New Media Age*. London: Routledge.

Kress, G. and van Leeuwen, T. (1996) *Reading Images: The Grammar of Visual Design*. London: Routledge.

Lam, W.S.E. (2000) L2 literacy and the design of the self: a case study of a teenager writing on the Internet, *TESOL Quarterly*, 34(3): 457–82.

Lanham, R. (1994) The economics of attention. Proceedings of 124th Annual Meeting, Association of Research Libraries. sunsite.berkeley.edu/ARL/Proceedings/124/ps2econ.html (accessed 2 July 2000).

Lanham, R. (1995) Digital literacy, *Scientific American*, 273(3): 160–1.

Lankoski, P., Heliö, S., Nummela, J., Lahti, J., Mäyrä, F. and Ermi, L. (2004) A case study in pervasive game design: the Songs of North, in A. Hyrskykari (ed.) *Proceedings of the Third Nordic Conference on Human-Computer Interaction*, pp. 413–16. New York: ACM Press.

Lankshear, C. (1999) Literacy studies in education, in M. Peters (ed.) *After the Disciplines: The Emergence of Culture Studies*, pp. 199–227. Westport, CT: Bergin and Garvey.

Lankshear, C. and Bigum, C. (1999) Literacies and new technologies in school settings, *Pedagogy, Culture and Society*, 7(3): 445–65.

Lankshear, C. and Knobel, M. (2003) *New Literacies: Changing Knowledge and Classroom Learning*. Buckingham and Philadelphia: Open University Press.

Lankshear, C. and Knobel, M. (2006) Digital literacies: policy, pedagogy and research considerations for education, *Nordic Journal of Digital Literacy*, 1(1).

Lankshear, C., Peters, M. and Knobel, M. (2000) Information, knowledge and learning: some issues facing epistemology and education in a digital age, *Journal of Philosophy of Education*, 34(1): 17–40.

Lankshear, C. and Snyder, I. (2000) *Teachers and Technoliteracy*. Sydney: Allen & Unwin.

Latterell, C. (2006) *ReMix: Reading and Composing Culture*. New York: Bedford/ St Martins.

Leander, K. (2003) Writing travellers' tales on new literacyscapes, *Reading Research Quarterly*, 38(3): 392–7.

Leander, K. (2005) *Fieldnote Excerpts from the SYNchrony Project*. Nashville, TN: Vanderbilt University.

Leander, K. and Lovvorn, J. (2006). Literacy networks: Following the circulation of texts, bodies, and objects in the schooling and online gaming of one youth. *Cognition & Instruction* 24(3): 291–340.

Lehmann, E. (2006) Wikipedia firestorm spread quickly, *The Lowell Sun*, 7 February. lowellsun.com/ci_3484460 (accessed 14 February 2006).

Lent, A. (2003) Far out and mundane: the mammoth world of manga, *Phi Delta Kappa Forum*, 84(3): 28–41.

Lessig, L. (2004) *Free Culture: How Big Media Uses Technology and the Law to Lock Down Culture and Control Creativity*. New York: Penguin.

Lessig, L. (2005) Creative commons, paper presented at the 2005 Annual ITU Conference, 'Creative Dialogues'. Oslo, Network for IT-Research and Competence in Education (ITU), University of Oslo.

Lih, A. (2004) Wikipedia as participatory journalism: reliable sources? Paper for the 5th International Symposium of Online Journalism, Austin TX: University of Texas, 16–17 April.

Lunenfeld, P. (1999) Unfinished business, in P. Lunenfeld (ed.) *The Digital Dialectic*. Cambridge. MA: The MIT Press.

Machinima.com (2006) What is machinima? *Machinima.com*. machinima.com/ article.php?article=186 (accessed 14 February 2006).

Mäenpää, P. (2001) Mobile communication as a way of urban life, in A. Warde and J. Gronow (eds) *Ordinary Consumption*, pp. 107–23. London: Routledge.

McBride, K. (2004) Journalism in the age of blogs, *Poynter Ethics Journal*, www.poynter.org/column.asp?id=53&aid=71447 (accessed 18 October 2004).

McClellan, J. (2004) How to write a blog-buster, *The Guardian Online*, 8 April. technology.guardian.co.uk/online/story/0,3605,1187545,00.html (accessed 4 April 2006).

McManus, R. (2004) Tom O'Reilly interview Part 3: eBooks and remix culture. readwriteweb.com/archives/tim_oreilly_int_2.php (accessed 22 April 2006).

Martin, J. (1993) Genre and literacy: modeling context in educational linguistics, *Annual Review of Applied Linguistics*, 13: 141–72.

Martin, J. and Rothery, J. (1993) Grammar: making meaning in writing, in B. Cope and M. Kalantzis (eds) *The Powers of Literacy: A Genre Approach to Teaching Writing*, pp. 137–53. London: Falmer.

Mattila, P. and Fordell, T. (2005) Moop: using an m-learning environment in primary schools, paper presented at the 4th World Conference on Mobile Learning, Cape Town, South Africa, 25–28 October.mlearn.org.za/CD/papers/ Mattila.pdf (accessed 16 February 2006).

Memmott, C. (2005) Comic pages make room for manga, *USA Today*, 29

December. news.yahoo.com/s/usatoday/20051229/en_usatoday/comicspages makeroomformanga (accessed 29 December 2005).

Merchant, G. (2005) Digikids: cool dudes and the new writing, *E-Learning*, 2(1): 50–60.

Merchant, G. (forthcoming) Digital writing in the early years, in D. Leu, J. Coiro, M. Knobel and C. Lankshear (eds) *A Handbook of New Literacies Research*. Mahwah, NJ: Erlbaum.

Moore, R. and Young, M. (2001) Knowledge and the curriculum in the sociology of education: towards a reconceptualisation, *British Journal of Sociology of Education*, 22(4): 445–61.

Mortensen, T. (forthcoming) Of a divided mind: weblog literacy, in D. Leu, J. Coiro, M. Knobel and C. Lankshear (eds) *A Handbook of New Literacies Research*, Mahwah, NJ: Erlbaum.

M.P. (2005) The good, the bad, and the ugly in (game) fanfiction writing, *The Fanfic Symposium*, trickster.org/symposium/symp169.htm (accessed 8 October 2005).

Naismith, L., Lonsdale, P., Vavoula, G. and Sharples, M. (no date) Literature review in mobile technologies and learning, Bristol: NESTA Futurelab. http:// www.futurelab.org.uk/download/pdfs/research/lit_reviews/futurelab_review_11.pdf (accessed 22 June 2006).

Nardi, B. (2002) I'm blogging: a closer look at why people blog. Submitted to Communications of the ACM. home.comcast.net~diane.schiano/Blog.draft. pdf (accessed 12 July 2005).

Negroponte, N. (1995) *Being Digital*. New York: Vintage Books.

Oliver, B. (2005) Mobile blogging, 'Skyping' and podcasting: targeting under- graduates' communication skills in transnational learning contexts, paper presented to the 1st Microlearning 2005 conference. microlearning.org/ micropapers/MLproc_2005_oliver.pdf (accessed 28 January 2006).

Ooi, J. (2004) Blogs give Dan Rather '60+1 Minutes', *Screenshots . . .*, Sunday, 12 September. jeffooi.com/archives/2004/09/september_8_cbs.php (accessed 22 October 2004).

O'Reilly, T. (2005) What is web 2.0?: Design patterns and business models for the next generation of software.oreillynet.com/pub/a/oreilly/tim/news/2005/09/30/ what-is-web–20.html (accessed 4 April 2006).

Papert, S. (1993) *The Children's Machine: Rethinking School in the Age of the Computer*. New York: Basic Books.

Peretti, J. (2001) My Nike adventure, *The Nation*, 9 April. Reprinted at CorpWatch corpwatch.org/article.php?id=147 (accessed 7 March 2004).

Perrone, J. (2004) Random reality bites, *The Guardian Online*, 5 July. technology. guardian.co.uk/online/weblogs/story/0,,1254467,00.html (accessed 31 Decem- ber 2005).

Plant, S. (2001) *On the Mobile: The Effects of Mobile Telephones on Social and Individual Life*. Report prepared for Motorola. www.motorola.com/mot/ documents/0,,296,00.pdf (accessed 27 June 2003).

Plotz, D. (2000) Luke Skywalker is gay? Fan fiction is America's literature of obsession, *Slate*, slate.msn.com/id/80225 (accessed 19 November 2004).

Pool, C. (1997) A conversation with Paul Gilster, *Educational Leadership*, 55: 6–11.

Pownell, D. and Bailey, G. (2001) Getting a handle on handhelds: what to consider before you introduce handhelds into your school, June, *Electronic School.com* (accessed 4 April 2006).

Prinsloo, M. and Breier, M. (eds) (1996) *The Social Uses of Literacy: Theory and Practice in Contemporary South Africa*. Amsterdam and Johannesburg: John Benjamins and SACHED Books.

Pugh, S. (2004) The democratic genre: fan fiction in a literary context, *Refractory: A Journal of Entertainment Media*. 5. refractory.unimelb.edu.au/journalissues/vol5/pugh.html (accessed 27 December 2005).

Rezak, A. and Alvermann, D. (2005) Why choose one? Multimodality, identity, literacy practices of LiveJournal bloggers, paper presented to the National Reading Conference, Miami, FL, 2 December 2005.

Rheingold, H. (2002) *Smart Mobs: The Next Social Revolution*. Cambridge, MA: Perseus.

Roschelle, J. (2003) Unlocking the learning value of wireless mobile services, *Journal of Computer Assisted Learning*, 19(3): 260–72.

Rowan, L. and Bigum, C. (1997) The future of technology and literacy teaching in primary learning situations and contexts, in C. Lankshear, C. Bigum *et al.* (investigators) *Digital Rhetorics: Literacies and Technologies in Education – Current Practices and Future Directions*, Vol. 3. Children's Literacy National Projects, Brisbane: QUT/DEETYA.

Sanchez, F. (2003) HIST 101: History of manga. AnimeInfo.org – Anime University. animeinfo.org/animeu/hist102-11.html (accessed 24 November 2003).

Scholz, T. (2004) It's new media: but is it art education? *fibreculture: internet theory + criticism + culture*. 3. journal.fibreculture.org/issue3/issue3_scholz.html (accessed 7 November 2005).

Schrage, M. (2001) The relationship revolution. seedwiki.com/wiki/Yi-Tan/TheRelationshipRevolution.htm?wikipageversionid=417577&edit=yes&i=87 (accessed 4 April 2006).

Schwartz, J. (2003) Professors vie with web for class's attention, *New York Times* (2 January 2003).

Schwartz, P. (1991) *The Art of the Long View*. New York: Doubleday.

Scollon, R. and Scollon, S. (1981) *Narrative, Literacy, and Face in Interethnic Communication*. Norwood, NJ: Ablex.

Scribner, S. and Cole, M. (1981) *The Psychology of Literacy*. Cambridge, MA: Harvard University Press.

Shanmugasundaram, K. (2002) Weblogging: lessons learned, in Editors of Perseus Publishing (ed.) *We've Got Blog: How Weblogs Are Changing Culture*, pp. 142–4. Cambridge, MA: Perseus Publishing.

Shirky, C. (2003) Power laws, weblogs and inequality, shirky.com/writings/power law_weblog.html (accessed 7 March 2006).

Sholle, D. and Denski, S. (1993) Reading and writing the media: critical media literacy and postmodernism, in C. Lankshear and P. McLaren (eds) *Critical Literacy: Politics, Praxis and the Postmodern*, pp. 297–323. Albany, NY: SUNY Press.

Smith, I., Consolvo, S. and LaMarca, A. (2005) Pervasive gaming: The Drop – pragmatic problems in the design of a compelling, pervasive game, *Computers in Entertainment*, 3(3): 4–8.

Somogyi, V. (2002) Complexity of desire: Janeway/Chakotay fan fiction, *Journal of American & Comparative Cultures*, Fall–Winter: 399–405.

Spector, R. (2000) *Amazon.com: Get Big Fast*. San Francisco, CA: Harper Business.

Squire, K. (forthcoming) Video game literacy: a literacy of experience, in D. Leu, J. Coiro, M. Knobel and C. Lankshear (eds) *A Handbook of New Literacies Research*. Mahwah, NJ: Erlbaum.

Stalder, F. and Hirsh, J. (2002) Open source intelligence. subsol.c3.hu/subsol_2/contributors2/stalder-hirshtext.html (accessed 16 February 2006).

Steinkuehler, C. (forthcoming) Cognition and literacy in massively multiplayer online games, in D. Leu, J. Coiro, M. Knobel and C. Lankshear (eds) *A Handbook of New Literacies Research*. Mahwah, NJ: Erlbaum.

Stone, J. (2006) The 'unofficial' literacy curriculum: popular websites in adolescents' out-of-school lives, paper presented at the Annual Meeting of The American Educational Research Association, San Francisco, 11 April.

Street, B. (1984) *Literacy in Theory and Practice*. Cambridge: Cambridge University Press.

Street, B. (ed.) (1993) *Cross-Cultural Approaches to Literacy*. Cambridge: Cambridge University Press.

Street, B. (2001) Introduction, in B. Street (ed.) *Literacy and Development: Ethnographic Perspectives*. London: Routledge.

Taylor, C. (2001) All your base are belong to us, *Time*, 157(9): 4.

Thomas, A. (2005) 'Fictional blogging and the narrative identities of adolescent girls', Unpublished manuscript. personal.edfac.usyd.edu.au/staff/thomasa/AngelaThomasBlogPaper.html (accessed 13 March 2006).

Thomas, A. (2006) 'MSN was the next big thing after Beanie Babies': children's virtual experiences as an interface to their everyday lives, *E-Learning*, 3(2).

Thomas, A. (forthcoming) *e-selves | e-literacies | e-worlds: Children's Identities and Literacies in Virtual Communities*. New York: Peter Lang.

Thorne, S. (2003) The internet as artefact: immediacy, evolution, and educational contingencies, or 'the wrong tool for the right job?' paper presented to the American Educational Research Association Annual Meeting, Chicago, 21 April.

Tunbridge, N. (1995) The cyberspace cowboy, *Australian Personal Computer*, December: 2–4.

Unsworth, L., Thomas, A., Simpson, A. and Asha, J. (2005) *Children's Literature and Computer Based Teaching*. Maidenhead: Open University Press.

US Department of Education (2002) No Child Left Behind Act. ed.gov/nclb (accessed 24 April 2006).

van der Heijden, K. (1996) *Scenarios: The Art of Strategic Conversation*. Chichester: John Wiley.

Vavoula, G. and Sharples, M. (2002) KLeOS: a personal mobile knowledge and learning organising system, in M. Mildrad and U. Hoppe (eds) *Kinshuk: Proceedings of the IEEE International Workshop on Mobile and Wireless Technologies in Education*, pp. 152–6. Vaxjo, Sweden, 29–30 August.

Wack, P. (1985a) The gentle art of reperceiving, *Harvard Business Review*, September–October: 73–89.

Wack, P. (1985b) Scenarios: shooting the rapids, *Harvard Business Review*, November–December: 139–50.

Walker, J. (2005) Weblog, in D. Herman, M. Jahn and M. Ryan (eds) *Routledge Encyclopedia of Narrative Theory*. London and New York: Routledge.

Webb, R. (1955) *The British Working Class Reader*. London: Allen and Unwin.

Wexler, P. (1988) Curriculum in the closed society, in H. Giroux and P. McLaren (eds) *Critical Pedagogy, the State and Cultural Struggle*, pp. 92–104. Albany, NY: SUNY Press.

Whybark, M. (2004) Hopkin explained. 22 November. mike.whybark.com/archives/001951.html (accessed 9 March 2005).

Wikipedia. en.wikipedia.org/wiki/Main_Page. See entries for: Anime; Audioblogging; Blog; Blog fiction; Fan fiction; i-mode; Manga; Mindset, Photoshopping; Podcasting; Remix; Vlog.

Wilkins, J. (1998) What's in a meme? *Journal of Memetics – Evolutionary Models of Information Transmission*. 2. Jom-emit.cfpm.org/1998/vol2/wilkins_js.html (accessed 1 March 2005).

Wired (2002) Nigeria e-mail suckers exist, *Wired*, April. wired.com/news/culture / 0,1284,51725,00.html (accessed 7 March 2005).

Wright, M. (2003) *YOU Back the Attack: WE'LL Bomb Who We Want!* New York: Seven Stories Press.

Wright, M. (2005) *If You're Not a Terrorist . . . Stop Asking Questions*. San Diego, CA: Xlibris Corporation.

Wright, M. (2006) *Surveillance Means Security*. NY: Seven Stories Press.

Wright, T. (2004) Blog fiction. *trAce: Online Writing Centre*, 16 January. trace.ntu.ac.uk/Process/index.cfm?article=91 (accessed 13 March 2006).

Name index

Subject index